GIANTS
OF CORK SPORT

Dave Hannigan

Published 2005
by Evening Echo Publications
a Thomas Crosbie Holdings Ltd. Company

ISBN
0-9528856-6-2

To my father Denis

Acknowledgments

In October, 2003, a UCC soccer club alumnus called Eddie Murphy rang me up. We had both worn the skull and cross-bones in different eras (him with far more distinction than me) and though we had friends in common had never previously met. At our first meeting, it was he prompted me to embark on this, and with the subsequent assistance of Tom McCarthy and Niamh O'Shea at Cork 2005, the project took off.

At the Evening Echo, Dan Lenihan, Maurice Gubbins and Diarmuid O'Donovan supported it with their customary mixture of enthusiasm and humour from the moment the manuscript crossed their desks; Robert O'Shea and Barry Woods did a fine editing job, and Marguerite Kiely's exceptional work on the design and layout is evident in your hands right now. John McHale, Sports Editor of the Evening Echo, is my continuing link with the newspaper and has been a great supporter. Special mention to the Library staff of the Evening Echo / Irish Examiner particularly Anne Kearney, Declan Ryan and Pat Good for their research and help with the images in this book. The Marketing Department of the Evening Echo led by Marketing Manager Orla Keane has been instrumental in coordinating all the activities of this book from planning, proofing, print liaison, distribution and promotion. Without Orla's persistence this book would never have been published.

It would require several more pages to list the rest of the people who assisted in some form at different stages. Since pressure of space and fear of omitting anybody prevent me from doing that, I would just like to say a heartfelt thank you here to everybody who poked out an ancient book or a musty article or a phone number over the past two years. To my circle of friends especially, I will be gladly repaying your favours for decades yet.

This book would not have been possible but for the love of Cork in general and Cork sport in particular handed down to me by my parents, Theresa and Denis. They are remarkable people, they are my heroes and everything I aspire to be. I would like to express my gratitude also to my brother Tom, my sisters Denise and Anne, niece Kadie, and parents-in-law, George and Clare Frost.

A very special tribute is due to my wife Cathy without whose love, patience, encouragement and understanding, none of this would be very much fun. Her own courage in the face of considerable adversity is a daily inspiration to me.

Last but definitely not least, my darling son Abe was born in Dublin, is growing up in New York, and, though he owns three red jerseys, has not yet fully grasped how special it is when one of the teams in any match is called Cork. There will be a special joy in teaching him that.

Dave Hannigan
Rocky Point
New York,
October, 2005

Contents

Icons

Olympians

Moments

Footprints

Exiles

Prologue

Jerry Moynihan's teaching career brought him to Cloyne National School in 1933. An inter-county footballer with Cork, he borrowed a field on the Ballycotton Road known as the Groomeen, imported a couple of dozen new hurleys and began organising matches for the schoolchildren. Christy Ring always had hurling in his family, but he didn't have proper games until Moynihan came to town.

When Sonia O'Sullivan fetched up at Cobh Vocational School nearly half a century later, she tried every sport on offer. Once it became apparent she had some aptitude for athletics, a teacher called Jim Hennessy invested time and effort beyond the call of his profession in helping her develop. Decades later, she'd recall how Hennessy drove her to races the length and breadth of Munster so she could measure herself against the best in the province.

Around about the same time, Roy Keane was starting to learn his trade at Rockmount. Having followed his brothers and uncles into the club, he fell under the spell of Timmy Murphy and Gene O'Sullivan. Murphy and O'Sullivan pooled together a schoolboy soccer team of some talent, christened their energetic under-sized midfielder 'boiler-man' and every time scouts passed him over, assured the youngster that one day his gifts would finally be recognised by somebody.

In the fables that are the sporting lives of that trio, Messrs. Moynihan, Hennessy, O'Sullivan and Murphy play truly heroic roles. Would Ring have become the greatest of all time if Moynihan hadn't arrived and revitalised hurling in the village? What were the chances of Sonia winning silver in Sydney without Hennessy fostering her dreams as a teenage novice? How differently might Keane's career have turned out if he hadn't come under the wings the orbit of two great mentors?

This is a book about Cork's most famous stars, their greatest achievements and most impressive feats. If there is one thing many of them have in common, it is that somewhere along the way to the Pantheon they were assisted by teachers, coaches and that never-ending army of unpaid volunteers that are the lifeblood of every sport in the city and county. The four people mentioned above merit footnotes in this history because they crossed paths with greatness and pushed it in the right direction. The vast majority however, spend entire lifetimes working below the waterline, their names never writ large via the exploits of a former pupil or player.

These characters are the foundation stones upon which Cork sport was built and still thrives. In every code and every game, there are so many men and women who selflessly devote their days and nights to clubs, buffing and polishing talent when it appears, using ingenuity and enthusiasm to overcome deficient resources and inadequate facilities. They line pitches, wash jerseys, referee matches, man committees, sell tickets, and do whatever it takes to keep kids' dreams alive. There is no money in it, often precious little glory and definitely not enough appreciation.

Some of us may never meet our heroes, but we'd do well to remember that every time we go to a sporting event, we run into the unsung heroes. They deserve our gratitude and so much more.

1

By one definition, an icon is a person regarded as a symbol of a belief or cultural movement. These are the people whose exploits have mapped out and defined the progress of sport in Cork through generations. Synonymous with the games they bestrode, we know them by their first-names and can recite their achievements like cathecisms.

Icons

Ring

In the thirtieth minute of the 1946 All Ireland final between Cork and Kilkenny, Paddy Donovan's clearance dropped around centre-field where Christy Ring had come foraging for possession. In a flash, he controlled the loose sliothar and embarked on a solo run, the ball hopping on his hurley. His first instinct was to find space and he headed towards the corner to shake off the pursuing defenders. One Kilkenny back would say later the only way he could have possibly checked Ring's progress at that point was by throwing his arms around him and hauling him to the ground.

As Ring gathered momentum, the crowd noise grew louder with anticipation that something special was afoot. After outstripping the initial cover, he changed direction on the 21, cutting inside towards goal. He ghosted past Kilkenny's captain Mulcahy, and sidestepped Walsh and Butler. Having travelled nearly 70 yards, he was near enough then to the target. His left-handed shot flew over Jim Donegan's right-shoulder and billowed the roof of the net. Both sets of fans rose to give him a standing ovation. The following day, one newspaper described the goal as a 'wonder', another preferred to call it a 'miracle'.

'When you pick up a ball in the All-Ireland final you don't know where you are going to end up,' said Ring in an interview with Donnacha Ó Dulaing on RTE. 'Well, anyway, I picked up the ball and started to run and I suddenly found out that I had shaken off most of my opponents but was in the wrong place, so then I decided that I could move across the goal and picked my spot and hit it into the roof of the net. I don't know what you'd call it but I hadn't any idea what to do when I picked up the ball first, but suddenly I realised I was clear. I suddenly decided that I could score a goal.'

No matter what was happening around him, Christy Ring never took his eye off the ball. He is seen here in action against Dublin in the National Hurling League at the Mardyke, Cork.

There are so many awesome goals, so many breath-taking cameos that the task of profiling Christy Ring for a Cork audience is akin to trying to synopsise the life of Jesus for Evangelical Christians.

By 1946, Ring was 26 years of age, playing his seventh senior championship and reaching a peak he would maintain for more than a decade after. The Cork four-in-a-row team of 1941-1944 had fragmented a little, and now, Ring was not only captain, but the undisputed leader of the attack, a role he would underline at another crucial juncture in that final when his determined solo run set up Mossie Riordan for the goal that finally clinched victory and Cork's 16th title.

'Up to that point," said Con Murphy, full-back that day and later president of the GAA, 'Christy Ring was regarded as a very good player on a very good team. From '46 on, he was seen as a match-winner in his own right.'

There are so many awesome goals, so many breathtaking cameos that the task of profiling Christy Ring for a Cork audience is akin to trying to synopsise the life of Jesus for Evangelical Christians. How is it possible to decide which of the miracles to leave out? Are any of the parables involving him less worthy of inclusion than others? The biblical language is appropriate about somebody whom Archbishop Morris from Tipperary once described as 'the devil himself'. From a man of the cloth whose people had suffered at Ring's hands, that sort of blasphemy is of course a kind of praise.

Before one particular Munster final, Jim 'Tough' Barry was going through his final instructions in the dressing room as the Cork players readied themselves for Tipperary. After Barry spoke his piece, Ring took the floor and delivered a rabble-rousing oration that had his team-mates fired up and desperate for battle. A priest lurking in a corner of the dressing room wasn't too pleased with Ring's ardent tone or his choice of colourful vocabulary and he ventured to complain.

'My dear Christy,' he said, 'I'm sure you never read that in the New Testament.' 'The men who wrote the New Testament,' replied Ring, 'never had to play Tipperary.'

Of all the stories attached to his legend, this one resonates because Ring was a devoutly religious man himself. Upon moving to Cork city, he was a daily communicant at the Society of African Missions Church in Blackrock, his faith the foundation stone of his character. He was scrupulously honest, and fiercely loyal; a true Catholic of impeccable moral virtue. When he did a good turn for a friend in need or any charitable act, he did so privately and always without display. In Val Dorgan's wonderful phrase, he was a 'secret humanitarian'. He later donated his eight All-Ireland medals and a selection of other mementoes to St. Augustine's Church so they could be melted down and recast as part of a chalice.

Nicholas Christopher Ring was born in the townland of Kilcrone, just outside Cloyne on October 30, 1920, the fourth of five children. He had two sisters and two brothers, and the family can reportedly trace its lineage in that part of East Cork back to at least the 14th century. His father, Nicholas, a gardener by profession, was a hurling zealot who would cycle all over the county to matches. Once Christy was deemed old enough, he was given the space on the crossbar and a glimpse of the sporting world beyond the town they'd moved into a few weeks after his birth. Christy was just 16 when his father died but by then he'd inherited his fervour for the game.

'Cloyne bore no relation to Las Vegas,' wrote Denis Walsh in The Sunday Times on the 25th anniversary of Ring's death. 'Outside of hurling, entertainments were scarce. Like all of his peers, Ring was a member of the Catholic Young Men's Society in the village. In the society's rooms the lads had access to billiards and darts and table tennis, at which Christy was imperious. Members joined in their teenage years and stayed on into their 20s.

'All of the lads in Cloyne started off as pioneers but few of them maintained a pledge for life as Christy did. An old lady in Mrs Motherway's shop, known to everyone as Aunt Jo, introduced temperance to every 11-year-old in the village with what was known as a penny pioneer pin. Then, after 12 months, you graduated to be a probationer. Christy never bothered with drink or pubs. Hurling was his liquor and in Cloyne he drank deeply.'

He won his first proper hurley when he was 10, a prize awarded to the student with the best results in the school's six classes. To that point, he'd made do with an adult stick his father had trimmed down for him and the rudimentary crookeens that he and his brothers, Willie John and Paddy Joe would fashion from ash they gathered themselves. The basic equipment was enough to start honing the talent, and so began a legendary devotion to self-improvement and mastering the skills. The old chestnut about him practicing by hitting the ball into a bucket dangling from a tree thirty yards away may not be historically accurate. Every word about how hard he worked however, is.'There is no such thing as practice,' said Ring in a rare interview with the Cork diocesan magazine "The Fold" 'There is such a thing as hard work. Hurling is hard work, it's like carrying one hundred bricks before you put one up. You must learn to carry them first. Then you'll put them up. You must work step by step. The hardest things that you must do in training will

serve you well in the game because you'll never be asked to do them as hard again. I got down to hard training and I eventually wound up enjoying doing the hard thing. And when you are talking about hurling, the easy way happens in a game. But of course it only seems easy because you have been doing the hard things in training.'

Previous page: Christy Ring, wearing the colours of his club Glen Rovers, drives the sliotar goalward against UCC during 1955 County Senior Hurling Championship game at the Athletic Grounds.

In the latter stages of his career, a broken arm put him out of work for three months so he left his flat on the Grand Parade and went home to Cloyne to recuperate. Locals testify to seeing him out in the field, one arm in a sling, the other swinging a hurley. Whatever portion of his talent came from on high, it was overmatched by the desire to maximise every ounce of it that came from within. Inexplicably kept on the bench by the county minors in 1937, the following year he was playing right half-back in the All-Ireland final when Cork were clinging to a two-point lead late in the game. Without being asked, he sprinted from his defensive outpost to blast a 21-yard free to the net and finish off Dublin.

'Modesty is not saying you're no good when you know you are,' said Ring. 'It's knowing how good you are and what your weaknesses are.'

Twenty-four years after his first appearance at Croke Park, he wore the red jersey for the last time at the same venue, scoring 1-5 of Cork's total of 1-8 in a defeat by Kilkenny in the 1962 National League final. A few months short of his 42nd birthday, all but one point of his contribution came from play. Even still, he returned to Jones's Road once more with Munster the following spring, collecting his 18th Railway Cup winner's medal in his 22nd consecutive final. This was in an era when that competition was a vital event on the GAA calendar and many directly trace its decline to the departure of Ring from the scene. The Railway Cup record will never be matched and though his tally of eight All-Ireland medals was equalled, the Tipperary man who did so put it in proper context.

'Ring won eight All Irelands for Cork,' said John Doyle. 'You'd have to say that my lads won eight All Irelands for me.'Ring played with some of the greatest hurlers of his time but Doyle's point is well made. So often he was the difference between Cork winning and losing. If the goal in 1946 is remembered by many as his finest work, there was another in the closing stages of the 1944 Munster final replay that, while not as aesthetically pleasing, was even more dramatic.

'It was the effort of an athlete who would not accept defeat,' wrote John Power in the "Cork Book of Champions". 'An effort the like of which occurs perhaps only once in a lifetime. There were Limerick, winners it seemed, all the way. And Cork desperately battling against time to bring down that lead. Point by point, Cork narrowed the score. There was brave Mick Mackey dashing from goal to goal, playing several men's parts to uphold the lead. Then well back in his own half, the unconquerable Ring snapped up the ball. Tim Ryan went for him, Christy tapped the ball on his hurley and sailed around him.

'On for twenty yards went the Corkman still tapping the ball on his hurley. Out came Jackie Power, then Cregan, then McCarthy, then Power again. Christy Ring still had the ball. Suddenly, he stopped, steadied and swung his hurley. Like a bullet the ball flew straight and true. Hurleys flashed to meet it but there it was, dead in the back of the net. 'Tense and dramatic. It was seconds before the crowd had realised the truth. A few moments later, the game was over – Limerick defeated.'

Twelve years later, he broke Limerick hearts again in another Munster final. They were leading by five points with 15 minutes to play. Ring only needed five minutes to turn the game on its head by scoring three goals. The first was palmed to the net at the end of a run that saw him fight off two desperate challenges en route. The second was the culmination of a solo run, the third the result of a sleight of hand as he snatched the ball from between two Limerick hurleys. He tacked on a point too in perhaps as mesmerising a 300-second spell as hurling has ever seen.

When Wexford beat Cork in the All-Ireland final that year, Art Foley carved his own place in folklore with a wonder save from Ring three minutes from the end. It was a miss that in time has become as famous as any of his goals.

'Well actually I blocked it with the hurl,' said Foley. 'The ball went straight up in the air. Then it was just like a camera: you're looking around to see who's around. (Josie) Hartnett and (Gerry) Murphy were coming in at full belt so I blocked it out to (Jim) Morrissey. Christy was full sure he had a goal and that's the whole idea of it. He came rushing in after it and when he saw the ball wasn't in the net the first thing he did was stuck out his hand and says "You little black bastard, you're after beating us".'
Even in defeat, Ring was the story as Nick O'Donnell and Bobby Rackard chaired their vanquished opponent off the field that day. It was an incredibly magnanimous gesture that illustrates the regard his peers had for him. Not all of them were fond enough of him to ever pay him the compliment the Wexford duo did that day but they all respected the fact they were in the company of someone special.

'Except among truest friends, the immensity of his generosity and intellect remained well wadded in reticence,' wrote Kevin Cashman in the Sunday Independent in December, 1995. 'That changed utterly at every throw-in of a sliothar. He would exhort and goad his own, and seek to disconcert and down-face the other lot, with trenchant wit and colour.'

Christy Ring collected the Liam McCarthy Cup for the third time and won his eights All-Ireland medal when Cork defeated Wexford in the 1954 All-Ireland final. To the left of Ring is Jim 'Tough' Barry, trainer of the team and in to the right is Andy Scannell, chairman of the Cork County Board.

Some of the onfield exchanges have passed into folklore. 'I'll open you the next time the ball comes in here,' threatened one opponent.'If you're still here,' replied Ring.

The physical cut and thrust of hurling in the forties and fifties exhilarated him. Although some in Galway still nurse a grudge about the incident with

Mickey Burke in the 1953 All-Ireland final, and nobody has yet established beyond reasonable doubt if it was Ring who hit Tipperary's Tom Moloughney in the 1961 Munster decider, most of his rivals testify he was, in that classic cliché, hard but fair. Even if hard but fair was open to a considerably more robust interpretation then than now, he certainly wasn't considered dirty.

'During my playing career, I met a lot of players that were faster, taller and better in several ways but to be a good hurler, you have to have something the others haven't got,' said Ring. 'I had that strength. I never met anybody physically stronger than myself. I achieved this strength by hard, physical training. Allied to this, I had fierce determination when going for a ball. I would go through a stone wall to get a fifty-fifty ball. I would stop at nothing. My strength was largely hidden because I wasn't a big fellow. I never weighed less than 13 stone. I knew that weighing 13 stone and travelling at speed, I could take on any player. I only used my strength when needed.

'All round physical strength was my best weapon. I never did weightlifting or anything like that to develop this strength. I had it automatically and I'd say it was in the mind. Seventy-five per cent of everything is in the mind and it's mind that counts. Most times, if you get the better of your opponents, the rest takes care of itself. When you are playing games a while, you have great confidence in yourself, if you are really a great player. 'You actually put it up to the other fellow. It's like saying to your opponent "that's the ball and I am going to get it". You let him make up his own mind but if you are really good you'll get it... you have eight or nine skills that you have really perfected and you decided that you are going to use one or more of them. The game is all about confidence in what you have learned.'

His supreme confidence and inordinate strength also came infused with passion. He hated to lose and was always conscious of the record books. As he was being carried shoulder-high following the victory over Tipperary in the 1952 Munster final, blood was leaking down his face but when he saw Eamonn Young approaching, he manically shouted 'For the Doc... For the Doc'. Young's brother Dr. Jim Young had been one of the Cork four-in-a-row team, and Cork's win had ended Tipp's gallant attempt to emulate that feat.

'The greatest win we ever had was against Tipperary in the 1952 Munster final,' said Ring. 'We went into Limerick in 1952 and we had trained hard, we had ten changes from the year before. From a Corkman's point of view, we said we were going out there to play for Cork, and when you play for Cork there's no looking back. We played that day in Limerick but it was with a heavy heart we came to Carrigtwohill that morning, when Mattie Fuohy said he wasn't playing.

'Mattie, I reckon, is the best man on our team. No doubt about it, Mattie is the man. We threw Willie John (Daly) back in the back line and we were short a forward, but when the full-time whistle blew in Limerick there were two points in it. I think that was a great achievement for this Cork team. There were some of them new and some of them never hit a ball in a Munster final but that day they hit them better than any Cork team that came before.'

That quote is taken from an interview with Ring done in Barry's Hotel on the morning of the 1953 All Ireland-hurling final. Three Cork fans, Ger Murphy, Sean O'Connor and Jim Ahern brought a basic dictaphone along to record some of the players, and Ring, intrigued by the new-fangled technology, agreed to speak to them. When Michael Moynihan wrote a piece about them in the Irish Examiner half a century later, the fresh quotes were a welcome addition to the canon. Ring gave few enough in-depth interviews in his time, although whenever he did speak out, it was always with a purpose. On one occasion, he called for the abolition of points, games of greater duration and the throw-in to be replaced by a puck-out.

Befitting his standing as a true Corinthian, he eschewed countless opportunities to cash in on his fame. He wouldn't allow a pub in New York to pay him to take his name in its title, rebuffed repeated lucrative offers from newspapers and publishers to write his life story and made do with his earnings from driving an oil truck. The oil truck from which he would alight in a field most lunchtimes with his hurley and ball to further work on his skills. Admirable as those decisions were from a quality of life point of view, they added to the eccentric view many had of him.

One afternoon in 1964, Ring was walking along Patrick Street with the journalist Breandán Ó hEithir when their progress was suddenly checked by the sound of jeers coming from across the road. At a safe distance, a gaggle of students were boldly chanting 'Dirty Ring!' in their direction, a mocking reference to an incident the previous Sunday in a county championship match where the UCC player marking the Glen Rovers' man had suffered a broken wrist. The result of a bad fall, the injury nevertheless spawned a false rumour about foul play, and spotting Ring in his civvies, these miscreants sought to milk the moment for all it was worth.

Duly rising to the bait, he fired back abuse at his assailants, his apoplexy only adding fuel to their fire. As Ó hEithir tried his best to calm him down, advising that the best policy was to ignore the taunts, Ring turned on him too. 'That's all you know then,' said the winner of eight All-Ireland hurling medals. 'You probably think I'm a respected man in this town. There are people in this town, boy, who think I'm locked up in the red house (the mental asylum on the Lee Road) on the hill all week and only let out to hurl on Sundays.'

At this remove, it's difficult to envisage anybody, even students under the influence of drink, speaking with anything less than awe about Ring. In life, he was adored but in death, he has been, rightly, exalted and venerated. That the bridge named after him abuts Cork Opera House and the Crawford Art Gallery is appropriate, a recognition that he was as much an artist as a sportsman. His brush may have been made of ash and his favoured canvas a vast green sward but anybody who has viewed Louis Marcus's poetic film of Ring teaching the game's skills would acknowledge the aesthetic quality to his play.

Perhaps the best summation of his standing among his own is Niall Toibin's account of meeting him for the first time. At a post-All-Ireland hurling final function at the Spa Hotel in Lucan in the seventies, Toibin had been invited along to do a turn. Although a selector by then, Ring was a surprise visitor to the dinner and when the seating was hastily rearranged to accommodate him, he was placed sitting across from the actor.

'You're Toibin, aren't ya?' asked Ring.
'Yes,' replied the actor.
'I like you.'

'I felt that I could relax,' said Toibin. 'He had sort of given me permission to stay.' A veteran of stage and screen, Toibin had wowed Broadway and lit up the West End but he knew was in a room where the imprimatur of only one man really mattered.

The last hurling match he ever attended was a Harty Cup tie between the North Mon and St Colman's in Buttevant, a game long since consigned to history but one that of course has yielded yet another delightful Ring moment.

'St Colman's came out on the field 20 minutes before throw-in and went through an elaborate pre-match routine,' wrote Enda McEvoy in The Sunday Tribune. 'Their calisthenics were keenly watched by Ring, who wasn't impressed by this exhibition of style over substance and immediately announced that they had "only two hurlers". A few moments later, one of the St Colman's mentors, a cleric, wandered over and solicited Ring's opinion. "Ah, Father," came the reply, "ye're wasting yer time. The Mon will beat ye by four goals." The priest departed, shocked. The game ended in a 2-14 to 0-8 win for the Mon.'

A couple of days later, Friday March 2nd 1979, Ring collapsed on the street outside the School of Commerce, A schoolteacher named Patricia Horgan was first to his aid and she whispered an act of contrition in his ear in the moments before he died. In an eerie coincidence, the pair had met before. Twenty-six years earlier a woman had been walking with her pram and baby behind the old Cork Athletic Grounds. As she made her way up by the Atlantic Pond a car turned in from the Marina. Seconds later another followed and tried to squeeze past. The possibility of her pram being crushed between the two cars flashed in front of the woman's eyes. The first driver spotted the danger and reacted. He pulled over on to the grass verge and made the other driver stop. The first driver was Ring; the infant in the pram was Patricia Horgan. As word filtered through the city centre that fateful afternoon, the Taoiseach Jack Lynch's state car stopped at Brian Boru Bridge so he could buy the Evening Echo. He rolled down the back window and the newspaperman, Johnny Chris Kelleher, told him the news about the death of his friend and team-mate.

'Oh no,' said Lynch, 'it can't be true.'

After an epic funeral that inspired comparisons with those afforded the martyred Lord Mayors, Tomas MacCurtain and Terence MacSwiney, in the twenties, they brought Ring back to Cloyne and buried him in a graveyard that had been one of the beloved playing fields of his youth. Around Ring's wife Rita and his children Christy and Mary, was a crowd containing perhaps the greatest collection of hurlers ever gathered in one place together. They had come from all over to pay their final respects.

'As long as the red jerseys of Cork and the blue of Munster and the green, black and gold of Glen Rovers, colours that Christy wore with such distinction, as long as we see these colours in manly combat the memories of Christy's genius and prowess will come tumbling back with profusion,' said Lynch, in his graveside eulogy, his voice crackling with emotion. 'We will relish and savour them for we will hardly see their likes again. And men who are fathers and grandfathers now will tell their children and grandchildren with pride that they saw Christy Ring play. The story will pass from generation to generation and so it will live.'

So it will live.

Danno

The sepia print of Danno O'Mahony's arrival on the dock at Cobh in the summer of 1936 is a snapshot of a matinee idol coming home. His hair is immaculately coiffured, a tailored two-piece suit hangs perfectly from his broad frame, and a sheepish grin is breaking across that lantern-jawed face. Men are swarming around him with their hats aloft in triumph, young boys are jostling to get closer to the hero, and the few women present are smiling beatifically. He looks like he's just stepped off a sound-stage in Hollywood.

At this remove, it's almost impossible to grasp what O'Mahony must have meant to Cork people when he wrestled his way to a world title. The hurlers were in the middle of a ten-year long famine, the footballers hadn't won an All-Ireland in nearly a quarter of a century and the soccer clubs were struggling on the national stage. The country was fighting an economic war with Britain and the only glint of sporting success to lighten the gloom had been Dr. Pat O'Callaghan's second hammer gold in 1932. Then, Danno went to America and came home a champion.

'A reception committee, travelled to Wilton to welcome Danno to Cork,' wrote Sean Beecher in "Day by Day; A Miscellany of Cork History". 'From an earlier hour, huge crowds thronged the route of the procession and thousands congregated at Victoria's Cross. It was a reception, The Cork Examiner stated, 'of a size unique in Cork's history'. The official party took their seats in an open landau [a four-wheeled horse-drawn carriage], decorated with the tricolour and Old Glory, and led by ten bands, with another bringing up the rear, it proceeded down the Western Road and Patrick Street to the Lower Glanmire Road.'

Danno O' Mahony know as "the Irish Whip" is greeted by friends and supporters at Cobh after he arrived home from America where he won the World Wrestling Championship.

At a massive banquet in the Arcadia Ballroom, the Lord Mayor, Alderman Sean French, presented the wrestler with a silver tea-set and gave his wife Esther – an Irish-American from Massachusetts – a Tara Brooch. Although another lavish formal dinner was held in his honour at the Hibernian Hotel in Dublin, the most emotional celebration of the return was in his native Ballydehob. Photographs of the scenes in the West Cork town show flags and bunting draped across the width of the main drag and locals dressed in their Sunday best thronging the street waiting to gaze at the diamond-encrusted championship belt worth a reputed $10,000.

Imagine their pride. Danno O'Mahony had been born at Dreenlomane, three miles outside the village on September 29th, 1912. At his baptism, Father James O'Donovan supposedly remarked to the proud parents, Big Dan and Susan, that he was one of the strongest babies the curate had ever baptised. Maybe he did say that. Who's to know? When a boy goes out into the world and reflects glory back on the home place like he did, colourful details are inevitably appended to the birth of the legend. What is not in dispute is that he certainly inherited good sporting genes. A farmer by trade, his father, Big Dan, was also a noted jumper and weight-thrower at athletic meets, and Danno's own brothers were all good athletes; Florence, a national champion several times at the 56lb weight throw, was the best of them.

At the age of 21, Danno and Florence both enlisted in the Irish Army where they quickly distinguished themselves in the athletic rather than the military sphere. In any case, one brother was to have his time in uniform prematurely ended. On leave from The Curragh one weekend, Danno came upon Father Cashman, the local priest from Ballydehob, in a spot of bother down the hill from the O'Mahony homestead. The curate's car had skidded off the road into a ditch and he asked the young soldier if he might be able to quickly source a horse to pull the vehicle out.

There was no need for that. Twenty years after another man of the cloth had praised his strength at the baptismal font, O'Mahony took hold of the rear bumper and lifted the car clean out. Suitably bowled over, Cashman recommended the broth of a boy think about wrestling as a career and put him in touch with a coach up in Cork city. Of course, another version of this anecdote has O'Mahony dragging the vehicle out of the ditch when he was just 12

Danno with family and friends at his home village of Ballydehob.

years old and not yet fully grown. The stories are to be relished and passed on rather than held up to forensic examination.

His life certainly took a fortuitous turn in 1934. Three thousand miles away, in a country in the grip of the Great Depression, Paul Bowser, a promoter and horse-trainer from Worcester, Massachusetts, happened upon a scheme to help improve flagging attendances at wrestling events. With the memory of the popularity of the great 19th century Irish-American boxer John L. Sullivan still fresh in his mind, Bowser decided that with proper management, an Irish wrestler might just turn into a box-office smash.

Bowser dispatched Jack McGrath, one of his trusted lieutenants, to sail across the Atlantic and bring back an instant boost to the sport's fortunes. After two-time Olympic hammer gold medallist O'Callaghan refused his advances, O'Mahony hovered into view. The remainder of his contract with the army was bought out and following a training stint in London, designed presumably to knock the edges off the neophyte wrestler, the pair of them returned to America. There, Freddie Moran, a veteran trainer in New York, was enlisted to intensify the education of the new boy.

'A new face has appeared near the top in big league wrestling, the direct answer to Paul Bowser's prayers,' wrote Boston sportswriter Doc Almy previewing O'Mahony's American debut. 'Daniel O'Mahony of Ireland will disport in the feature bout at Boston Garden in the first week of the New Year. It is fitting and timely that a performer of undoubted merit should show his wares in one of the greatest cities for real sport on the map. Best of all as we see it, O'Mahony is a genuine Irishman with a delightful unfeigned brogue, plenty of wit, gentlemanly manners outside the active part of his profession and plenty of strength when engaged in it.'

In the first week of January, 1935, Danno O'Mahony (with an e inserted into his last name by the Americans) climbed through the ropes at the Boston Garden and took his first professional bow. Before 14,000, he defeated Ernie Dusek from Nebraska with a straight falls win in 15 minutes and 50 seconds. The bout marked the first appearance of The Irish Whip, the manoeuvre in which he grabbed his opponent's arm, held it straight out at the side and rotated it in a full circle before flipping him over his head.

It would become his trademark, his nickname on the posters and the sign over the bar he later opened in Santa Monica, California. Over the next seven months, he fought and won 54 times at some of the most fabled arenas in American sport as his march to the title gathered pace.

'In one short year in the United States, matman Danno O'Mahoney appeared in more towns and cities, drew more money and wrestled before more people than the highly touted and praise-agented "Dynamite" Joe Louis,' wrote Marcus Griffin in "Fall Guys: The Barnums of Bounce, The Inside Story of the Wrestling Business, America's Most Profitable and Best Organised Professional Sport". 'During that period, after all expenses were deducted, O'Mahoney made 150,000 dollars clear for his own particular pocketbook. While Louis earned much more in the same period, training expenses and the division of his earnings among various piece-men and racketeers who cut in on him, brought his net earnings to approximately 100,000 dollars.'

The way in which Griffin compares the wrestling champion and the boxer who eventually took the heavyweight title in 1937 point up the sport's popularity in America at the time. Although box offices were down – how else could they be in a country with such a depressed economy – wrestling was still a lucrative business for the top performers, and O'Mahony's relentless march towards the top of the profession gathered pace throughout the first half of 1935. It culminated in two fights in three days that completed his trip from obscurity to world champion.

On June 27th at Fenway Park, home of baseball's Boston Red Sox, O'Mahony defeated Jim 'The Gorgeous Greek' Londos with a scissors hold and took the New York version of the world heavyweight title. When news of that triumph filtered back to Ballydehob, locals held a torchlight procession through the town and at the bottom of Staball Hill, Father Coffey gave a speech outlining the achievements of the 23-year-old exile. Three days after besting Londos, O'Mahony went across Boston to another baseball diamond, Braves' Field, to take on Ed Don George in what was classed as a bout to unify two rival world title belts.

The final act of a bruising 90 minute contest came when O'Mahony flung George – another from the Freddy Moran stable - over the ropes and out of the ring. Apparently knocked out, George struggled to climb back in by the count of 20 and the Corkman was declared the winner. Inevitably, the vanquished wrestler complained about the way the count was conducted but the objection wasn't sustained. Within a month, O'Mahony successfully defended the title for the first time against the veteran competitor Ed 'Strangler' Lewis in Boston but was soon back on the road, bringing his new billing with him to venues far and near. By the end of that year however, his reign was under critical attack.

'Danno O'Mahony and Everett Marshall, top ranking heavyweights, continue to forge ahead, each in their own individual territory,' wrote Jim Amann in Ring magazine, the boxing bible which then also covered wrestling. 'O'Mahony, the real champion, insofar as successorship is concerned, should meet the LaJunta claimant (Marshall) and end all the squabbling which isn't doing the wrestling game any bit of good.'

Not everybody felt wrestling was a legitimate sport. While the story that a drunken press officer sent out the results of one evening's contests before they begun has never been proven, there are numerous instances where sportswriters correctly published the outcome of matches in the early evening editions of newspapers, hours before the wrestlers even entered the ring. Often, aggrieved promoters would feed this information to friendly hacks to scupper rivals trying to sell tickets in their town. In this regard, most wrestling matches were almost certainly decided long before the two competitors entered the ring. So too was the destiny of the champions.

'The dethroning of O'Mahony is scheduled to take place between now and the Irishman's return to his native land in March,' wrote Harry Grayson, in

Danno O' Mahony beating Yukon Robert at the Boston Gardens in 1936.

Galesburg Daily Register-Mail, an Illinois newspaper on December 3, 1935. 'O'Mahony has served his purpose and even the clan [the promotional alliance running the sport] is commencing to object to his being the head man.The most damaging indictment against the former soldier is that he cannot be brought back to the more important centres at a profit. O'Mahony had little or no experience when Jack McGrath, of Worcester, imported him.

'Danno obtained a lot of publicity through the introduction of the Irish Whip but it generally was agreed that Jim Londos presented the title to him in Boston last summer. Danno was quite an attraction for a time, particularly with the Irish of South Boston, but lost appeal with each appearance. The grappling lords basked in the glow of O'Mahony's sucker money for a time, but have emerged with a painful sunburn.They fumbled with the gates when they tried to stuff Danno down the patrons' throats. He does not look the part of a champion, and shortly began to attract unfavorable press notices. This is fatal to a star pachyderm.'

The journalists were on O'Mahony's case. One New York writer described the Corkman as knowing no more about wrestling 'than John Quincy Adams did at the age of three'. In Detroit, another critic asserted that the champion 'looked like a high-school tackle trying to make the (grid-iron) team. The background to all this is that wrestling was essentially divided into rival conglomerates at the time. On one side there was the Wrestling Trust, a quintet of promoters, including O'Mahony's sponsor Paul Bowser; on the other, there were rival promoters Jack Pfeffer and the Johnson Brothers battling for a slice.'

'O'Mahony wasn't another Jim Londos (the Greek was acknowledged as one of the greatest of all time) but he was a short-term improvement at the box office,' wrote Steve Yohe on "The Other Arena", a wrestling history website. 'Then disaster fell on the Trust, as on March 2, 1936 Dick Shikat double-crossed O'Mahony in Madison Square Garden and stole the title. Pfeffer and Al Haft backed Shikat's double cross. An injunction was filed against Shikat, taking him to court. The trial started in April 1936 in Columbus, Ohio and the first witness called was Jack Curley, described as "the leading sports promoter in the country. The trial that was going to "blow the lid off pro-wrestling" never really got started as Shikat was "upset" and lost the World title to Ali Baba in Detroit on April 24, 1936.'

Regardless of the legal action and the disputed nature of his defeat, O'Mahony fought on. A month later, he was in Detroit to take on Dynamite Gus Sonnenberg and in the newspaper previews of the contest, he is described as holding a version of the world title. Indeed, much was made of the fact that O'Mahony was bringing the diamond-encrusted belt with him to the match. The sport had essentially splintered and belts proliferated at the same pace they did in boxing in more recent times.

Five years after losing to Shikhat, records show the Irish Whip fought three times in ten days at venues as far apart as Toronto, Philadelphia and Minneapolis. That he did well financially in the time before America's entry into World War 2 effectively ended his career is evident from the fact O'Mahony opened a bar and nightclub in Santa Monica, California. Even from that distance, he was a regular visitor to Ireland. On one such trip, on November 2nd, 1950, the car he was driving hit a lorry outside Portlaoise and he died that night. Survived by his wife and four children, the 38-year-old is commemorated in his prime by a 6 foot-five inch life-size bronze statue that stands sentry in Ballydehob.

Revisionist histories may force us to re-examine the exact nature of his world title win but what can't be disputed about O'Mahony's career is this. Plucked from obscurity and catapulted into the highest echelon of a sport that was then one of the biggest entertainment industries in America, he more than held his own. Long after the reverse by Shikat, he was good enough to make serious money plying his wares at massive arenas all over the United States. It wasn't his fault that he signed up (perhaps unknowingly) to a game that was fundamentally corrupt, in a profession where his own destiny was often more than likely out of his own hands.

'Gerard Egan, a sports promoter, staged a number of spectacular wrestling contests in Long's Field at Victoria's Cross,' wrote Tom McElligott in "Six O'Clock All Over Cork". 'In one of these Danno was billed to wrestle Charlie Strack, an 18-stone American. At one stage of the contest, the latter was seated on Danno's back, occupied apparently in methodically gouging out his eyes. Such cruelty, even in wrestling, was thought to be excessive and after the referee had sought in vain to separate them, Danno with a mighty heave displaced Strack and in the best tradition of a thriller film was free. He then began to swing Strack round and round before slamming him not once but many times face downwards on the mat.'

The account of a contemporary Cork observer working as a steward at the event, it may be the best way to remember him.

Dr. Pat

After the sports meet had ended, Pat and Con O'Callaghan loaded up their bicycles with the prizes they had won. An alarm clock, a penknife, a barometer, an enamel bucket and a rose bowl were among the booty garnered. As they made their way along the roads back towards their home in Derrygallon, darkness began to fall and they chanced upon a dance in a village hall. Deciding a break was in order, they parked the bikes and spent a couple of hours enjoying the festivities.

They resumed their journey in better fettle and cycled on through the night towards north Cork. Dawn broke and with it, came a rumbling in their stomachs. They hadn't eaten since the athletics the previous afternoon and with no houses in sight, were forced to improvise to sate their hunger. Following a starter of wild blackberries gleaned from a bush, they feasted on turnips that Pat picked from a nearby field and prepared with the pen knife won earlier. The meal was then washed down with milk that Con had coaxed from a cow and gathered in the rosebowl.

Historians can quibble with the veracity of the detail but we think you get the idea. Ireland's greatest ever Olympian came of age in a simpler era. One biography lists his childhood hobbies as poaching, hunting and playing football in Cronin's Field. What other lifestyle would have contributed so naturally to his aerobic conditioning than one in which 30-mile cycles were considered the norm? How much joy and fun must himself and his brothers have knocked out of tramping the highways and byways in search of fresh competition? Can we even visualise the rural idyll which fashioned O'Callaghan and sent him out to bring back two gold medals to a brand-new nation?

'All the competitors were sitting on the bench, awaiting our turn to throw,' said O'Callaghan of the scene at the 1928 Olympic Games in Amsterdam. 'I was a bit back after the first round, sixth or seventh? I was happy to make the final and then in the fourth round, I went into the lead ahead of Ossian Skjold and that was the end of it."

That was the end of it. And the beginning of the legend. Two years previously, he'd seen the hammer for the first time. Thirteen months earlier, he'd made his competitive debut in the event. Now, he was the world's best. It was the kind of wondrous feat only within the remit of a natural athlete. He was certainly that. Known as a brilliant hurdler, jumper and discus-thrower via his feats in the red vest of Banteer AC at the various sports held around the country, he didn't pick up his first hammer until his medical studies brought him to Dublin.

Dr Pat O'Callaghan competing in the Hammer event at a meeting in North Cork.

'At the UCD grounds in Terenure, he spied a man throwing this highly unusual and costly object at the end of the field,' wrote Johnny Watterson and Lindie Naughton in their book "Irish Olympians". 'This prized hammer was jealously guarded by its owner – but when O'Callaghan discovered that

Olympic gold medal winner Dr Pat O'Callaghan and Bob Tisdall are paraded through the street of Cork following their arrival home from the 1932 Los Angelus Olympic Games.

he kept it in the gatekeeper's lodge, he found a way of "borrowing" it for some exploratory throws. His main goal in life was now to find himself a similar implement. During the summer, a pile of cannonballs outside Macroom Castle caught his eye. He managed to acquire a couple and then made his own hammer with the help of the local blacksmith, by boring a hole in the ball and inserting some steel clothes line.'

He spent the summer of 1926 in Knockardsharrive. His mother's relatives had a farm there and his expressed purpose was to hone his hammer skills while based there.

'He set out a throwing circle in the front field and with the determination and total concentration that was his trademark he worked up his new technique,' wrote the Castlemagner Historical Society. 'It was an exhilarating time for all concerned as the hammer came in for rough handling, frequently breaking to threaten life and limb and involving many tedious searches in heavy summer undergrowth for the elusive ball.'The training was regularly interrupted for farm work interspersed with impromptu cross-country races, fiercely contested over hedges and 5-bar gates. When he introduced quantities of raw eggs and bloody raw steak to his diet, the charm of his deep blue eyes and shock of fair hair was not enough to offset the disgust of the women of the household.'

With coaching input from Superintendent Dinny Carey, trainer of the Garda team, and advice garnered from three-times Olympic hammer champion, John J. Flanagan, the training paid off. In 1927, he threw over 142 feet and defeated reigning champion Tipperary's Bill Britton to take his first national title. He still hadn't mastered the art however, and upon returning to Dublin for his studies, he was waylaid outside the anatomy room of the Royal College of Surgeons by a small, immaculately dressed man named John Tallon. A professional tailor who had studied the science of the hammer and gauged O'Callaghan's speedy development into a top-class thrower, Tallon came to offer him his services as a technical coach.

Despite knowing full well this character had never competed as a thrower, O'Callaghan was somehow convinced he could do with his advice. Within the year, he was travelling to Amsterdam, along with his brother Con who had been selected as a decathlete. A romantic entanglement truncated Con's experience of the ninth Olympiad but Pat was in top form going into competition. Coming off the back of a sustained run of success which had seen him throw over 171 feet in Kanturk just weeks earlier, he only needed to go as far as 168 feet and seven inches to narrowly beat out Skjold for the gold.

The first man from the Irish Free State to win an Olympic title was born in the North Cork townland of Derrygallon on September 15th, 1905. The third and youngest son of Paddy and Jane O'Callaghan, a farmer and a nurse respectively, he was blessed with good bloodlines. Jane's brother Tim Healy was a national sprint champion who had played for Cork/Dromtariffe in the 1893 All-Ireland football final, a rancorous game later awarded to Wexford after Cork walked off in protest at crowd interference.

Older siblings Sean and Con were both keen sportsmen and Pat dabbled in everything. Apart from athletics, he played football for Dromtariffe, hurled for Castlemagner and was apparently training for the university boxing championships when distracted by the hammer out in Terenure that fateful day. An ecumenical approach became his hallmark. Huge crowds greeted him upon his return to Kanturk from Amsterdam and although he confirmed his new-found pre-eminence in the discipline by subsequently shattering the Irish record at the Tailteann Games in Croke Park, he was soon assisting the town in another code. Whatever the truth of the well-known yarn about him converting a penalty from 75 yards out, he and Con definitely bulwarked a dominant pack as Kanturk won the County Cup final against Bandon at The Mardyke on April 21st, 1929.

At six foot one, and 16-and-a-half stone, O'Callaghan was the quintessential athlete. Apart from his dexterity with the oval ball and his supremacy in the hammer, he won three consecutive Irish championships in the High Jump and, at various times, was also national champion in the discus, the 16lb shot, the 56lb weight throw. Not bad going for somebody juggling the demands of a burgeoning medical career. Having qualified as a doctor at the age of 20, he served in the RAF Medical Corps between 1926 and 1928 because he was too young to be licenced to practice in Ireland.

Having paid his own fare to the Netherlands four years earlier, by the time the 1932 Olympics came round, the elite Irish athletes were being treated more professionally. Sponsorship had been secured from Guinness and a church gate collection also carried out to fund the prohibitive cost of sending them 6,000 miles to Los Angeles. General Eoin O'Duffy, president of the National Athletic and Cycling Association of Ireland, even assembled the Irish squad for three weeks collective training in Ballybunion in Kerry before sailing to America.

There had been a slight doubt cast on O'Callaghan's participation. By that point in his professional career, he was working at Clonmel Mental Hospital, and the Mental Hospitals' Committee initially requested he pay for his own replacement at the facility for the duration of his absence. The authorities eventually saw sense and with three months' leave granted, he decamped to Kerry to work on his conditioning and technique. In truth, neither probably needed much improving.

The years since his first Olympic triumph had seen him hit the form of his life. At the 1930 National Championships, O'Callaghan won the hammer, the shot put, the discus, the high-jump, the 56lb over-the-bar throw, and the 56lbs without-follow. More than once, he'd come within an inch or two of breaking the world high-jump record, and had travelled as far as Sweden to

Dr Pat arrives at Newmarket, North Cork after the 1932 Olympics.

meet and inevitably beat his old rival Ossian Skjold in an international hammer invitational.

During the epic train journey across the width of the continent to Los Angeles, the Irish party stopped in Chicago and Denver to break up the arduous trip with work-outs. When they finally arrived at the Olympic village in Baldwin Hills overlooking the city, they were struggling with the intense heat of high summer in California. Despite adhering to his usual breakfast of six raw eggs, O'Callaghan still found himself shedding pounds in weight. At least he was faring better than team-mate Bob Tisdall, the 400m hurdler was spending most of his time in bed because of the oppressive weather.

On August 1st, the pair of them entered the Los Angeles Coliseum and in the space of less than an hour brought home two gold medals. Tisdall had been first up, coasting to victory in the final of his event. As that was going on, O'Callaghan was struggling. Unaware that the surface of the throwing circle in the arena was hard cinder, he'd worn shoes with steel spikes more suited to grass or clay. With the footwear playing havoc with his crucial third turn, he'd just managed to qualify for the final. Then, he'd borrowed a hacksaw and a file from a groundskeeper to try to make emergency repairs.

Fresh from his own victory, Tisdall joined him in the infield.'We held up the whole Olympic Games while we filed Pat's spikes down,' recalled Tisdall later.

Finland's Ville Porhola had taken advantage of O'Callaghan's difficulty and held the lead when the Corkman came to the circle for his final throw. The last of the spikes had been pared down, and rid of the final obstacle, he produced the effort of his life, hurling the steel ball and chain just an inch shy of 177 feet. With his title on the line, he had oustripped the Finn's best mark by over five feet.

'I felt then that I would be a very poor Irishman if I didn't rise to the occasion,' said O'Callaghan later.

The dramatic manner in which O'Callaghan had come from behind to retain his title brought the crowd to their feet.

'There was pandemonium in the stadium,' said Tisdall. 'Speech was impossible for almost five minutes and the few who did not appear to be Irish were shouting, if not for the significance of the achievement, for the manner of its doing. It was indeed a great achievement for Ireland.'

Among the Irish entourage on hand, former Olympic long jump champion Peter O'Connor – present as a judge and an NACA delegate – declared afterwards that the Corkman was 'unquestionably the most outstanding and popular figure in LA'. Certainly, he had caught the eye of Hollywood moguls, and having been persuaded to take a screen test, he was reputedly offered the part of Tarzan in a movie by Sam Goldwyn himself. O'Callaghan turned down that opportunity and once the team traversed the continent again, sailed out of New York on the Majestic, the largest liner then operating.

'On their arrival in Dun Laoghaire, government cars transported them to the RDS, where an impressive parade had assembled,' wrote Mark Quinn in "The King of Spring". 'Led by the Number One Army Band, veteran athletes including Peter O'Connor, the Garda Motor Cycle Corps, army athletes, boxers, and over 100 gardai marched towards the city centre. At the Mansion House, O'Duffy, O'Callaghan and Tisdall were met by Lord Mayor Alfie Byrne... From the Mansion House, the party continued to the Gresham Hotel on O'Connell Street where, once outside the hotel, O'Duffy, O'Callaghan and Tisdall stood on a motor car and took the salute of the passing parade. Upwards of 250,000 people are thought to have thronged the streets in celebration.'

Four years later, O'Callaghan was sitting in the stands in Berlin when he should have been defending his title, a victim of the NACA's battle for recognition from the IAAF. Not the first or the last great Irish athlete to suffer because of the workings of sports politicians. The pity was there looked to be every chance he could have made it three in a row. He'd begun experimenting with a new four-turn technique that had helped him to a new European record in 1935. And a year after Hitler's Olympics, he broke the world record in Fermoy. The throw was never recognised, ironically because the hammer he was using was heavier than standard.

Following a tragic accident in which his hammer struck and killed a young boy at Mallow in 1938, O'Callaghan retired from the sport. He emigrated to America for a short time where he dabbled in professional wrestling, a mooted bout against Danno O'Mahony never coming off. Though he dallied for just a little while in professional wrestling, O'Callaghan left his mark there too. According to one account, he picked up a 17-stone opponent in a bout, did three spins as if readying to throw the hammer and then flung the man out across the first rows of seats in the auditorium. Apocryphal? Probably only to those of us who never saw him in his prime.

Upon his return from the US, he established a General Practice in Clonmel, hometown of his wife Kitty O'Reilly. The couple raised four children there, and for nearly half a century, he was a revered doctor in the town. Perhaps inevitably, Clonmel Commercials GAA club enlisted his help in 1964. Between then and his death in 1991, he served as club chairman, vice-chairman, president, doctor, trainer, and was a selector on a fabled team that won three consecutive Tipperary county senior football championships. O'Callaghan retired from the medical profession in 1984, and spent his superannuation hunting and fishing near his home. The passions of his youth in Derrygallon became the pastimes of his old age.

Dr Pat O'Callaghan enjoyed an active retirement at his home in Clonmel until he died in 1991.

O'Brien

An hour before the race, Vincent O'Brien and Aubrey Brabazon went to the bar and ordered stiff brandies and ports. The Cork trainer had never been to Cheltenham before and now that he was about to send the Kildare jockey out on Cottage Rake, a 10-1 outsider in the 1948 Gold Cup, he needed to calm his nerves. Resolve suitably hardened, and the clock ticking down, O'Brien led the six-year old horse out on to the course himself. When they finally parted ways, he decided the best place to watch the outcome would be down at the final fence.

From that vantage point, he saw Martin Molony on Happy Home jump a length and a half clear of Cottage Rake and things didn't look good. But O'Brien didn't notice that Brabazon was grinning as he landed, confident his horse had the pace for the uphill finish. In those days, the course didn't have a P.A. commentary and befitting his quiet demeanour, O'Brien walked around behind the stands without asking a single punter which horse had actually won. Only when he came within sight of the winners' enclosure did Brabazon spot him and touch his cap to signal victory.

'The greatest moment of my life had just become a reality,' said O'Brien of that one-and-a-half length triumph. On March 4th, 1948, a few weeks shy of his 31st birthday, the most illustrious training career in history had taken its first significant step into the big leagues. The wider world had just caught a glimpse of his ability to spot something special in an unfancied animal.

The homecoming was an epic. Thousands greeted the horse's arrival on the train at Buttevant station, from where a nun and a pipe band led the parade

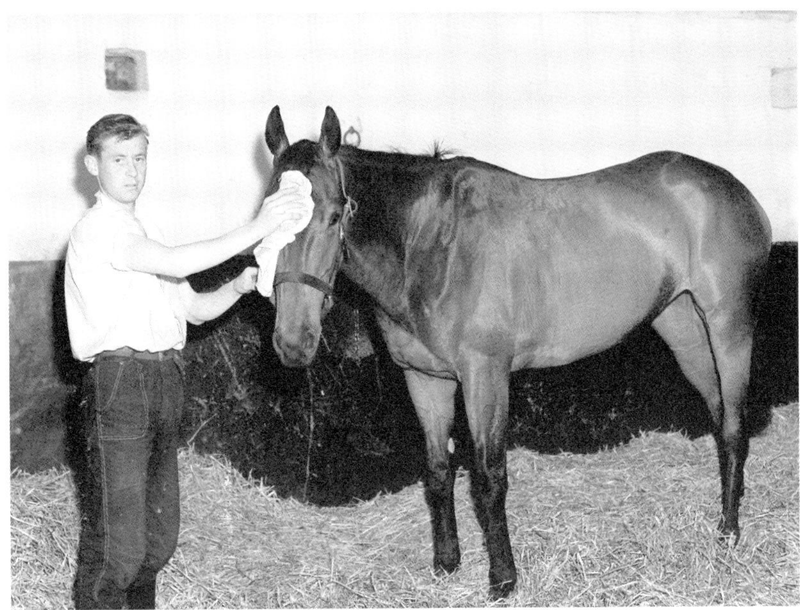

Vincent O'Brien at his stables at Rosegreen, Cashel, Co Tipperary in 1959.

six miles back to Churchtown. O'Brien's home place was already en fete. Acting on a tip-off from Cottage Rake's owner Frank Vickerman, the publicans had stocked up with barrels of porter because he assured them he'd pay for everything from the horse's winnings. A bonfire blazed and from the centre of the crowd, the local curate spoke and solved the problem of the celebration falling in the middle of Lent.

'All you who have made resolutions to abstain from such things as cigarettes, sweets and above all, the booze, can forget about it this night and indulge yourselves,' said the priest. 'You can renew your resolutions when the bell rings tomorrow at noon.'

Cottage Rake took home the Gold Cup the following two years and Brabazon later described the horse's supporters in North Cork as 'a semi-religious movement'. It was around the trainer, however, that the phenomenon had begun to wrap itself. The Corkman had won the first five races he entered at Cheltenham, and four of the following seven. Not just any old races either. Hatton's Grace, known as 'the ugly duckling', delivered him three successive Champion Hurdles between 1949 and 1951 and by the time he quit training jumpers in 1959, 11 trips to the Festival had yielded an astonishing 22 winners.

Cheltenham hadn't been the only happy hunting ground. One Friday night in 1955, four jockeys gathered for a meeting in O'Brien's room at Liverpool's

Adelphi Hotel. With each about to ride one of his horses in the Grand National at Aintree the following afternoon, he showed them film of Early Mist and Royal Tan winning the previous two Nationals. After they had watched the races again and again, the trainer spoke at length about the areas of the course he needed them to avoid and the most advantageous track to take. Three of his horses managed to finish, and when Pat Taaffe steered Quare Times to victory, O'Brien had completed another treble; he'd trained three different horses to win the Grand National in three successive years.

For most trainers, a decade of success like the one O'Brien enjoyed following Cottage Rake's first Gold Cup would represent a lifetime's work. For him, it was merely an exciting opening chapter to a sizeable tome that would engross readers so much that towards the end of the book, they could easily forget exactly how it had all begun. If his achievements with jumpers heralded the arrival of a great, it was on the flat that O'Brien surpassed all that had come before him in the sport.

'I rode my first winner for Vincent nearly 40 years ago,' said Lester Piggott in 1994, of the man with whom he'd shared 15 classic triumphs in Ireland and England. 'He has been part of my life ever since. In my opinion he is the greatest trainer of all time.'

From the greatest jockey, that is some praise. Taken in tandem with his National Hunt career, his record of 44 classic winners, among them six Epsom Derbys, has long rendered moot all arguments about his pre-eminence. There is no Mackey to this Ring. Atlhough he handed in his trainer's licence and retired in 1994, O'Brien finished first in a 2003 Racing Post readers' poll to establish the top 100 personalities in the history of British and Irish racing. Almost thirty per cent of voters plumped for a man who walked off the racecourse for the final time nine years earlier.

'This is a great lift for me,' said O'Brien of the honour. 'It's come as a surprise and is a tremendous thrill. I am really touched, especially by the fact that it was a readers' phone vote. It is like winning a couple of Derbys. We followed '100 Racing Greats' here in Australia with great interest. It's a great honour.'

He was speaking then from Perth on the west coast of Australia, the latest location for his retirement, the home country of his wife Jacqueline. The couple were engaged three weeks after they first met at a dinner in Dublin's Russell Hotel in 1950. She knew nothing about horse racing except that her father, an MP back home, didn't approve of horse trainers. When the time came to inform him of her new romance, she told him she'd fallen for an Irish farmer. Well, that was kind of true.

O'Brien was born on April 9th, 1917 at Clashganiff House, near Churchtown where his father Dan farmed and trained a small string of horses. A selling yard where money was tight, Dan's biggest winner came when Solford took the Irish Cambridge in 1939. In time, Vincent became his assistant and after his father's death in 1943, took out a licence. Supposedly, the only other career option available to him was as a butcher. His elder stepbrother had inherited the house and the gallops, so the 26-year-old leased them back, picked up a couple of horses, and laid the foundations for an empire.

In his first season, Good Days won the Irish Cesarewitch and Drybob dead-heated for the Irish Cambridgeshire. But for the dead-heat it would have been an 800-1 double. The betting would have factored into O'Brien's day too. His relationship with the bookmakers begun as a boy when he put £4, the proceeds from selling a greyhound he'd bred himself, on a 10-1 winner. Although his every move in the later stages of his career came with corporate backing, there was a time when O'Brien needed wins for reasons other than padding the most illustrious record in the history of the sport.

At a time when he was still largely unknown in England, he was so certain Hatton's Grace could take the 1949 Champion Hurdle that the stable started backing the horse ante-post at 33-1. By race time, he went off at 100-7. It scarcely mattered then because they'd got on him at all points in between. Although O'Brien lost his licence for three months in 1954 for alleged discrepancies between the English and Irish form of his horses, it took a few years for the bookies there to fully comprehend that every O'Brien horse was a contender.

Not every betting coup ran smooth. While accepting the prestigious Sir Peter O'Sullevan Award – recognition of a lifetime's contribution to the sport - on behalf of his father in 2001, Charles O'Brien told the story of the 1958 Prix de l'Arc de Triomphe. Having wagered a tidy sum on his runner Ballymoss, O'Brien and O'Sullevan spent the time before the race frantically running around the course trying to lay-off those bets. The ground had come up soft and they feared had spoiled the chances of Ballymoss.

'Can you imagine Saeed bin Suroor and Aidan O'Brien running around Longchamp to do the same today?' asked Charles O'Brien.

That Ballymoss won despite the going was one more tribute to his father, the man who formed a perfect bridge between the two different eras in the sport. He came of age when it was still possible for the small-time trainer to make a huge impact, but by the date of his departure, the game had changed irrevocably into a sport where billionaires dominated. O'Brien's own role in the transformation was, of course, significant.

At the Keeneland Sales in Kentucky in 1972, he was introduced to Robert Sangster. He'd once been advised by the Irish-American owner Jack Mulcahy 'to get a piece of the action' himself. In a partnership that turned Coolmore Stud into a major player in international breeding, O'Brien, Sangster and John Magnier decided upon a simple plan. They would find potential stallions to syndicate for big money. British racing would never be the same again.

'He almost goes into a trance studying a yearling,' said Sangster later. 'I've watched him in the heat of Kentucky at over 100 degrees in the shade standing looking at a horse for a quarter of an hour. He's visualising what it's going to be like as a three-year-old. He can see the future better than anyone.'

Arguably the greatest example of his ability to spot potential was The Minstrel. At Keeneland in July, 1975, they saw him first, a small, chestnut-coloured yearling with four white legs out of Northern Dancer.

'He stared quietly into the yearling's eye,' wrote Patrick Robinson in his book "Horsetrader". 'And the little horse stood stock still, staring back. Vincent smiled at him, pulled his ear gently, ran his hand down the horse's neck . . . "He's more than 14.1 hands," he said. "But not much. He could just be big enough, but only just".'

They forked over $200,000 for him that day and nobody else in the room felt they'd got a bargain. After a dodgy enough start, The Minstrel won the English Derby, the Irish Derby, and the King George VI and Queen Elizabeth Stakes at Ascot in the summer of 1977 and they later syndicated him for $9m. Storm Bird, a less impressive performer on the course, turned out to be such a great horse at stud that they sold him for $28m. He'd cost them $1m.

'The Irish have a natural affinity with horses,' wrote Sangster in a piece for The Sunday Times the week O'Brien retired in 1994. 'With Vincent, though, it was a unique gift. He always told me it was in the eye. He'd stare at

Vincent O'Brien in a pensive mood in April 1984.

a horse's head and would be able to read something, look down into its soul. I tried to learn from him by following him around for seven or eight hours a day but soon realised that I had better rely on him. He was also brilliant with pedigrees. He knew the idiosyncrasies of every family; for example, whether a particular family was too excitable and needed a steadying influence. That was why his advice on matings was invaluable.'

Although his natural instincts were enhanced through the decades by experience, there were a few failures too, the most spectacular being $13m they wasted on Seattle Dancer in 1985. Even before he and his cohorts revolutionised the bloodstock industry, O'Brien had won four Derbys and enjoyed enough of a reputation that Sangster admitted to being awed in his presence at their first meeting. By that point, O'Brien was known to all as 'The Master of Ballydoyle', the Tipperary stables to which he had moved back in 1951. Renowned for his attention to detail, employees at the complex called him 'The Fuhrer' because the place was run like a military operation.

'He worries about the small things,' said the American jockey Cash Asmussen once, 'but the important small things.'

The results of such precision were self-evident. After temporarily losing his licence for a horse testing positive for a banned substance in 1960, Larkspur brought home his first Epsom Derby two years later and from then on the procession of champions consisted of names that would define the sport for a generation: Sir Ivor, Nijinsky, Roberto, The Minstrel and Alleged. Of them all, Nijinsky, is usually acknowledged as the finest he ever trained.

O'Brien had initially gone to Canada to inspect a colt named Ribot for one of his owners, Charles Englehard. Unimpressed by that prospect, he spotted Nijinksy in a field at EP Taylor's farm in Canada and recommended this son of Northern Dancer be bought instead. More brilliant than any he'd ever worked with, the colt was also highly strung, tough to handle and needed to be handled carefully. Under the tutelage of O'Brien and with Piggott on board, Nijinsky would land the Triple Crown of 2000 Guineas, Derby and St Leger in an unforgettable summer in 1970. The role of jockey and trainer in the success was paramount.

'Nijinsky was the horse they were born to share,' wrote Brough Scott in his obituary of the horse in The Independent in 1992. 'A giant of a beast, as light on his feet and taut in his temperament as his spring-heeled namesake, he seemed the complete runner that their combined riding and training talents were one day bound to spawn. This time, we thought, Lester and Vincent were bringing us the ultimate. They had brought us so much already.

'In 1970, Piggott was 34; O'Brien, 53. Both were at the absolute height of their powers and the only truly acknowledged geniuses in their respective professions. They were both great actors, O'Brien playing the shy, studious perfectionist on whose soft-spoken words millionaires and punters alike would ponder; Piggott was even more sparing of speech and mercurially difficult to understand, both on a horse and off it. As a double act, Vincent and Lester brought mystery to match the excitement.'

Ten years after Piggott had finished as O'Brien's stable jockey, they enjoyed a unique postscript to their partnership. Their last great fling came at New York's Belmont Park in the Breeders' Cup Mile. For the trainer whose best days were gone – the arrival of the major Arab owners had dried up the supply of brilliant young horses throughout the eighties - the jockey came out of a retirement punctuated by a year in prison to ride Royal Academy to a sen-tional victory. Although College Chapel gave him his 25th Royal Ascot winner in 1993, many regard the Belmont triumph as the crowning achievement of his career.

'Racing has been very good to me,' said O'Brien the day he announced his retirement. 'It has enabled me to pursue a career which combined work with pleasure. When I started training the bloodstock industry in Ireland was still developing. Now we are one of the major racing and breeding countries in the world. I have had the good fortune to have had many wonderful horses and owners, and have been ably assisted by dedicated staff down the years. To these and all my friends in racing I am most grateful.'

The feeling, we suspect, was mutual.

Nijinsky ridden by Lester Piggott being led to the enclosure by Vincent O'Brien at Ascot in July 1970.

Kiernan

At the age of five, Tom Kiernan was the mascot for a schoolboys' rugby match at Cork Constitution. Led on to the field by international referee Dickie McGrath, the child was given the task of starting the game with a ceremonial kick-off. When he swung his foot that day, Kiernan didn't even manage to connect with the ball. Like most kids probably would have, he missed the target and kicked air. Not quite quarter of a century later, the same boy would be responsible for 35 of the 38 Test points scored by the 1968 Lions on their tour of South Africa. The start may have been inauspicious but his journey through the sport was an epic.

He captained UCC, Cork Constitution, Munster, Ireland and the British Lions, and for a long time was the most capped full-back in the history of the sport. He pocketed 13 Munster Senior League medals and seven Munster Senior Cups, and for those living in the Heineken Cup era, it is important to note that those competitions meant something big back in the fifties, sixties and seventies. For those living in the Heineken Cup era, we might also point that Kiernan was one of those who basically invented the European competition that has made red Munster jerseys so fashionable on the streets of Cork this past few years.

'What he contributed on and off the field, and the circumstances in which he achieved what he did at administrative level, marks him down as arguably the greatest figure in the history of the game in his country,' said Syd Millar, a former colleague on the field with Irish teams and off it in the committee rooms of the IRFU. 'Most people do not know, and in many respects that is understandable, what he contributed and the manner in which he handled

the most critical situations. Some of the happenings could have led to the demise of the Five Nations and the European Cup. Tom Kiernan held European rugby together in those troubled times."

Previous page: Tom Kiernan kicks three points for Ireland against Wales at Cardiff Arms Park in 1969.

After finishing as a player, he carved out two further careers in the highest echelons of the sport. He coached the Munster team that became the first Irish side to defeat the All Blacks at Thomond Park in 1978, and four years later brought Ireland out of the wilderness to win the country's first Triple Crown in 33 years. Having become president of the Munster Branch in 1977, he also served terms as president of Cork Constitution and the IRFU, as chairman of ERC (European Rugby Cup), honorary treasurer of the IRB (International Rugby Board), and member of just about every heavyweight committee in Irish rugby up to his retirement in 2000.

That his career will never be replicated goes without saying. There will be other great players and other progressive administrators but in the professional domain, none could possibly make the transition from one role to the other the way he did in his own time. Not to mention that the demarcation of the game now would prevent anybody from impacting at so many different levels. The greatest irony may be perhaps that though he played and coached in the amateur era, his instincts on the field were always so professional. This much was evident from an early age.

Tom Kiernan shakes hands with President of Ireland, Eamon De Valera at Lansdowne Road in February 1968 .

Although he won Munster Junior and Senior Cup medals at Presentation College, Kiernan wasn't selected on the provincial schools' team to play against Ulster at Ravenhill in 1957. On the morning of the game however, his friend and schoolmate Jerry Walsh had to withdraw from the selection and Kiernan was promoted to the starting XV. To that point, the Munster students had never emerged from Belfast victorious and that year's northern crop was formidable, bulwarked by Willie John McBride.

'Tom came into the side and it really was his cuteness that won the day for us,' recalled Jim Riordan, another member of the side, in The Limerick Leader. 'At half time we were 9-0 down and we came back in the second half with 14 men to beat them 9-10. Whenever we were under pressure in the backs Kiernan, would shout: 'go down injured'. This caused Ulster a lot of frustration, these interruptions in play.'

Imagine the maturity involved. A teenage boy with the wherewithal to know achieving victory in difficult circumstances often requires far more pragmatism than romance. That he was on the first Munster schools team to defeat Ulster on their home patch is appropriate because historic firsts were a -hallmark of his sporting life. Apart from the overturning of the All Blacks in 1978, he captained the first Irish team to win a Test in Australia in 1967, was full-back on the first Munster team to defeat Australia later the same year, and kicked the winning score the first time Ireland bettered South Africa in 1965.

'It went so low over the crossbar,' said Kiernan later of his 75th minute penalty that clinched the 9-6 victory at Lansdowne Road, 'that it was like a two-iron golf shot.'

Thirty years after he last played for Ireland, the rugby fans elected him full-back on the Lansdowne Legends XV, a selection of the best Irish team ever. How others viewed him tells its own story too.

'The Grey Fox belonged in the old last-line-of-defence school of full-backs whose priority was to catch well and find an unerring touch,' wrote Gareth Edwards in his book 100 Great Rugby Players. 'He could kick goals under pressure, and although he lacked the speed to enter the three-quarter line regularly and decisively, he recognised that this was a skill full-backs would have to cultivate, and tried to get up with a centre or a wing from time to time. Also on the field, it has to be said that nobody tried harder, or gave more than Tom Kiernan, a captain who led by example. It goes without saying that, as an opponent, Tom was one of the men Wales respected above all in my time.'

That he was on the first Munster schools team to defeat Ulster on their home

Born in Cork on January 7th, 1939, Kiernan's father Michael, a Westmeath man, had married Eileen Murphy from Tory Top Lane. A cousin of Noel Murphy, her brothers all played for Cork Constitution and the bloodlines going through her side of the family ran thick with rugby. The family home was on the Mardyke, and from a young age, Tom Kiernan was steeped in the sport he would later bestride.

By the time he walked into Presentation College, his older brother Jim was an established star at the school and the path had been laid out in front of him. The only curiosity of his stint there is perhaps that he once lost a vote for the job of vice-captain. Pres would be the only team in his career he never led. Just two years after his Leaving Cert, while still playing for UCC, he won his first Irish cap against England at Twickenham.

'Although Ireland lost by 8-5, all the tension was for the innocent-faced Cork boy with the button nose and crinkly fair hair from Presentation College, in his first international,' wrote Frank Keating in The Guardian, who travelled to the match as a spectator with his uncle John Kearney from Cork. 'He played a nerveless humdinger at full-back and the joy of my uncle's group was unconfined - and, of course, Tom Kiernan went on to be the world's most capped full-back, captain of the Lions and Munster's coach when they beat the All Blacks in 1978. And I was to grow up and become a friend of his until we stupidly fell out - completely my fault.'

Keating's mistake was to write, years after the fact, about how back in 1982, he spent the Friday night before Ireland played Scotland in the game that clinched Triple Crown in a pub drinking with Kiernan and some senior members of the Irish team. That Kiernan didn't appreciate the journalist's revelation about the unorthodox and relaxed preparation of his side was inevitable. The ability to unite his players and to have them believing themselves capable of great things was a feature of his coaching style. Keating had breached the inner sanctum.

patch is appropriate because historic firsts were a hallmark of his sporting life.

'The first time to do anything is hard,' says Gerry McLoughlin in Stand Up and Fight, Alan English's classic account of the 1978 victory over the All Blacks. 'First Cup medal. First time to play for your country. First Irish team to beat the All Blacks. It's only human to have doubts. You don't know if you can do it or not. Outside of Munster, people made you feel you weren't good enough. But Kiernan put the belief into us. He convinced us we could do it.'

In the build-up to that game, Kiernan had reinforced the idea in their heads that the New Zealanders were not superhuman. Sure, they had the reputation and the tradition but they were actually just fifteen men. He'd seen a Munster team robbed by the All Blacks at the Mardyke when he was just nine years old, played on a side that drew with them at Musgrave Park in 1973. He knew they were beatable on any given day. Part of his unique approach that afternoon in Limerick involved a long period of silence during the team meeting, a ruse designed to force the Munster players to think those thoughts for themselves.

Elsewhere in that book, English recounts a wonderful exchange between Kiernan and Martin Walsh, a Dubliner who was one of the touch judges in Thomond Park. With three minutes remaining on referee Norris White's watch, Walsh was officiating a line-out on halfway when he heard a voice behind shouting 'Martin, Martin...' When he turned around he saw Tom Kiernan, no longer able to sit in the stand as the final whistle loomed.

'If he asks you what time is left, tell him it's all up,' said Kiernan

'As if I wouldn't,' replied Walsh.

That little cameo epitomises Kiernan's attitude. Twelve points up and the clock ticking down yet no room for complacency. Even the soiree in Sean Lynch's pub on the eve of the triumph over Scotland in 1982 can be viewed – much like Brian Clough's celebrated use of the same tactic on the eve of a

European Cup final with Nottingham Forest – as one more canny strategy to get his players in the best frame of mind possible. Ollie Campbell has always maintained that Kiernan's approach to the Scottish game, including holding a then unheard of behind-closed-doors training session on the Thursday, meant he was never more relaxed before a crucial fixture.

'He (Kiernan) was an absolute rock,' said Campbell. 'People forget that going into the Welsh game we had lost seven and drawn one of our previous eight games. We had been whitewashed the previous season but as Moss Keane said, it had been Ireland's best ever whitewash.'

The Triple Crown had always lain out of Ireland's reach during his stint at full-back. He played 54 internationals but his best chance of a Triple Crown or a Grand Slam was scuppered in 1972 by Scotland and Wales refusing to travel to Dublin because of the political situation in the North. He was unlucky too with the Lions. Having travelled to South Africa in 1962, he returned as captain six years later, favoured for the post over Scotland's Jim Telfer. They lost three Tests and drew one but two of the defeats were by just five points, and Kiernan's contribution with his boot had basically kept them in every match.

'Kiernan's captaincy came slap in the middle of the period when coaches were taking over the direction of rugby matches from captains, and I often enjoyed late-night conversations with the Cork accountant on the validity of the new system,' wrote Gareth Edwards. 'On the Irish tour of Australia, he would argue, he had been in sole charge of coaching and also of tactics during matches. Suddenly, he found himself having to play a subservient role to Ronnie Dawson, appointed as the Lions' first-ever coach. This gave rise to a few misgivings on his part. After the tour had been underway for a few weeks, however, he was prepared to admit that there was much to be said for the new regime.'

Dawson and Kiernan later soldiered together in the committee rooms of Irish and international rugby. The administrative phase of his life was to prove as productive as the other two before it. His chairmanships of the Five Nations and the ERC came at particularly contentious junctures when, more than once, northern hemisphere rugby looked like splitting in two. Having been involved in its conception, many cite his stewardship in particular as crucial to saving the European Cup from early extinction, most especially during the self-imposed exile of English clubs.

'His career has been without parallel in the history of the game in this country,' wrote Edmund Van Esbeck in an Irish Times' piece on the occasion of Kiernan's retirement from the IRFU and the IRB in 2000. 'What he has given to the game - not just here but globally - most certainly deserves to be recognised and more widely appreciated than, I believe, it is. It could be said that, in every facet of the game that he embraced he made a profound impact. Rugby officials very often come in for criticism and sometimes it is justified. Likewise, there are occasions when credit is not given were it is due.

'Kiernan knows well what it is to be the recipient of severe criticism, particularly when he was chairman of ERC (European Rugby Cup). Some of the criticism he took, from across the water, was a subjective tirade from those whose agenda was prompted by self-interest and those who wanted to fashion the competition to suit themselves.'Kiernan's place at the pinnacle of Irish rugby will not depend on tradition, legend, hearsay or deceptive and exaggerated claims. The facts speak for themselves, for his has been a career without equal in the history of Irish rugby.'

Without equal. Without parallel. Van Esbeck said it best.

Tom Kiernan was coach of the Munster when they famously defeated the New Zealand All-Blacks 12 - 0 at Thomond Park in October 1978. Here he is seen engrossed in the action during the game.

Bruen

On the 14th tee at Royal Birkdale, Jimmy Bruen stood 3-up against America's Bob Sweeney with five holes to play in the final of the 1946 British Amateur. The championship was almost within his reach but Sweeney, an experienced competitor who'd won the title back in 1937, kept hanging in there. Until now. Playing into the wind, with driving rain cascading into his face, Bruen drove the green 520 yards away in two. The American's spirit was finally broken. They shook hands on the next hole.

'This is what I have always dreamed of, to take this back to Ireland,' said Bruen upon receiving the cup from FDB Hill, captain of Birkdale. 'It has been my life's ambition.'

Hundreds of fans had waited around in the inclement conditions to witness the ceremony, their joy at seeing the first Irish victory in the event heightened perhaps by the club's coup in having a plentiful supply of Scotch whisky – a rationed commodity up to then because of the war – on the premises. Bruen's triumph was all the more remarkable because he was driving the ball so far the course actually played harder for him than for most others. On Birkdale's many dog-legs, his tee shots invariably carried way past the traditional safe landing zones and forced him into audacious recoveries.

'James Bruen of Ireland is a lusty young champion if ever there was one,' concluded an editorial in Fairway and Hazard magazine. 'He is possessed of great strength and hits the ball vast distances not only from the orthodox places but from the unorthodox places as well. The fact that he broke three iron clubs in the week will probably go down to posterity. Yet it is not what happened to the club which is the least bit important but what happened to the ball. Bruen's powers of recovery are amazing.'

An amateur success of this ilk is often the springboard to greater things but Bruen never won a major. He never played professional golf. Yet, whenever the discussion turns to trying to identify the best player Ireland has ever produced, his name is right up there. Sometimes he wins the argument. Other times he doesn't. That he even figures in the debate is a tribute to what a brief but stellar career he enjoyed. His best years were stolen by World War II, his subsequent shot at redemption hampered by injury, yet a biography was written about him 25 years after his death and a prestigious amateur trophy is named in his honour.

Very often in sport, a truncated or shortened career lends itself to an exaggerated legacy. People remember an athlete or a player performing feats far beyond what they actually managed. In time, stories are passed down and ridiculously enhanced en route. They grow legs and tails and it becomes difficult to distinguish between what somebody did and what their supporters imagine them having done. With Bruen, this is not the case. We know this because the contemporaneous press clippings prove the veracity of what is now said and establish his greatness beyond doubt. Paeans had been written to him long before his moment of glory in Southport.

'At the risk of having a shower of controversy poured on my head, I make bold to say that Bruen was the best player in the field,' wrote Laddie Lucas, a

Jimmy Bruen (left) against Dr Billy O'Sullivan in the Irish Senior Cup at Douglas in 1939.

distinguished amateur player and journalist in the Sunday Express following the 1939 British Open where the 19-year-old Corkman had finished eight strokes behind the leader. 'In three years time, he will, I believe, be standing out in golf as emphatically as Bobby Jones did in his day. You can't say why he is so good. It is nature, of course. But what the boys do think is that he has a more accurate sense of distance than anyone else playing golf. Whatever it is, Bruen now stands alone, wonderfully alone and it is only a question of time before the golfing world is at his feet.'

The boy dubbed 'The Hibernian Wonder Golfer' by the Scottish media for his displays at St Andrews in that Open was born on May 8th, 1920 in Belfast. His father James J. Bruen was originally from Wilton in Cork city but after serving with the Connaught Rangers in the British Army, the Munster and Leinster Bank posted him to the northern capital. He and his wife Margaret moved back to Cork not long after christening the child James O'Grady Bruen. An injury sustained playing rugby at Presentation Brothers College in the Mardyke forced him to give up on the oval ball and his hurling career and to focus on his other sporting love. By 15, he was playing off six at Muskerry and Cork golf clubs and was ready for a bigger stage.

A close up view of Jimmy Bruen in action.

At the British Boys' Championship in 1935, he was defeated in the second round. One year later, he returned to win the trophy in impressive style at Birkdale, taking the final by 11 and 9. There followed the most impressive three years put in by any Irish teenage golfer. He won the Irish Close (twice), the Irish Amateur Open, and everywhere he went, served notice of his talent. Top amateur at the Irish Open three summers running, he held a share of the first-round lead at the 1938 British Open in Sandwich and finished leading amateur 12 months later at St. Andrew's.

In between all that, he became the youngest player to make a Walker Cup team, a record he held until Ronan Rafferty broke it in 1981. Bruen was still a student at Pres when in 1938 he was invited to the May trials used to select the team. With ten places up for grabs, and 24 aspirants, he made quite the impression during his time in Scotland. On the first day of official competition, he equalled the St Andrew's course record of 68 shot by Bobby Jones in 1927. It was a score that launched a thousand newspaper comparisons with the great American. More importantly, he went round four times in just 282 to cement his place in the side.

In the previous nine editions of the competition, Great Britain and Ireland had never won the Walker Cup. Moreover, only twice in that time had they even made a match of it. Things had reached such a sorry pass during their 1936 defeat by 10 and a half to one and half that the celebrated golf writer Henry Longhurst confessed to the nagging thought that he'd never live long enough to see the Americans beaten. Despite the obvious home advantage provided by St. Andrew's, the cream of British and Irish golfers weren't fancied in June, 1938 either.

As is so often the way in team golf, it wasn't a comprehensive win but an inspirational comeback that built the platform for a famous upset. In the first foursome of the competition, Bruen and Harry Bentley were three down with ten to play against Johnny Fischer and Charles Kocsis. Having been hyped beyond belief by the British press, Bruen had struggled for most of the match until he came good down the stretch. He holed a ten-foot putt on the 11th to reduce the deficit to one and his perfect approach to the 17th green clinched a famous draw that infused the whole team with confidence. Although that half was the only tangible contribution Bruen made to GB and I's subsequent victory – they would not win again until 1971 - his input in other ways is best described by a team-mate.

'Bruen gave the Americans a bit of an inferiority complex,' said Cecil Ewing, a Walker Cup team-mate from Sligo. 'They had heard of his phenomenal scoring on the old course before they arrived. In practice, he would continue to do these scores. The Scots are pretty hardened golf watchers. Only the best will do them. During the practice, they deserted the Americans to go and watch Bruen. He kept on going around in 68. He should have won a single but I made a mistake. I knew that (Johnny) Goodman, their champion, was playing badly but I thought he would still play top and put Bruen in against him. But they paid us the ultimate compliment of placing (Charlie) Yates who had just won the Amateur at number one and he beat Bruen narrowly.'

At 17, Bruen set a course record at Muskerry with a seven-under par 65. Over the following two seasons, he laid claim to the official course records at

Portmarnock, Royal County Down, Royal Portrush, Muskerry (again), Baltray, Little Island, Macroom, St Andrew's Old Course, and St Andrew's New Course. Dermot Gilleece –doyen of Irish golf writers - ranks a seven-iron he hit to the 15th green at Royal County Down during the 1939 Irish Open as the second best shot in the history of Irish golf. Eyewitnesses claim to have seen him drive the first three greens at Portmarnock. All this was achieved with a swing so bizarre it was christened 'The Bruen Loop'.

'Bruen drew the club back outside the line of flight and turned his wrists inward, to such an extent that at the top of the swing the club-head would be pointing in the direction of the tee-box,' wrote Pat Ward-Thomas in Masters of Golf. 'It was then whipped, no other word describes the action, inside and down into the hitting area with a terrible force. There was therefore in his swing a fantastic loop, defying all the canons of orthodoxy, which claims that the back and downswing should, as near as possible, follow the same arc. There must have been a foot or more between Bruen's arcs of swing.'

His first flush of success was interrupted by the outbreak of World War II and part of that enforced hiatus from serious competitive golf allowed him the opportunity to attempt to iron out the kink in his swing. Once the kink disappeared so did some of his genius and he reverted back to the method that had made his name. Apart from winning a couple of Cork Scratch Cups, Bruen got on with the other side of his life. He began working in the insurance business and, in 1943, married Eleanor Cremin, a Dubliner who by a strange quirk of fate he had played his first game of golf with as a child on holiday in Bundoran, County Donegal.

Having made such a triumphant return with his win at the 1946 British Amateur, Bruen's next move was surprising. He declared in an interview that he was looking forward to going sailing for the rest of summer and wasn't sure he'd play any more championships that year. He skipped the British Open and the Irish Amateur and citing the pressure of establishing his own Insurance Brokerage, restricted his golfing mostly to his home club. On fine days, he used to row across river from the house he and his wife bought near Blackrock Castle to Cork GC. The idyllic image that conjures offers perhaps one more clue to his lack of desire to participate regularly at the highest level in the post-war years.

'While there is no doubt that he was very involved in building his business, I do feel that there was something deeper,' wrote George F. Crosbie in his exhaustive biography "The Bruen Loop." 'I felt at the time, as I do now, that the real trouble was that Jimmy had lost his appetite for the rough and tumble and strain of championship golf. He never actually said so – but then Jimmy never said a lot about himself. Nevertheless, I don't really feel that Jimmy Bruen any longer had his heart in golf. He did, of course, make a number of appearances and inevitably showed that most of his skill was there, but these were isolated appearances. He was, in fact, a true amateur and even though he practiced quite a lot, he really was only a weekend golfer from this point on. I think it's true to say, that fame did not rest too easily on his shoulders, and while the public clamoured for more and more Bruen, he felt that, being an amateur, he should be free to lead his own life.'

Whether or not his appetite would ever have returned in full, his ability to mix it at the highest level was undermined further by a serious injury to his right wrist sustained in 1947. That cost him the whole of the 1948 season. The following year, he made the Walker Cup team again for the trip to Winged Foot, New York but at the same event two years later in Birkdale, his wrist collapsed completely on the first day of play. It is a testament to the size of his talent that he still figured on those selections at a time when golf took second place to his other interests in life.

He could still summon up the old magic when required. After a 17 year absence, he returned to the Irish Close at Killarney in 1963 and reached the semi-finals. At that stage, Joe Carr had to go 18 holes before finally defeating him, their epic contest long since entering the realms of folklore. Only a couple of years younger than his opponent, Carr had dominated the Irish amateur scene for two decades by then, winning 40 titles and amassing the sort of career record many once felt would be Bruen's.

'I have no hesitation in acknowledging Jimmy as the best Irish amateur I ever saw,' said Carr in Dermot Gilleece's "Breaking 80: The life and times of Joe Carr". 'No doubt about that. I played him three times but I thank God it wasn't in his heyday. People talk about John Burke, but he didn't have the shot-making talent of Jimmy, who, from 1938 until about 1942 was among the six best players in the world, amateur or professional, in my view. There was nobody in this country in the same class as him at that stage, myself included. Though I never felt I had to emerge from his shadow, I have no hesitation in saying that in his hey-day, Jimmy was better than me. And as a holer-out, he was probably better than me, even at my best.'

Like so much about Bruen, that remains a matter of conjecture.

Jack

The location was a pitch in Bandon known as 'The Bog' on the last Sunday in November, 1938. The occasion was the county senior football final between Clonakilty and St. Nicholas. On a dirty, wet afternoon, St. Nick's were having the better of it against a West Cork side determined not to lose its sixth such decider in seven years. They were leading 2-1 to 0-2 with the clock starting to wind down, when an attempted clearance by a Clon defender got caught in the wind and blew into a flooded stream nearby. The conditions had already finished off one ball and the future of the game was suddenly cast into doubt.

This was roughly the point when Jack Lynch assumed control. Demonstrating the leadership skills of a future Taoiseach and the desperation of a man who knew little football glory to that point in his career, he waded into the gushing waters, swam after the ball, recovered it and promptly returned to man his position for the time remaining. What else could he have done? He and half his team were chasing a county double, and just up from intermediate ranks that season, probably didn't fancy giving the more experienced Clonakilty side a replay the following week. The Northsiders and Lynch hung on for their first football title.

Not quite seven years later, Lynch was standing at the Number 16 bus stop in Kenilworth Square, Terenure on the Sunday morning of the 1945 All-Ireland football final. Several packed buses had passed him by when he finally flagged one down and pleaded his case. He needed to get to Croke Park to play in the match against Cavan. The novelty of the story so amused the driver he allowed him to board. When Lynch finally reached the dressing-room

Facing page: Jack Lynch leads his football club, St Nicholas in the parade before the 1947 County Senior football against Clonakilty. Dave Creedon ■ walking behind him.

A minor hurler and footballer at the callow age of 13, he was first picked for the Cork senior hurling team while still in fifth year at the Mon.

Despite losing his hurley Jack Lynch continues to head for goal against Tipperary in the 1948 National Hurling League final at Croke Park. Cork won the game 3 -3 to 1 - 2

where his anxious colleagues were already dressing for the fray, the door was opened by Jim Hurley, a selector, who greeted the arrival: 'Hello, Jack Lynch,' said the Clonakilty man, 'you were great to come'.

Two hours later, Cork had bridged a 34-year gap, taken possession of Sam Maguire and made Lynch the first man to bring a football All-Ireland back to Blackpool. There are so many victories that it just seemed appropriate to start with two of the most colourful, a pair of football triumphs amid all that hurling glory.

His career with St Nick's, Glen Rovers and Cork yielded five All-Ireland hurling medals (four in a row, of course), one All-Ireland football, 10 Cork county senior hurling championships (eight in a row), three National Hurling Leagues, three Railway Cups, two Cork county senior football championships, and a Dublin senior football title with Civil Service. Listing his achievements takes nearly a whole paragraph, when most would need only a sentence.

'First and last, Jack is a hurler,' wrote a contemporary observer, John Power in The Cork Book of Champions in 1945. 'To him the art of the camán is an open book. Fast ground play, open, overhead hurling, attack, defence – Jack has mastered them all. His game is ever clean, no shouting, no nerves, no fraying temper. He can give and take hard knocks as part of the game and being grassed – which indeed has been very seldom – can pick himself up with as charming a smile as you could wish to see. A hurler of the old and new schools, Jack Lynch seems to be to typify the kind of Irishman Cusack, Croke and those others had in mind when they brought back the hurling to Ireland.'

If he was indeed the archetype of what the founding fathers of the GAA had envisaged, it was kind of ironic that he learnt much of his football skills playing with a soccer ball on the streets around Shandon. Often, the only ball available belonged to his uncle, Mick O'Donoghue who was chairman of the Munster Football Association. When not kicking that into an improvised goal by the entrance to the Butter Market, he and his pals would buy 'shape-outs' from the woodmills on Leitrim Street that they would then convert into hurleys.

'As we grew older, we moved up to the open spaces of the Fair Field where others joined us from the surrounding areas, many of whom later went on to achieve fame with Glen Rovers and Cork,' wrote Finbarr Lynch in a moving contribution to "Where We Sported and Played", Liam Ó Túama's celebration of Lynch's life. 'Many thrilling games were played on the hard surface and it was here that Jack further developed his hurling skills. When the games were over, we washed ourselves and drank water from the pump at Mickey Sullivan's pub and made our way home in time for tea and some homework for school the next day.'

Born on August 15th, 1917, the boy who would become famous as Jack was christened John Mary Lynch and was the youngest of seven children. His father Dan, a tailor, hailed originally from Baurgorm, near Bantry, and his mother Nora's family were from Glounthaune. Schooled at St. Vincent's and The North Monastery – with whom he won three successive Harty Cups – his extra-curricular education began after he took the same path as his older brothers down to Glen Rovers around the age of ten. On and off the field, he was a stalwart for them thereafter.

In 1953, Lynch, by then a local TD, went to the Munster and Leinster Bank to apply for a loan of £10,000 on behalf of the club. They needed it to fund the construction of a new premises. A tidy sum for the time, the bank manager asked him what he proposed to put down as collateral. 'The people of

Blackpool are my collateral,' he replied. On becoming Taoiseach thirteen years later, a Dublin journalist asked him why he'd chosen to return to the Glen Hall to celebrate his election: 'Sure in the name of God,' he answered, 'where else would I go?'

Where else but the club he began starring for in his early teens. A minor hurler and footballer at the callow age of 13, he was first picked for the Cork senior hurling team while still in fifth year at the Mon. That many adolescent prodigies in every sport fail to deliver on early promise makes the subsequenty length of his stint at the top – 15 years with the county alone - one more remarkable element of his persona. More impressive still, Lynch achieved all this success in two codes while pursuing a serious academic career. From secondary school through studying law by night to qualifying for the bar, he managed to somehow balance the different sides of his life.

The juggling act reached a ridiculous level on February 20, 1944. That was the day he togged out for three different matches in Dublin. His first was a league game for Civil Service against Eoghan Ruadh at Islandbridge. In order to conserve energy, he started in goal but for once he wasn't a natural. To atone for a couple of errors, he played the second half out the field and chipped in 1-2 to his side's victory. From there, it was into town and on to Croke Park for the Railway Cup semi-finals. At a time when that competition was still a prestigious date in the GAA calendar, he contributed a point to Munster's victory over Ulster in the hurling. A change of jersey later, he took

Jack Lynch is seen here speaking in Cloyne at the unveiling of a statue to commemorate his great friend and teammate, Christy Ring.

the field again and scored two points for the province's footballers in their defeat by the northerners. A curious entry in his career log, it is one that reeks of his commitment.

The irony of his intercounty career was that for a time he had no luck at all with Cork teams. His years in the minor grade coincided with the emergence of Tipperary who dominated that age group then. His early days on the senior scene were equally uninspiring. After three premature Munster championship exits in his first three summers as a first-choice, his luck changed in 1939. Cork came out of Munster and reached their first All-Ireland final since 1931. The opening game of the '31 trilogy marked his first trip to Croke Park as a fan. On the weekend that the world went to war, he returned to Dublin as captain of his county in a game that would enter the annals as the 'Thunder and Lightning final'.

'It was a raging storm and the rain came down like stair rods,' said Lynch in an interview with Mick Dunne on RTE Radio. 'At times, it was impossible to see more than 20 yards away from you. Conditions were almost unplayable. The ground conditions themselves were very difficult and we felt a bit strange as we had not been to Croke Park before, at least not as a senior county hurling time. Kilkenny had been there many times and they seemed to settle in far more quickly.'

A one-point defeat was made worse for the captain by the fact he'd missed a goal chance near the end, first-timing the ball over the bar. The circumstances of the loss – arguments still rage about whether Kilkenny's winning 70 was taken from the right line – reinforced Lynch's own concern that he might never win an All-Ireland. How wrong he was. The circumstances in which he snagged his first Celtic cross against Dublin in 1941 were so comfortable that towards the end of that 5-11 to 0-6 rout, Lynch and John Quirke went down "injured" in order to allow Bobby Ryng and Paddy O'Donovan to be introduced to the fray.The two teams met again a year later, and in the build-up to that encounter, there was an incident which demonstrated the different conditions Lynch and his peers laboured under at the old Athletic Grounds. They togged out for training in an area under the old stand, with an earthen floor, and wooden planks on upturned boxes served as seats. Having hung their clothes from nails that were driven into the seats of the stands above their heads, they returned from the field to find every item they owned soaked through with rain. With each player using a solitary tap to wash the mud from their legs, they were soon up to their ankles in sludge.

As captain, Lynch left the session and made it to the regular Tuesday night meeting of the County Board in time to voice the players' anger about the conditions under which they were training. However eloquent he put their case, the reaction of the delegates and officials was unanimous. 'I'm afraid I got short shrift,' he wrote later. Despite the board's unwillingness to do something about the standard of facilities, Dublin were duly dispatched again, and as captain, Lynch lifted Liam McCarthy.

'I was marking Jack in that game,' recalled Dublin's Harry Gray in Tim Horgan's magnificent history 'Cork's Hurling Story'. 'And I must say it was a pleasure to play on him. He was a great ball-player, very clean and had wonderful anticipation. Jack would move into position as soon as the ball was struck at the end of the field, and he always picked the right spot to be under it. My gambit was to pull in the air as the ball landed. Otherwise I might as well say goodbye to it.'

The next September, Antrim shocked Kilkenny in the semi-finals but playing into the wind in the first half of the final, the northerners were 3-11 to 0-2 down at the break and the game was over as a contest. Later, Lynch would often speak of the sympathy he felt for his opponents that day, more especially when a couple of them informed him they'd often been prevented from getting to training by the authorities. When Taoiseach in 1969, at the height of the troubles, he stepped in to ensure the Antrim under-21 footballers could get to Cork for an All-Ireland semi-final. With roadblocks blocking their path to the south, he organised for them to fly down.

En route to the four-in-a-row, Cork's most difficult games were always in Munster. They were actually defeated by Tipperary in the 1941 provincial final – the game was played after the All-Ireland because of a foot-and-mouth outbreak - and at least three of Lynch's team-mates made the unwise decision to stop off in a Croom pub on the way to the re-fixed Munster final. They needed a replay and a wonder goal by Christy Ring to get past Limerick in 1944 and though strong at the time, Dublin never seemed able to bring their best form on the days it mattered most. In '44, they did make a promising start to their third appearance in four deciders, and kept Cork scoreless for the first ten minutes.

'Lynch's 70s were going wide of the mark but he collared one and double-turned swiftly to hit a darling ball off his left,' wrote Carbery. 'Sixty yards out, it travelled all the way above the bar and Cork's procession of scores was underway.' Six points clear at the interval, Cork won by 14. For the one and only time, a county had managed four All-Ireland hurling titles in a row and Lynch had been one of nine players to play in all four finals.

'It's a funny thing,' said Lynch. 'But I always felt at a loss on the football field. I didn't know what to do with my hands, being so used to holding a hurley. It was a strange feeling which one got over only after many, many matches.'

When the hurlers were caught by Tipperary the following summer, Lynch continued a remarkable run by returning to Croke Park with the footballers. According to popular lore, he had protested upon first being selected for the county team years earlier that he was 'no footballer at all'. To which the trainer Jim 'Tough' Barry responded: 'But you have the brains'. At a crucial point in the All-Ireland victory over Cavan, Lynch was moved from corner-forward to centre-field and told not to field but to break every ball towards Mick Tubridy. From exactly one such ball came Derry Beckett's goal that clinched the triumph over a fancied Cavan.

'He could play well, facing the ball or doubling on it,' said Eamonn Young. 'Reflexes faster than normal, a mature shrewdness and an ability to keep cool, allowed him not only to see what way the tide was flowing but to take advantage of that flow by adjusting his own play or suggesting changes. Never one for spirited exhortations, he led more by example than by word. Anything he had to say was said in that quiet determined level-toned voice which became so familiar to the entire nation later on.'

The record-setting sixth consecutive All-Ireland medal – a feat nobody is ever likely to match - came via victory over Kilkenny in the 1946 final. With typical modesty, Lynch always claimed it would have been seven if he hadn't missed a couple of easy points against the same opposition the following year. There had been just one bump in the road on the path to that sixth medal.

In January, 1946, Lynch and Paddy O'Donovan attended the final Irish international rugby trial at the Mardyke. Lynch's brother-in-law John Harvey, a full-back with UCC, was among those trying to convince the selectors of his merits in that game. For this 'crime', the duo incurred an automatic three-month suspension from the date of the offence. This cost Lynch his place on the Munster football team for the Railway Cup, and although he and O'Donovan began an appeal against the fact they hadn't been allowed appear in their own defence, that was soon dropped. By the business stages of the National League, both were back in the fold.

The defeat by Kilkenny in '47 heralded the end of the good times. Lynch spent three more summers with Cork and indeed near the finish of his inter-county career, made one of his most memorable cameos. Towards the end of a first-round tie against Tipperary 1949, Cork were trailing by four points when his wonder goal set them up to snatch the draw.

'It took the old master, Jack Lynch, to display a flash of his superb genius,' wrote Carbery. 'Ranging upfield as the time was ebbing, he took the law into his own hands. Showing surprising speed, the ball in perfect hopping control, he bore his weaving way through the staggered Tipp backs and 15 yards out, he let fly with a short, sweet, wrist-snap. The net bulged.....'

Rarely included in the barstool debates about the greatest hurlers of all time, Lynch endured enough to figure alongside Lory Meagher at centre-field on the team of century in 1984 and the team of the Millenium in 1999. As the decades passed, he also appeared to have carved out a unique place in the affections of people across the country. As his political career flourished, Professor Dermot Keogh once wrote of how a distinguished Fianna Fáil scion described campaigning with Lynch as 'like walking into a town with Cuchulainn'. And witness the reception he received when introduced during the on-field ceremonies preceding the 1984 All-Ireland hurling final.

'The biggest cheer at the centenary hurling final was evoked not by the Cork team, or even Offaly but by Jack Lynch,' wrote Stephen Collins in The Irish Press. 'The entire crowd – Offaly supporters as well as those from Cork – erupted in sustained applause when Mr. Lynch made his appearance as one of the 38 All-Ireland-winning captains.'

Long into retirement, sport coursed through his very being. In 1972, Lynch became the first western head of state to invite Muhammad Ali – in town to fight Al 'Blue' Lewis at Croke Park - to visit the seat of government, an honour gratefully acknowledged by the boxer in his autobiography 'The Greatest'. The two men sat on a couch in a Leinster House room normally reserved for cabinet meetings, and with typical modesty, Lynch quipped: 'I played many times, Muhammad, on that field where you will be boxing.'

He had grown up at a time when young boys made their own hurleys and thought nothing of sitting on the crossbar of a bike for a five-mile journey to play or watch a match. The friendships he made through sport were so

Even when he was Taoiseach of Ireland, Jack Lynch loved to come home to Cork and to puck an occasional sliotar when the opportunity presented itself.

unique and special that in his history of twentieth century Ireland, Professor Joe Lee justifiably speculated that after the death of Christy Ring in 1979, Lynch seemed to lose his appetite for politics. There was certainly a noticeable catch in his voice when delivering the eulogy at his former team-mate's graveside

After his own death in October 1999, the funeral procession that carried his coffin from the North Cathedral through the city to St. Finbarr's Cemetery in Glasheen was clapped every inch of the way by onlookers. One more round of applause for the favourite son. The headstone over the grave where he is buried contains a single quote: 'Happy is the man who finds wisdom'.

Roy

Very few people remember where they were on Tuesday, August 28th, 1990. It's just another date at the end of a joyous summer during which a nation had giddily followed its soccer team on an unlikely and thrilling journey to the quarter-finals of the World Cup. At Anfield that night, the first steps were taken in a professional career that would obsess the country for most of the next decade and a half. As Liverpool cruised to a handy 2-0 win over Nottingham Forest, the visitors' 19-year-old debutant should have been booked for a wild challenge on David Burrows in the 20th minute. Despite most of his team-mates not knowing his name by that point in the match, Roy Keane did enough to catch the eye of one man sitting in the stands.

Manchester United's chief scout Les Kershaw took a note of the newcomer and reported back to Alex Ferguson the next day that Forest had given a start to a young midfielder who might be worth watching for future reference. That his first performance on Broadway merited just a footnote in the Irish papers was ironic because very soon, everything he did on and off the field would be magnified and occasionally distorted by the constant media glare. He would grow into a bigger and more enduring story than every one of the heroes of Italia '90. He would win more medals, garner more headlines, and divide the loyalties of Irish fans like no player ever before.

His transformation from one more promising young midfielder to once-in-a-generation icon happened relatively quickly, and coincided with such a change in the prevailing media culture of his homeland that he truly became the first superstar of Ireland's tabloid age. It was perhaps the only title he

never wanted and the one that presented him with most difficulty. A boyhood preparing for on-field glory never included any courses about how to negotiate the off-field perils of fame. In the summer of 1996, Keane had paparazzi stalking his trail and taking intrusive photographs of himself and his kids outside his parents' house in Mayfield. This was back when David Beckham hadn't even yet been introduced to Posh Spice.

Unlike his erstwhile United colleague, Keane never courted that sort of publicity, rather he openly bristled at it. Moreover, his evolution into one of those outsize characters who transcend the game they play was never a consequence of slick marketing or canny advertising. It was merely an unfortunate by-product of the magnificent displays he produced almost every time he togged out and crossed the white line. Nobody ever warned him that aspiring to be the best would yield so much baggage. Some are not fazed by celebrity, others embrace it. Keane detested it.

A fellow Irish international once confessed that the sight of the Manchester United captain walking into the team hotel on the week of games instantly lifted him. His thinking was that, no matter the quality of the opposition, the presence of this one player immediately gave Ireland a chance of winning the match. Over time, other countries singularly associated him with the nation the way we ourselves used to associate Romania with Gheorghe Hagi, or Bulgaria with Hristo Stoichkov. He was the national symbol. Accordingly, opponents respected the Irish team when Keane was in the line-up and reckoned it extremely vulnerable if he was absent.

Of course, Hagi and Stoichkov never won any popularity contests in their own dressing-rooms, and from what we know of Keane's standing among his Irish, and indeed his United peers, he too embodied the age-old belief that the most important player on any team is rarely the most beloved and often the most controversial. Co-existing with contemporaries unable to reach the same heights on the field is never easy. When that tension boiled over in Saipan in May, 2002, the very fact many people described the fall-out as "a civil war" was itself indicative of the ridiculous hyperbole that had begun to infect modern Irish discourse.

Such exaggeration was less common in the Ireland in which Keane came of age, and the country he left in the summer of 1990 was markedly different from the place he divided twelve years later. Apart from the economic boom, interest in the game had – not least because of his own rise - exploded in the interim. Robbie Keane's goalscoring debut for Wolverhampton Wanderers in August, 1997 immediately garnered double-page spreads in tabloid newspapers. Earlier that year, a David Connolly hat-trick against Liechtenstein had caused some Irish journalists to seriously compare him to Ronaldo. Very few people even noticed back when a Corkman, a couple of weeks past his 19th birthday, became Brian Clough's last great hunch.

The timing of Keane's arrival into Clough's orbit was fortunate. At that juncture, the belief among many people working at the City Ground was that Steve Hodge had more interest in preserving himself for England international duty than playing week in, week out. When the first team travelled to Liverpool for their second match of the season, Hodge announced he had another of his famous niggles so Clough decided to call his bluff. The coaching staff told him the most suitable candidates to replace Hodge in midfield were the new kid Keane and Phil Starbuck. As it turned out, both of them travelled late and both started the match.

Famously, Keane was trying to look busy in the dressing-room, helping to put the jerseys out when Clough turned to him and said: 'Irishman, put the number seven shirt on. You're playing.' That the game here owes Clough a debt for that bold decision is without question. Although the teenager seized his opportunity like few others before or since, the role the then Forest manager played in his rise can never be overestimated. Even if the boss may have been half in the tank when he picked him to play that evening, would any other manager in England have thrown a callow novice into the fray against Liverpool the way he did? Considering the Liverpool team sheet read: Grobbelaar; Hysen, Burrows, Venison, Whelan, Gillespie, Beardsley, Houghton, Rush, Barnes, and McMahon, it's probably safe to say no. Might Keane's entire professional career have turned out very differently if he hadn't found a manager crazy enough to gamble he could cope with the atmosphere at Anfield? Almost certainly.

'People said I'd flipped my lid,' said Clough of his punt on Keane, 'but he did well and after that even Enid Blyton couldn't have written a better script.'

The background to the debut is classic Clough too. Playing for the club's Under-21s in a pre-season tournament in Holland, Keane had excelled at right-back, right-wing, centre-half and midfield, confounding the coaches with his performances in every new position they tried him in. Intrigued by the dispatches, Clough sidled along to a couple of reserve games to see what all the fuss was about. Frustrated to see Keane on the bench at one of those,

Roy Keane became an instant hit with the fans at Nottingham Forest.

he waited until half-time before informing the reserves' manager Archie Gemmill to replace his son Scott with 'the Irishman'. Gemmill ignored that request until, with 20 minutes remaining, Clough vaulted the hoardings and issued an order: 'Get your son off, and put the Irishman on.'

What did Keane do in the time available? What did Clough see that impressed him?

'Brian was such a genius at spotting youngsters,' said Alan Hill, then the club's chief scout. 'He could always spot something that the rest of us couldn't. I think he saw Roy make a couple of forward runs and then stick somebody on their backside and that was enough. Afterwards, he told me: "The kid has everything, you just have to encourage him".'

Keane's adolescence had been spent on a Rockmount team that was one of the most gifted schoolboy outfits the city of Cork had ever seen. So gifted indeed that he was not even the brightest star in the firmament. Alan O'Sullivan, the sort of mercurial winger who catches the eye of scouts, was snapped up by Luton Town years before Keane arrived at Forest. Paul McCarthy, a burly centre-half with an eye for goal from set-pieces, turned professional at Brighton and Hove Albion and even tried to persuade his new club that his former colleague was worth pursuing.

Brighton looked into it and were told by an Irish scout that the kid in question was too small, had a dodgy temperament and wasn't worth looking at. The same month in 1997 that Keane won the third of his seven Premiership titles, Brighton lost the Goldstone Ground and narrowly avoided relegation to the non-leagues. In failing to recognise the gift horse being placed before their mouths, Brighton weren't alone. A legion of scouts tracked that Rockmount team season after season and none ever saw fit to take a chance on Keane. The letters he wrote to every English club begging for a trial never elicited a single plane ticket.

Later, many around the game in Ireland would claim they were on the verge of making just such a recommendation when Noel McCabe spotted him excelling in a losing effort for Cobh Ramblers' youth team in an FAI Cup match at Fairview Park. Keane was a few months into a FAI/FAS soccer apprenticeship course in Dublin, and just starting to evince the physical benefits of full-time training. Others on that scheme would testify later that from the first day there, he was working harder than the rest, running further and faster. The picture of a guy striving to get on is appropriate because Keane had no real fall-back by that point in his life.

School had never been his milieu so further education wasn't an option. With Cork still recovering from a decade of factory closures and economic depression, jobs were scarce. Like every other house in Cork, his family knew the spectre of the dole, though the later tabloid attempts to portray his life as some rags to riches yarn were insulting and misguided. Until McCabe sauntered into view however, the best Keane might have hoped for was combining the part-time earnings of a League of Ireland player with some menial job. Little wonder then that when the scout mentioned the possibility of a trial at Forest, he thought the teenager was 'so eager and enthusiastic that I felt here was a boy who would swim to England if I asked him to.'

The preface to Keane's professional career is important because it's obvious how much it shaped everything that happened after. There has always been about him the sense of somebody manically afraid of failure. The incredible determination and sheer force of will that dragged Manchester United to the 1999 Champions League final and (almost single-handedly) qualified Ireland for the 2002 World Cup finals can be equally interpreted as the desperate brilliance of somebody unwilling to contemplate or accept losing. What is most impressive about this is the zealousness never once waned, even as his salary mushroomed to a reported £100,000 per week and his personal fortune soared into the tens of millions. It is worth remembering that he chose United over Blackburn Rovers, even though Ferguson was then offering a smaller wage packet than the one being dangled by Kenny Dalglish.

The 'driven bastard' he once described himself as can also be glimpsed in the way he outstripped so many of his contemporaries at different stages. At Forest, Gemmill was thought to be his equal once, and even when he moved to United in the summer of 1993, he wasn't reckoned the brightest young thing on view. Back then, Ryan Giggs threatened to replicate all the good stuff from George Best's repertoire and serious pundits fancied Lee Sharpe's chances of winning 100 caps for England. If Sharpe is a tell-all book waiting to happen, Giggs didn't exactly live up to his advance billing either. As defined by the old soccer truism, great players come good in big games, and the bigger the game the better they play. Has Giggs done that often enough? How often of late? Not half as often as Keane.

Roy Keane in action for Ireland.

'Keane is a great soccer player,' said the legendary Juventus and Holland midfielder Edgar Davids. 'He is one of the best midfielders in the world. Keane is what a great player really is. I don't look up to him, because I don't look up to anybody, but he's fantastic.'

Although he was, by some distance, Ireland's best player at USA '94, it was Gary Kelly, Jason McAteer and Phil Babb who arrived home to an exaggerated fanfare, their charismatic personalities off the field almost obscuring Keane's achievement on it. While they immersed themselves in the demimonde of pop biographies and celebrity lifestyles, he simply became the best combative midfielder in the world. The way that players like Babb and Sharpe, McAteer and, to a lesser extent, Kelly squandered so much of the promise they once engendered is anathema to Keane.

He cannot cope with people ostensibly showing less commitment than he does. This is what makes him such an indefatigable force on the field and such a troubled figure off it. The very stuff that makes him great has also proved his undoing on the many occasions he overstepped the mark, those cameos when the red mist descended and fervour gave way to foul play. It appears impossible to have one without the other.

A less intense individual might have looked at the FAI's slipshod attitude to preparation, decided it was hardly fair to compare their approach to that of Manchester United, one of the leading sports franchises in the world, and got on with the job in hand. A less intense individual wouldn't have been half the player he is. Alex Ferguson accepted that he had to take the good with the bad and never once complained about the deal. He knew the positives far outweighed the negatives, something emphasised by Keane's colossal role in bringing seven Premierships, four FA Cups and of course the Champions League to Old Trafford.

Even that night in Barcelona when suspension forced him to wear a suit rather than a jersey, the way in which Keane celebrated afterwards gave an important clue to his character. In contrast to the animated antics of non-playing substitute David May, there was no real joy on the captain's face when he perfunctorily lifted the trophy at the Camp Nou. For somebody who has always measured himself by his contribution once the whistle blows, watching his own team snatch victory right at the death must have been scant consolation. The competitor only ever wants to be in the arena competing. That is, after all, what he does.

In a similar vein, the saddest element of Keane's departure from Saipan was that it cost him his last chance of playing in a World Cup at somewhere close to his peak. He was right about the laxity of Ireland's approach but wrong to speak out then and ultimately deprive himself of his own day on the biggest stage. Subsequent revelations about the extent of his hip problem at the time lent credence to a conspiracy theory that maybe his unhappiness had its root in his own fear of failure. When a man has spent his entire career living up to the incredibly lofty standards he set himself, it's reasonable to speculate he knew that this time round his body would not hold up as he would have wanted.

His eventual return to the Irish fold was equally significant. Throughout his career, Keane has shown the capacity to develop and evolve. The slight figure with ample space in the red jersey of Forest grew to fill out every one of United's myriad strips. His physical enhancement was matched by his growth as a player. Within 12 months of his arriving at Old Trafford, Ferguson knew that he, rather than Paul Ince, would become the heartbeat of the side. The Guvnor only lasted one more campaign. Over time too, the nightclub-hopping, jowly young pro flitting over and back to Cork turned into the wise old owl, who preached the virtues of rest and yoga and became a contented family man.

Like anybody who leaves a city at 18 and then spends his entire adult life elsewhere, Keane's relationship with his home town has been a complex and fluctuating entity. This is, after all, the city where Seán Ó Faoláin counselled that to succeed, 'you have to have the skin of a rhinoceros, the dissimulation of a crocodile, the quality of a hare, the speed of a hawk'. When a native departs and covers himself in so much glory, for all those that applaud his achievement - witness UCC conferring him with a degree and his freedom of the city - there will be always some available to begrudge it. Such has been the way with Keane, at least until, in the bitterest moments after Saipan, there appeared to be a groundswell of support that started in Mayfield and washed down over the city.

'Like most Cork people, I am inordinately proud of my roots,' wrote Keane in his autobiography. 'When asked about their origins Cork people invariably reply with a mischievous grin, 'Irish by birth; Cork by the grace of God.' A superiority complex is the mark of a sound Corkman.'

At the start of the 2004 season, Keane was the only one of the 13 players who saw active service in Giants Stadium the day Ireland humbled Italy in 1994 to still be playing in the top-flight of English football. By then, he was also one of just two of the 13 used by Alex Ferguson when clinching the 1994 double at Wembley to be plying their trade in the Premiership. For a footballer whose job has always necessitated a blood-and-guts element to his play, who has battled the sort of personal demons that curtailed so many other sporting lives, that longevity is one more arbiter of his greatness.

'He's an incredible man, he really is,' said Ferguson after another gargantuan Keane performance at the age of 33 in February, 2005. 'When you are talking about Manchester United in 50 or 500 years from now, Roy Keane will still be regarded as one of the greatest players ever at this club.'
Nothing more to be said.

Leader of the Pack. Roy Keane seen here wearing the captain's armband will always be synonymous with the famous red jersey of Manchester United.

Billy

When Mikey Sheehy somehow inveigled a goal from an impossible angle to over-turn a two-point deficit in the final moments of the 1987 Munster football final at Páirc Uí Chaoimh, Billy Morgan fell to the ground, prostrate on the sideline in front of the covered stand. With his team moments away from victory, he'd been following the action so intensely that he was almost parallel with the action as it unfolded. At the prospect of a title being snatched from Cork's grasp, Morgan keeled over. A snapshot of his commitment, the image was that of a man so tortured by the possibility of losing that his emotions overpowered all other senses.

No sooner had the late John Kerins evinced the wherewithal to take a quick kick-out that culminated in Larry Tompkins pointing the equalising free at the other end than Morgan showcased the other side of his genius. The man tormented by the drama morphed back into the manager with a job to do. Having dispatched everybody else from the chaos of the post-match dressing-room, he gathered his squad around him and began talking about the replay. As he spoke animatedly, he hand-passed a ball around the room asking each man what they planned to do to Kerry in the replay down in Killarney. The responses increased in fervour until finally, the masseur John Kid Cronin fumbled a pass.

'Jesus Christ, Kid,' shouted Morgan, 'will you concentrate?'

Facing page: Cork captain Billy Morgan calls at the toss before the 1973 All-Ireland Senior Football final. Also in the picture are Liam Salmon, Galway Captain and referee John Moloney.

To paraphrase Nick Hornby's famous line about Liam Brady's relationship with Arsenal, if you cut Billy Morgan, he would bleed Cork. The county has had great servants in both codes for over a century but it's difficult to find

Billy Morgan rises above corner back (no 4) Brian Murphy to fist the ball clear during Nemo Rangers against UCC in Cork County Senior Football final of 1972. This was Nemo's first senior county championship victory.

anybody, apart from Christy Ring, to whom the jersey meant quite as much. First-choice goalkeeper for 16 years, captain of the 1973 All-Ireland winning team and manager during the most successful decade in our Gaelic football history, every triumph of the modern era has had Morgan's fingerprints all over it. Even during those spells when he didn't have an official title, there was no off-button to his passion.

'When Cork were six points ahead at half-time in their first-round championship game against Clare in 1997, Morgan took it upon himself to wait outside the dressing room in Ennis, just to remind Larry Tompkins that Clare had come back from a heavy deficit the previous year too to force Cork into extra-time,' wrote Kieran Shannon in The Sunday Tribune. 'Morgan watched the second half of that game in the press box, kicking every ball. Anyone who saw his face after Martin Daly's last-second goal would swear that had there been more room in that press box, Morgan would have fallen to the ground in disgust, just as he did after Mikey Sheehy's in Páirc Uí Chaoimh 10 years earlier.'

Born on February, 2nd, 1945 – a good year for Cork football all round – Morgan grew up in Tonyville Terrace off High Street. His father Tom,

The Cork team lines up to greet the President of the GAA before the start of the 1973 All-Ireland Senior Football final. Billy Morgan is on the right also in the picture are Frank Cogan, Humphrey Kelleher, Brian Murphy, Kevin Ger O'Sullivan (partly hidden) John Coleman and Connie Hartnett.

originally from Mullagh in East Galway, had been posted to the city as a guard. At Coláiste Chríost Rí and UCC, and with Nemo Rangers, the young Morgan first showcased his potential as a talented centre-forward, the position from which he started picking up honours. Although he had dabbled between the posts from the age of 16, he played half-forward on the Cork minors that lost to Kerry in the 1963 Munster final replay.

That was the point Tramore Athletic lured him away from the GAA for a season but after Dr. Dave Geaney in UCC asked him to keep goal for the college Sigerson team, the path of his Gaelic football career was set. W. Morgan (UCC), as he was officially listed, began his 16 year-stint as Cork custodian on the side that lost the 1966 All-Ireland semi-final to Galway by just two points. The following year, they went one stage further but couldn't get the better of Meath in the final. By the time he played in his second decider in '73, Morgan was captain. That honour came by virtue of Nemo winning their first county the previous autumn, and his role in that victory was, inevitably, outsized.

Upon graduating from UCC, he'd supplemented his teaching qualifications with a physical education degree from Strawberry Hill College in London.

What he learned there, he'd implemented in Nemo when he was put in charge of the senior team at the age of just 27. He revolutionised their training methods with increased emphasis on ball-work and imaginative drills to improve technical skills. The club's faith in him was rewarded as, wearing the twin hats of captain and coach, he led that side to their first All-Ireland club title. Thirty-one years later he guided a Nemo team, most of whom weren't even born then, to their seventh crown.

While the Cork team of 1973 was laden with stars, the final against Galway was a tight enough affair until eight minutes from the end when Jimmy Barry Murphy scored the goal that finally clinched victory and gave birth to his legend. As the ball hit the back of the net, Morgan slumped to his knees at the other end in a gesture of thanks.

'I suppose it was a spontaneous reaction,' said Morgan in Vincent Power's Voices of Cork. 'I remember saying to myself: 'We have it now, we're not going to lose it'. I realised we were going to win an All-Ireland.'

When the All-Stars were named later that year, there was no other nomination for the goalkeeping, and he also became the first Corkman to win the Texaco Footballer of the Year. The accolades were deserved because apart from his shot-stopping, he also brought a new awareness to the position. On every team he played for, Morgan was the last line of defence and first line of attack. Once the ball was in his grasp, he was immediately looking to pass directly to a waiting colleague instead of going for the traditional hoof down the field.

'I always believed in possession football,' said Morgan. 'I could not understand a goalkeeper saving a ball and then punting it downfield between one of his own players and a rival. He was giving the opposing player a 50-50 opportunity of gaining possession and I felt this was wrong. So with Nemo first and then my Cork colleagues, I worked on and developed the short pass to an unmarked team-mate.'

Kerry were beaten in 1974 and the Cork side so expertly pieced together by Donie O'Donovan were living up to their billing as the team of all the talents. But then, a shock loss to Dublin in the All-Ireland semi-final started their decline. Morgan would finish his career without ever winning another Munster medal. For seven consecutive summers, he had to give best to Kerry, the sort of cumulative losses that no doubt fueled his later manic desire to put Cork back on top.

There must have been times in those dark years when his mind harked back to the summer of '69. A superlative display against Kerry in the Munster final somehow segued into the offer of a month's trial with Jock Stein's Celtic. His trip to Glasgow had to be a clandestine affair because The Ban was still operating, and after a week at Parkhead, he was faced with a tough decision. The club wanted three more weeks to evaluate him but staying in Scotland would cause him to lose a teaching job in Cork. He chose the guaranteed career, and although further flirtations with soccer included signing forms for Waterford United, Cork Celtic and Cork United, he never actually played a League of Ireland match.

In any case, during the late seventies, he found other outlets for his enthusiasm. Before the 1979 Munster final in Killarney, he walked into the Cork minor dressing-room as they readied themselves to face the old rivals in the curtain-raiser. Already in his match gear, Morgan delivered a fiery speech to the teenagers, the central thrust of which was how nauseating it was to lose to Kerry at any time, in any game. What the youngsters knew of the orator in their midst ensured every word carried more weight.

Billy Morgan as coach of the Cork senior football team in 2004.

'At the end, I just wanted to give my all that day for Cork,' said Colman Corrigan, a minor that day. 'I thought then how I'd love to play with him.'

It's not surprising that somebody who cared enough to take time out of his own preparations for a crucial fixture to try to drive the minors on was often at odds with officialdom. Morgan didn't suffer fools. Consumed by the desire to win, he wasn't interested in politicking and couldn't abide those unwilling to assist the cause. When Adidas came calling with an offer of free gear and boots in 1977, the amateur sportsman who'd always given a professional commitment collided with authority. At a time when Cork players had to supply their own socks and shorts, Morgan saw it as an opportunity for the team to at least start receiving the same treatment as their rivals in other counties.

Suspected of being a ringleader in the affair, he was one of those suspended after the team wore the Three Stripes gear in the Munster final. Three years later, when Cork beat Kerry in the League final, he was effectively player-manager. Except for one crucial detail. The county board gave him the title of coach, still making him pay for his insolence. In 1986, they appointed him manager but initially, he had no official say in the selection of players. Incredibly petty behaviour towards somebody so devoted to Cork football, the inference that a price had to be paid by any maverick ruffling feathers is obvious.

'His relations with the Cork county board have often been bad,' wrote Denis Walsh in The Sunday Times. 'In the autumn of 1991, Morgan's enemies rounded on him. The county board executive drummed up 13 incidents of allegedly unbecoming behaviour or bad practice, which they felt ought to prevent Morgan continuing as the team manager. Cork players were outraged and the pressure to re-instate Morgan was irresistible. Morgan's relationship with his players was critical to Cork's success. He regarded them as his friends and wanted them to look on him in the same way. He seemed more comfortable with footballers and football people than with anybody else.'

At this remove, it's mind-boggling to consider people were seriously trying to oust a manager who had just presided over Cork football's most fecund five years ever. Objective viewers might have thought that leading the county to two titles from four consecutive All-Ireland finals, not to mention its first three in-a-row in Munster would have guaranteed the man the job for as long as he so desired. His detractors – some of whom still contend that Cork team should have won more - had obviously forgotten how bad things were when Morgan took over.

'It bugs me a little when people write we should've won more,' said Morgan. 'We won two All-Irelands, the same amount as Meath but no one would ever write or say that about Meath. We should've won All-Irelands in 1988 and 1993 but for a few refereeing decisions, and that's something I'll never be persuaded from. The equalising point Meath got in '88 (from a free) and, in '93, Anthony Davis's sending off, which was rescinded after the game.'

In his first campaign as manager, he had orchestrated the defeat of the greatest team in history. When his side fell short against Meath that year, he revamped it. Working all the time towards a winning formula, the side that lost the replay to the same opposition 12 months later had six new faces including the returning prodigals, Dave Barry and Dinny Allen. That Allen and Barry would scarcely have come back for anybody else is relevant too because man-management has always been Morgan's forte. He would have considered it part of his remit to occasionally drive the length of the county to privately help a player with a problem, whether sporting or personal.

'I don't know if Billy had to do the same with other players, probably not," said Danny Culloty, 'But he took me aside and had a couple of long chats about the problem of my kicking. It was going all over the place like and it was embarrassing. Billy forced me to lay it off soft and short all the time. I wasn't allowed stray outside of the area between the two 50-yard lines for a long time. I'd get the ball and lay off short passes to guys around me. They'd know to make themselves free.'

American-born Culloty mightn't have had the finesse with the boot that came naturally to those who'd grew up in the maw of the game but Morgan knew the Newmarket man had something to contribute. A more snobbish manager might have baulked at the lack of such a fundamental skill but not this one. His background in physical education (he gained another qualification from New York University in the early eighties) had always made him more open-minded towards every aspect of the game. As late as 2000, Morgan went to England to study training methods of soccer and rugby teams there. At a juncture in life when most people would have assumed he was winding down, there was still a zest for knowledge. Under his tutelage, the Nemo panel at that time could often be found playing a game of tip rugby or a full match with four sets of goalposts.

For all the thinking that informs his preparation of teams however, Morgan's hallmark is passion and commitment. More than once, his temper has neared critical mass on the sidelines of big matches but his fans will point out every occasion was justified. In the 1987 final, he got involved with a couple of Meath players because Jimmy Kerrigan had been struck off the ball. For a manager who kicks every ball with his team, remaining divorced from the fray isn't ever an easy option. There's a reason why long after retiring from the Cork colours, Morgan, in his mid-forties, could still be found wearing the black and green of Nemo, trying to sate the competitive thirst even then.

'I always felt that since the early 1960s when Cork started to produce good underage teams - and since 1961 I'm thinking Cork are up there in terms of winning minor and under-21 All-Irelands - that we should be up there at senior. In my own playing days we weren't properly managed with the exception of Donie Donovan and people like that. There were people coming in as selectors who had no real interest in us winning and didn't really believe in us. If Cork were properly organised, they'd be competing every year for All-Irelands. I like to think we did that in the late 1980s and half way through the 1990s. Cork should be competing. Look at the clubs and the size of the county.'

That guiding philosophy explains why after a career of so much achievement as player and manager, Morgan succeeded Tompkins as Cork manager in 2003. After the first championship of his second tenure was an unmitigated disaster, it became apparent that the task of bringing Cork back to national prominence remains an enormous one. If the climb will be steep, nobody knows the terrain quite as well.

Colm O'Neill is consoled by Billy Morgan after he was sent off during the 1990 All-Ireland football final against Meath. Cork went on to win the game.

Sonia

At Stuttgart's Gottlieb Daimler Stadium in the summer of 1993, three Chinese women finished ahead of Sonia O'Sullivan in the 3000m final of the World Athletics Championships. Supposedly fuelled by nothing stronger than some highly-secret concoction of caterpillar fungus and turtle blood, Qu Junxia, Zhang Linli and Zhang Lirong denied the Cobh woman what had seemed a certain medal over the last lap and a nation harrumphed at the injustice of it all. O'Sullivan had performed brilliantly to finish fourth at the Barcelona Olympics a year earlier but this was about the point when she started on her way to becoming one of the national sporting obsessions.

Coached by a mysterious figure called Ma Junren, the Chinese contingent had never really been heard of before, and that particular trio were rarely seen on the international stage again. But O'Sullivan's response to the whole brouhaha about alleged cheaters was telling. She knuckled down, returned to the track six days later, and grittily took silver in the 1500m. Resisting the urge to echo the chorus of people claiming her opponents were doping, and to possibly seek excuses for her defeat, she simply got on with the task of becoming the first Irishwoman to win a medal at a World Championships. Very soon, Sonia O'Sullivan would be just Sonia, on first-name terms with the entire nation.

The way O'Sullivan handled herself, on and off the track, that week in Germany catapulted her into the public imagination. For the next 11 years, she remained there and so many of her races became appointment television. In the same manner that they did for international soccer or rugby matches or All-Ireland finals, people with no interest in track and field made sure to be near a screen when she ran. They followed her progress from Stuttgart to Sydney, Atlanta to Athens. That the journey wasn't always smooth simply made her more compelling still. With every dramatic failure, she took on another layer of fascination and became an even bigger icon.

'Did you see Sonia?'

'That was terrible what happened to Sonia?'

'Will she do it the next day?'

Born on November 28th, 1969, Sonia was the eldest of John and Mary's three children. Her athletic endeavours began with the daily run between the family home and St. Mary's primary, and led her on a familiar path through the Community Games. Once she arrived in Cobh Vocational School, sport took on an even more competitive flavour under the aegis of a teacher called Jim Hennessy. Although she dabbled in basketball, camogie and volleyball, athletics began to predominate from the moment in first year when she took her first Munster Colleges' cross-country title. She couldn't sprint like the others but over the longer distances she always seemed to endure.

'I used to run to school all the time and when I was coming home from school I'd run between the light posts and race the cars coming behind,' said O'Sullivan in 2002. 'It's difficult to think that kids will go out and run around the fields like I used to because there are so many other things to do. Now I think it's a bit more scary out there for people and they don't like their kids to walk to school or home from school. Most kids get driven to school and picked up every day. I make Ciara (her eldest daughter) walk places all the time. My big thing was that she'd go somewhere where I could walk her to school. It's only 400 metres but we'll walk there every day. Then I'll go off and do my run and come back and get her at lunchtime. You can definitely see how it's much easier to drive them but you've just got to make the effort and take the time."

Despite the obvious promise she was showing at schools level, the most remarkable thing about her career may have been her initial motivation for joining Ballymore Cobh AC. She was one of a group of teenage girls who signed up principally because they wanted to be allowed entry to the club's weekly discos. Although there are conflicting accounts of how talented she was at that stage, the fact she seriously improved once under the remit of local coach Sean Kennedy is not at issue. In her final year in school, she shocked a star-studded field to win the BLE national senior cross-country. By then, an athletics scholarship to America had already become the next logical step. In picking Villanova University, she had chosen to follow in the footsteps of Delaney, Coghlan and more recently, another Cork exile.

Sonia with her 5,000m World Championsip gold medal that she won in Gothenburg, Sweden.

'Donie Walsh called me up and said this little girl from Cobh, same name as yourself,' said Marcus O'Sullivan, 'this girl will be the greatest thing that ever hit the women's scene.'

She arrived in Pennsylvania in 1987 carrying a stress fracture. Not the best of starts and it got worse from there. Her first couple of years were injury-prone and difficult. Unable to get fit enough for long enough to measure herself against her American peers, she repeatedly butted heads with the college coach Marty Stern about his training methods. Their fractious relationship was such that more than once she resolved to go back home. Eventually, a peace deal was struck between them that involved her being allowed to train on grass, and crucially, in the midst of her most troubled spell, Ronnie Delaney had visited the campus and sat her down for a private chat.

'He told her he thought she could emulate him and be Ireland's next great Olympic runner,' said Stern. 'He told her if she could stay injury-free for two years she could be the best. What a prophecy."

In time, a prolonged period of fitness ensued and the talent began to shine through. Having annexed a slew of American collegiate titles, she set a world 5000m indoor record in January, 1991, the first real international benchmark of her progress. Later that year, she won the 3000m at the World

Sonia O'Sullivan celebrates her victory in the 2004 1500m race at the Cork City Sports.

Student Games in Sheffield and suddenly started to be regarded as a potential contender rather than just a competitor at the following summer's Barcelona Olympics. Her subsequent fourth-place finish at those Games was disappointing yet also positively construed as evidence of a great career in prospect.

That much certainly proved true. Her suffering at the feet of Ma's Army in Stuttgart might have depressed any other athlete trying to compete at the elite level. In O'Sullivan, it sparked something different because it prompted two years of utter brilliance when her legend gained real lustre. At the World Championships in Gothenburg on August 12, 1995, she carved out a unique slice of athletic history by winning the first-ever running of the women's 5000m. She ran the last lap around the Ullevi Stadium in 61.5 seconds as she outstripped Portugal's Fernanda Ribeiro down the back straight to prevail quite handily by the finish.

'Success has been seized at last and her achievement has been tailored to her own specifications,' wrote Tom Humphries in The Irish Times about her victory in Sweden. 'After Barcelona, we hailed her as a heroine for her brave running, leading a field of Olympians all the way to the home straight. While we were basking, O'Sullivan was spending the rest of the summer slowly picking off the three runners who had finished in front of her in that 3,000 metres final. By September she had beaten them all. She's a slow burning obsessive, fierce and prickly.

'In the past week her excellence, her discipline and her competitiveness have been a thrill to watch. Already she is looking forward with laser concentration to the Olympics of next year, talking about how the timetable suits her, how she is heading with confidence for an attempt on the 1,500 metres and 5,000 metres double. Her determination is so deep, her character so singular, it's hard for anyone who loves sport not to look forward with her. Sonia O'Sullivan doesn't give us the open- top bus ride, and she doesn't stand to attention when somebody sings "you'll never beat the Irish". She gives us more than that. She gives everything.'

The Atlanta Olympics couldn't come soon enough for O'Sullivan or for a nation growing increasingly besotted by her feats. The anticipation in the twelve months between Gothenburg and her trip to Georgia only made what transpired all the more difficult to handle. The details are embedded in the national psyche. The stomach bug that thieved her strength, ran her off the track in the 5000m final and left her languishing in her 1,500m heat. The ignominy of the row about what gear she was allowed to wear, the politicking of amateurs infringing on the ambition of the ultimate professional. The crazed hyperbole that infected so much of the media and public reaction to the events.

'Nobody has died,' said John O'Sullivan famously to RTE's Tony O'Donoghue at one point in the melodrama. Her father won seven Munster Senior League titles as a goalkeeper with Cobh Ramblers. He knew competitive sport at a high level. He also knew how a country was going a little bit too over the top about his daughter and her travails. He was one of the few to retain a genuine measure of perspective.

In typical style, the Atlanta farce – and the inevitably Irish bureaucratic sideshow that would have drained the will of a lesser person - was followed by another rebirth; winning the short and long course titles at the 1998 World Cross-Country Championships in Marrakesh before bagging the 5,000m and 10,000m golds at the Europeans in Budapest that summer. Her narrative has always been more enthralling than all others because every cameo in which she departed sobbing appeared to be counterbalanced by an equally poignant episode where the tears are of joy. The victories seemed to come freighted with extra significance because every perceived failure was layered with so much emotion. It's not that she didn't seem to take any defeat easy, it's that, for a long time, she didn't seem to be able to take defeat at all.

The restorative triumphs of 1998 segued into a different type of drama. A few weeks after the birth of Ciara, her first child with her partner Nick Bideau, a priest in County Leitrim denounced O'Sullivan from the pulpit for giving birth out of wedlock. The public and the media were so outraged that both

Father Seamus Duffy and the hierarchy of the Catholic Church issued apologies. The vociferous reaction to this scurrilous attack on her character was one more demonstration of the cherished position she held in Irish society. The cleric may have figured he was calling out a celebrity athlete. He was actually insulting the nation's favourite daughter.

'The response to her birth by the people of Ireland, and the people of Cork in particular, has been unbelievable,' said O'Sullivan at the time. 'The house was filled with cards and presents for weeks. She certainly got more cards than I ever got when I won a race.'

Fourteen months after Ciara's arrival, her mother lined up for the start of the 5,000m final in Sydney and a nation held its collective breath.

'Right before the start,' said O'Sullivan. 'I wasn't sure how I felt. It was defnitely one of those situations where as soon as the gun went off I'd know how I was feeling. The gun went off and I was feeling really good. I was surprised at how good I felt.'The pace was slow but on the third lap she dropped back a little and by the fifth she was in trouble, 12th in the field, three from the back. It was early in the race but things did not look good. To the casual fan, this appeared an ominous development except for one crucial factor. She would tell reporters later that even though she'd slipped down the field, she was running well and feeling fine. With seven laps left, she moved up to sixth place and back into contention. Panic over.

Alongside her, the Ethiopians Geta Wami and Ayelech Worku were pushing the pace but their incessant talking to each other eventually took an argumentative turn. As the last lap loomed, Wami and Worku had failed to break away from the sprinters in the field. It had come down to a straight contest between the two fastest finishers, O'Sullivan and Gabriela Szabo, the Romanian runner who had once postponed her own honeymoon because she feared taking time off would allow her Irish rival to gain an advantage over her.

'When I came up on her shoulder,' said O'Sullivan, 'I felt she'd gone as well as she could and I thought I had it. Then she glanced over and she just moved up a little bit and that was it. There's a point when you're going as fast as you possibly can and you've run for so long and you're tired that you just can't get over the top of the person in front of you. It felt like the end of an 800m race where you're just getting to the line as quick as you can.' That the colour of her medal was silver rather than gold scarcely mattered. At the finish, it was only important that she had finally reached the podium at an Olympics. The nature of the contest made the achievement all the more remarkable. An Olympic record for Szabo; an Irish record for O'Sullivan, nearly 20 seconds inside the old Olympic record; seven runners under 14:50; 12 runners under 15 minutes: To that point in history, there had never been a better women's 5,000m race.

Athens brought closure of a different sort. The sight of O'Sullivan trudging through the last lap of the final of the same event in which she'd left her mark four years earlier was sad and yet inscrutably noble. Way off the pace, she could have been forgiven for stepping off the track and slipping away from the spotlight. Instead, she chose the more difficult option, to plough on regardless. And as that crowd began acknowledging her lone effort with more and more applause, we suddenly realised that over the years she'd been charming fans all over the world.

They might not have lived and died with her races like the Irish people but they saw what she gave to the sport. This is why they so vociferously cheered the contender turned backmarker. They knew this was a woman who'd travelled a long Olympic road and now that time had finally caught up with her in her fourth Games, the applause was an outpouring of respect and gratitude and solidarity. We expect people to celebrate the winners but the way that the crowd treated her in defeat that night offered a revealing glimpse of the place she held in their hearts.

'I didn't know that you could actually earn a living being a runner, didn't know that you could be a professional runner. Now I think people know a lot more, younger kids and I think it's one of the problems. They see people earn money running and they think about that before they actually think about being a good runner. It took me two years to even think that I could be in the Olympics and then when I was in the Olympics and finished fourth (in Barcelona), that was when I started to believe I really belong here, I can be competitive in these races, I can maybe even win these races. And that was when I really started to think that I could run for a living and become the best in the world.'

The privilege was watching her try.

JBM

With eight minutes remaining in the 1973 All-Ireland football final and Cork leading by five points, the ball broke in the centre of the field. All summer long, Donie O'Donovan had preached to his players about releasing the ball quickly and smartly so when Jimmy Barrett gained possession, he delivered a low ball into Ray Cummins. The full-forward sped out ahead of his marker to collect, and with a speed of thought and movement that gave the Galway cover no chance, Cummins immediately fisted a long arcing pass into the right corner where he knew Jimmy Barry-Murphy was lurking.

Pivoting out of an attempted tackle, Barry-Murphy started swaggering towards goal. As is always the case with the very best players, those around him seemed almost frozen as he soloed on the spot before nonchalantly firing home his second goal of the game and finishing off Galway. The economy of the entire move was a vindication of O'Donovan's philosophy, and the audacious final shot a tribute to his decision to blood a teenager. The tall, thin youth with the crew-cut raised his arms in triumph once after the ball hit the net and again as he trotted back to his position. Each time, the crowd noise grew louder and louder and somewhere in the cacophony, an icon was born.

'All I saw was net, the left-hand corner at the Hill 16 end and even though I knew Gay Mitchell, the Galway goalkeeper, was there, I couldn't see myself missing,' said Barry Murphy decades after the event. 'I delayed so much Micheal O Hehir actually said 'What's he going to do?' but I never felt there was any chance of missing. It was extraordinary. I was 19 and I didn't think in terms of taking responsibility, it was like, "Give me the ball, I want to get on with it".'

Jimmy Barry Murphy races past Ulster's Peter Mulgrew before shooting the first of his four goals in the 1975 Railway Cup inter-provincial football final at Croke Park.

Between those two Septembers in Croke Park, Barry Murphy won five hurling All-Irelands as a player, never featured on a losing championship team to Tipperary, and left us with a highlight reel like no other Cork hurler of the modern era. There were better exponents of both codes than him just none that had the impact on big games, the charisma or the flair for the dramatic.

Twenty-six years later, Barry-Murphy returned to Hill 16 in a very different moment of triumph. He clambered up the railings and with one hand clinging on to the fence, the other was raising the Liam McCarthy cup in front of a sea of red and white that ebbed and flowed up and down the terrace. Minutes earlier, in the culmination of five difficult years, he'd managed the youngest Cork team ever to win an All-Ireland, something that had seemed a distant prospect just months earlier. The identity of its architect, of course, just served to burnish his legend.

Between those two Septembers in Croke Park, Barry Murphy won five hurling All-Irelands as a player, never featured on a losing championship team to Tipperary and left us with a highlight reel like no other Cork hurler of the modern era. There were better exponents of both codes than him, just none that had the impact on big games, the charisma or the flair for the dramatic. Whether you called him Jimmy, JBM or Jimmy Barry, he seemed to be quintessentially Cork. Incredibly modest off the field and cocky enough on it in the way that the great ones have to be, he was the embodiment of so many virtues we like to prize as our own.

It's too easy to say that all of this was his birthright but the genes were undeniably promising. Born on August, 22nd, 1954, his father John won a minor All-Ireland in 1941 (on a Cork side that also included horse-trainer Ted Walsh's father Ruby), and his grand-uncle Dinny Barry-Murphy won four senior titles, including one as captain in the twenties and thirties. A versatile wing-forward or wing-back, somebody once wrote of Dinny that 'he'd take the ball out of your eye, boy, and he wouldn't hurt a fly, boy'. His two sporting passions were reportedly hurling and greyhounds, and both of those would obsess his grand-nephew too.

The nature of JBM's own potential was demonstrated by him making his senior championship debut for the St. Finbarr's footballers at just 16 while still a student at Colaiste an Spioraid Naoimh in Bishopstown. Later that year, he made his first appearance in Croke Park as the minor hurlers defeated Kilkenny. He subsequently lost the minor football decider to Mayo, and also started for St. Finbarr's in a bad-tempered county final defeat to Blackrock that October. A year later, the minor results were reversed and he gained his first football medal, contributing 2-1 in a one-goal victory over Tyrone.

Facing page: Jimmy Barry Murphy was the supreme dual star. On this occasion, October 1978, he lined out for both the Cork football and hurling teams in a National League double header at Portlaoise.

In the years after he retired prematurely from Gaelic football, some would have found it difficult to believe he was initially thought a better prospect in that game. After he wangled four goals and a point from just five touches of the ball in one Railway Cup final, Kerry County Board chairman Ger McKenna opined that if a transfer market existed in GAA, the Cork forward would go for a million pounds. Ironically, it would be the negative attentions of Kerry's Jimmy Deenihan and the myopia of various referees when it came to policing persistent foul play that would drive Barry Murphy to eventually concentrate on hurling.

'Jimmy has the quickest ball-playing sight I know,' wrote Eamonn Young in an appraisal of Barry-Murphy's footballing talent. 'The moment the ball has reached him the next move is already planned and half-executed. This natural reaction, anticipation and speed of foot make him a lethal man on the half-chance. I recall with delight the day down in the old Park when a high ball came back off the upright at the Blackrock end and JBM's foot stroked it home past Charlie Nelligan.'

After a sputtering start to his inter-county hurling career, the circumstances of his emergence from the Cork bench in the Munster championship in 1976 are covered elsewhere in this publication. The defining moment of that particular campaign however came at the end of the victory over Wexford. Having caught fire in the last fifteen minutes, scoring three crucial points, Barry-Murphy was the first player Christy Ring – a selector on that team – sought out at the final whistle. Historians differ on whether the hug took place beneath the Hogan Stand or in the centre of the field but commentators have properly parsed the significance.

A Glenman hugging a Barrsman in the middle of Croke Park and the icon of all icons publicly giving the newcomer his stamp of approval. He was never

Jimmy Barry Murphy celebrates Cork's third goal against Offaly during the 1984 Centenary All-Ireland Final

quite as great as his predecessor but for a generation to whom Ring was a story handed down from fathers and grandfathers, JBM was a living, breathing deity who walked among us. The day after watching him perform some wondrous feat, you might see him nipping out of Lennox's chipper on Bandon Road. He was real, he was genuine and he was, most importantly of all, ours.

'JBM became much more than a hurler,' wrote Denis Walsh in The Sunday Tribune in 1996. 'He became an idol, a darling and a hero. All the sophistication that Cork people like to ascribe to their hurling at its best resided in him. He was cute and cool and deadly. Terrorists forced him out of inter-county football halfway through his career, but his freedom of expression on a hurling field was never compromised for long.'

The most eloquent cameo of all came in the 1983 All-Ireland semi-final against Galway. John Fenton gathered a handpass from Dermot McCurtain in the middle of the field and drove the ball towards the 14-yard line where Conor Hayes was marking JBM. He thrived on the low intelligent ball usually delivered by the centre-fielder but this time Fenton had sent the ball in head high. Already a couple of steps behind the full-back, Barry-Murphy muttered 'Feck yeah, Fenton' as he noted the odd trajectory. Better-placed than his man, Hayes went up to block, at which point his opponent's stick came across him and somehow directed the ball to the back of the net. It moved far too fast for any camera to properly pick up its path but RTE's viewers voted it goal of the year anyway.

'In the following weeks – and years – there was no scarcity of sciolists to maintain that it was all "luck" or "chance",' wrote Kevin Cashman in The Sunday Tribune. 'It is pointless to explain to such people about the patience and practice and concentration and the unique natural gift of co-ordination of limb and eye which went to make that stroke. It is best simply to tell them that the greatest shots of Bobby Charlton and Ollie Campbell and Steve Davis and John Lowe were all luck and chance too.'

If the goal was one for the ages, the denouement of the championship wasn't. Kilkenny defeated Cork in the final for the second successive year and Barry-Murphy was held scoreless just like the previous September. As captain, the disappointment was made keener.

'I played the best hurling of my life in 1982 and '83 and bombed in the final both times,' said Barry-Murphy. 'I have often wondered what went wrong. I blame myself for not taking the game by the scruff of the neck, for not showing more leadership. But why didn't I do it? I desperately wanted to win those games but when it came down to it, I was hoping that one of my teammates would turn the game our way.'

Those were the low points of a career overstocked with virtuoso performances on so many different stages. Any of the 5,000 or so present in Páirc Uí Chaoimh on a wet summer's evening in 1977 when he inveigled three goals against what was a mighty Rockies team will still vouchsafe that was his best. Others, including the man himself, have cited his flawless display in the 1985 Munster hurling final in Thurles. Having brought Tipp to their knees from full-forward, he sunk to his own before the City End, the man and his people joined together in mutual embrace. Just one more indelible imprint on our psyches, one more reason why men who were teenage boys then would buy T-shirts bearing his visage two decades later.

Attempting to pick the definitive game is as pointless as trying to establish which W.B.Yeats poem or Beatles composition is the greatest of them all. It's a discussion that never ends. The respect and affection that Cork people bear him is also what made his elevation to manager in 1995 an impossible job. For no other reason than JBM had taken over, and could routinely perform miracles, fans believed the county would immediately rise again. It took longer, a lot longer than some expected but that only made the emergence from the wilderness in 1999 all the sweeter. Not to mention that Brian Corcoran winning his first medal on a team managed by JBM had a poetic ring to it. Very different hurlers yet, from his precocious beginning to his humble brand of excellence, there was a lot about Corcoran that reminded people of his manager in a different era.

'The medals are in a wardrobe at home, in the past as far as I am concerned, I have no interest in talking about the All-Irelands I won,' said Barry-Murphy during his time in charge of Cork. 'The one satisfaction I take from my career is the respect that I sense in people for the kind of player I was. I get this from my own countymen and around the country as well. That respect is the one achievement of my career.'

He won All-Irelands at minor, under-21, senior and club in both codes, amassed seven All-Stars, and yet, visitors to his family home will testify there isn't a single memento from the sporting half of his life hanging from the walls. There are simply the standard photographs we'd expect in a house where he and his wife Jean (daughter of Mick Kennefick, who captained Cork to an All-Ireland in 1943) have reared four kids, including a professional soccer player.

In 1973, Barry Murphy had a brief interlude at Cork Celtic. Inevitably, he scored on his debut and showed just enough to suggest he could easily have carved out at least a League of Ireland career. His son Brian would do just that and more, graduating from Cork City to playing in England with Sheffield Wednesday, Preston North End and Bury.

'I played everything until I was about 14 or 15,' said Brian Barry-Murphy. "But at that age I just decided to concentrate on football. My dad just let me decide for myself and didn't put any pressure on me to follow in his footsteps.'

Fittingly, Jimmy's last game for Cork was the 1986 All-Ireland final win over Galway. Before the match, he confided in team-mate Johnny Crowley that this was to be his last appearance. After a game, in which with typical aplomb, his parting shot was the final point of Cork's four-point win, he gave the hurley he used to team physician, Con Murphy. Barry-Murphy's distaste for winter hurling meant the official announcement didn't come until the following April and the news elicited the definitive article on him from a fellow Corkman, and doyen of hurling writers, Kevin Cashman.

'For all the immortal scores and passes he provided through the years, he is likely to be remembered for a ball he never struck at all,' wrote Cashman in The Sunday Tribune.'He had just come in as a sub in the league final replay of 1980 when he snapped a ball on the left wing some 60 yards from goal. He swerved past his marker and struck off on a solo which took that marker and another player with him. Then, after 20 yards he stopped and put his hands on his hips. The two Limerick players stopped playing too and well they might. For Barry-Murphy had dropped the ball on the ground on everybody's blind side as he swerved and Pat Horgan had picked it up and pointed it at his extreme leisure while three Limerick men chased after JBM on his sham solo.'

A fleeting moment where vision, class and touch were manifest in a sleight of hand nobody else would have even thought of. Classic JBM.

Lenihan

There were less than seven minutes left in the game when the cameras picked up Irish captain Ciaran Fitzgerald exhorting his team-mates, asking them 'Where's your f**king pride?' Michael Kiernan had just drawn them level with England at ten points all and their hopes of clinching a Triple Crown in 1985 had been reduced to one last desperate effort. The cudgels were taken up by Donal Lenihan in injury-time. On an afternoon when he and Brian Spillane had been especially prominent, Lenihan grabbed the ball from his comrade's take at the line-out and broke through the cover. The moment he laid it back, Michael Bradley swooped to feed Kiernan whose drop at goal split the posts and sealed the win.

Fitzgerald's rallying cry and Kiernan's calm kicking garnered most of the headlines, but the spadework in that final was done by the second row. Lenihan was 25 years old and his third season in international rugby had just yielded a second Triple Crown. Every team he'd ever played on seemed to win trophies and his arrival into senior ranks in 1982 had coincided with Ireland's first Triple Crown for 33 years. Nobody who followed the trajectory of his career would have expected anything different. When Lenihan played, his side didn't usually lose.

Gerald Lenihan came to Cork from Listowel, County Kerry and was a keen Gaelic footballer. Growing up in St. Luke's, his son dabbled in Gaelic football and hurling with Brian Dillon's and while at St Patrick's NS, he even played for Cork Primary Schools against Limerick at the old Athletic Grounds. Once he enrolled at Christian Brothers College, he embarked on a different path. Taking up rugby at the suggestion of Brother O'Reilly, he soon began amassing silverware. A Munster Junior victory in 1974 was followed by two successive Senior Cup triumphs in 1976 and 1977.

When he moved on to UCC he bulwarked a famous student side – including future Irish team-mate Spillane - that won the Munster Senior Cup, at a time when that trophy was still the ne plus ultra of club rugby in the province. Indeed, it was after he threw his lot in with Cork Constitution that the same trophy was brought back to Temple Hill for the first time in a decade in 1983. That was also the year Lenihan's run of success was interrupted by a dose of ill fortune. Having made the Lions' selection for the summer tour to take on the All-Blacks, the squad attended a reception at the New Zealand Embassy in London after which they went for their mandatory physicals.

Donal Lenihan rises highest for the ball while he is supported by Munster colleagues Ginger McLoughlin (in front) and Colm Tucker (behind).

The Ireland team that defeated England at Lansdowne Road to win the Triple Crown in March 1985. Back Row Mick Cuddy, Selector, Phil Orr, Philip Matthews, Brian Spillane, Donal Lenihan, Willie Anderson, Hugo McNeill, Nigel Carr, Jim McCoy. Front Row Michael Bradley, Paul Deane, Trevor Ringland, Michael O'Carroll President IRFU, Ciarán Fitzgerald, Captain, Michael Kiernan, Keith Crossan, Brendan Mullen, Mick Doyle, Coach.

Divided up along lines of nationality, Lenihan was the last of the 30 players examined by the doctor. Standing on his feet all day during the formalities had caused fluids and swelling to gather on a torn muscle and the medical staff misdiagnosed the problem as a hernia. He tried to persuade fellow tourist and international colleague Dr. John O'Driscoll to come up with another diagnosis but to no avail. In keeping with an effort to have the tour run on a professional footing, Lions manager Willie John McBride asked Lenihan to leave the hotel and fly back to Cork from Heathrow before breakfast the next morning in order to minimise the disruption in the camp. Following an injury to Bob Norster, Lenihan went out as a replacement towards the end of the tour but at the end of his career, the lack of a Lions Test appearance would be the only gap on his CV.

'I didn't play in a Test match and that is hugely disappointing,' said Lenihan in an interview with Gerry Thornley in The Irish Times. 'I would have made the Test team in '83. In '86, I played in the XV that started against the Rest of the World (in a one-off game because a proposed tour of South Africa was cancelled) so the likelihood is I'd have played in the Test team, and in '89 you moved into the era of 6 foot 8 inch locks.'

Even away from the main stage he left his mark on Lions folklore. In '89, he was appointed captain of the midweek team and his side – nicknamed 'Donal's Doughnuts' because they filled a huge gap – performed so well on and off the field that thereafter, they were held up as an example to all future tourists. The dictum is that Test teams are only successful if the players not playing in the glamour games have the right attitude.

'Donal is a super, super bloke,' said Scotland's Finlay Calder, captain of the Lions that summer. 'He went as fourth-choice lock behind Wade Dooley, Paul Ackford and Bob Norster and was at the tail-end of that bunch of men. He knew that, but he also knew the importance of touring and set about pulling the squad together. From day one he knew that success would be gained through the midweek team. He is a great rugby man.'

In that role, it obviously helped that Lenihan had a sense of humour.

'Donal, can I ask a silly question?' inquired Welsh prop Mike Griffiths at one meeting.

'There's none does it better,' replied Lenihan.

When RUC officer Jim McCoy joined the Irish squad in 1984, his initiation rite involved being made to sing 'The Sash My Father Wore' on the team bus. His rendition of the Ulster anthem was immediately followed by a rousing version of 'The Fields of Athenry' from Lenihan.

'At times I get annoyed with the inference, by an admittedly small minority, who feel, for some reason, that playing rugby make you less of an Irishman,' wrote Lenihan in his column in The Irish Examiner in 2004. 'I was privileged to play for my country in a sport that represents the entire island of Ireland. In the amateur era, I played alongside and shared hotel rooms with players who worked for the RUC and the British Army. From a playing perspective it was an issue that never raised a difficulty. Their presence meant our rooms required constant surveillance from armed units of the special branch from the time we assembled for a game. It was a very unusual environment from which to prepare for international competition.

'Yet, everybody just got on with it. Sacrifices were required on all sides. Of course it was disappointing to represent your country 12,000 miles from home without the reassurance of your national anthem to rival that of the opposition. In the aftermath of these games you faced the Irish community in the Irish clubs in such places, as Wellington, Auckland, Sydney and Brisbane and you understood their disappointment and frustration at its absence. In similar circumstances, players from Britain understand that "God Save The Queen" is not played at Lions Tests, as it does not represent the Irish contingent.'

When he was injured playing for Con the week before a Five Nations Game against England at Twickenham in January, 1990, Lenihan had to pull out of the Irish team and end a run of 43 consecutive international appearances; it was an incredible number for a second row. Two years later, on the day Lenihan started for the 52nd and final time for Ireland, the only other player on international duty that weekend who'd been around when the Corkman made his debut against Australia back in 1981 was English flanker Peter Winterbottom. Another fitting tribute to his longevity and physical conditioning.

Throughout the eighties, Lenihan managed to combine the demands of a professional career in finance with those placed on somebody wanting to compete at the highest level of an amateur sport. Very often, his desire to improve as a player didn't exactly dovetail with the prevailing structures in Irish rugby. Witness his account of preparing to captain the side in its first appearance at the inaugural World Cup in 1987.

'The players were hugely excited by the World Cup but the IRFU were not too keen,' said Lenihan. 'We'd all seen the soccer World Cup on television and we were excited about being involved in something like that. But the IRFU had opposed it right from the start and they didn't go out of their way in terms of preparation. I remember one evening driving up to Dublin with Brian Spillane to have a scrummaging session with the rest of the forwards, who were mainly based in the capital. We had to organise the session ourselves, it wasn't done by the IRFU.

'1987 was a totally different concept of a World Cup. Like, when you look back at it now, and you think about it, we were told not to play any matches for eight weeks before the competition – it was absolutely ridiculous. There was a lot of the same personnel as the side of '85 but way more experienced. So I have no doubt we lost an opportunity there through lack of preparation more than anything.'

Four years later, Lenihan was part of the side that came so close to defeating Australia in a World Cup quarter-final.

'I knew I was at the end of my career anyway, and to be within a minute or two of playing New Zealand in a World Cup semi-final at Lansdowne Road... I think we would have had a chance. We could have been in a World Cup final almost despite ourselves. Two weeks before, we had lost to Gloucester in a warm-up match but we were capable of one-offs. Eddie O'Sullivan was our fitness advisor, and briefly, we were as fit as most teams.'

Donal Lenihan in action for Ireland with fellow forwards Des Fitzgerald, Matt D'Arcy and Willie Anderson.

Having contributed to Con's victory in the inaugural All-Ireland league earlier that year, Lenihan's playing career was by then winding down. Following his retirement as a player in 1992, he was quickly on a management fast-track. A selector with the successful Lions in South Africa in 1997, he succeeded Pa Whelan as Irish manager in 1998. His three seasons at the helm alongside coach Warren Gatland were undistinguished, pockmarked by the 1999 World Cup defeat by Argentina, and he stepped down at the end of the 2000 campaign.

By then, he'd already been earmarked for another prestigious job. The morning after the announcement that Lenihan had been appointed manager for the 2001 Tour, a headline in the English Independent declared: 'Lions Entrusted To The Great Man of Cork'.

The Great Man of Cork. A nice ring to it.

Young

Shortly before togging out for the 1911 All-Ireland football final, Jack Young handed what money he had in his pocket to his travelling companion Con O'Regan for safekeeping. A pair of teachers, they'd come up from Cork together, one to play centre-forward, the other to watch the action from the terraces. As the afternoon wore on, Young was the fulcrum of an attack that garnered 6-6 on its way to a facile victory and the county's second title. Unfortunately, O'Regan hadn't been very stoic in his spectating.

At one point early in the contest, he'd become embroiled in some robust debate about the match with a group of Antrim supporters. When it was suggested he put his money where his mouth was, O'Regan had no hesitation. Cork had scored 8-11 and conceded just four points in the campaign to then so he ponied up the contents of his pocket, confident he'd be doubling his money by the final whistle. The only problem was that as the game wore on and his team's victory looked more and more assured, his excitement was so frenzied he forgot all about collecting the cash until he met Jack Young for the post-match celebration.

Without a coin in their pocket, the pair of them still managed to participate in the festivities. A kindly barman heard their story and took such pity that after plying them with complimentary whiskey for the evening, he even gave them the pewter cup he'd been using to measure the drinks. That vessel was filled and refilled the length of the train journey from Dublin to Cork the following day as they convinced people it was a replica of the All Ireland trophy. It took them two full days to get home to Barryroe where the pewter was, with great ceremony, presented to the owner of a pub.

Near enough nine decades later, Eamonn Young sat down to write the story of Cork's All-Ireland double of 1990 with that particular memento on his desk. His subsequent book 'Rebels at the Double' gave him a unique link to four of the county's five football triumphs in the twentieth century. Following in his father's footsteps, he had played centre-field on the winning team of 1945, and gone on to train the Cork side that lost in the 1956 and 1957 finals. Astute judges reckon he might just have been the best Gaelic footballer ever to emerge from the county.

When Jack Lynch was asked once to name the best footballers he'd ever seen, only one Corkman figured in his answer.

'Eamonn Young, for efficient application of football skill, would be hard to beat.'

Some may dispute that assertion but what cannot be argued is the way his story parallels the development of the GAA over its first 100 years. He started and finished his football career with Doheny's. Named for Michael Doheny, the Young Irelander who paid a fleeting visit to the town of Dunmanway while on the run from the authorities, it was the first West Cork club to affiliate to the new association in 1886. That the path wasn't smooth from then on is summed up by the fact Jack Young was playing for Nils at the time he won his All-Ireland, the GAA having briefly reached such a sorry pass in West Cork that the region's best players were recruited by city outfits.

'My father was a teacher and when he was coaching us he used to always say there was nothing to Gaelic football only catching the ball and kicking it straight,' said Young in an interview on RTE Radio. 'He emphasised the word straight. He wanted you to fetch the ball and drive it up in the air and over the bar from 35 yards.'

That simple philosophy guided Jack Young's son through his schooldays in Dunmanway and later at Good Counsel in New Ross, County Wexford. Towards the end of his secondary education, the name E Young started to figure on Cork minor teams in both codes. Like his older brother Jim, he hurled for Glen Rovers and garnered All Ireland minor medals in 1938 (playing centre-field on a team containing Christy Ring) and 1939. He also won a Munster championship with the minor footballers in 1939.

Although he made his senior debut for Doheny's while still a teenager, Young threw his lot in with Collins, the army team when he became a professional soldier. During the Emergency – as World War II was so quaintly called – the defence forces were stocked with some of the finest hurlers and footballers in the country. Four of the Cork team that brought home the Sam Maguire Cup, a bauble only 17 years in circulation, for the first time in 1945 were serving in the army or the Air Corps. Between 1949 and 1953, Young won three county titles with Collins.

'The Southern Command based in Collins' Barracks was fairly strong on the hurling and football fields,' wrote Young. 'And if the good Colonel James O'Hanrahan of happy memory, could coax a hurler from anywhere in the army to transfer to Cork and the Fourth Battalion so much the better. As already pointed out, that man's hurling might be no bar at all to promotion. One fine summer's evening, a tall, lean private, now at the end of his hurling career, was seen gazing steadily at the noticeboard over by the canteen. Slowly, shaking his head, he walked away and was heard to mutter in a quiet voice: "God help us.....96 McNamara....promoted to corporal...and that man never held a hurley in his whole bloody life.'

There were so many sporting soldiers that the Cork county board reacted to the demand to provide games for them by temporarily forming an Army division. They held their own championships and the winner competed in the county junior equivalent. It wasn't all fun and games for the enlisted men. Young often told the story of how he spent weeks on assignment in Tipperary in 1944, cutting turf from the bog of Killenaule and then to add further insult, was soundly beaten by the Tipp footballers in the Munster semi-finals.

Having defeated Kerry the previous summer for the first time in over thirty years, Cork narrowly lost the All-Ireland semi-final that year to Cavan. It was thought then a breakthrough was coming but following the Tipperary defeat, they found themselves back at the foot of the mountain in 1945. Their climb began with a slender one-point win over Tipperary, and following the dismissal of Kerry and Galway, they reached the county's first All-Ireland final for 34 years. Cavan were the opponents. A team that would go on to dominate football for nearly a decade had to give best on this occasion to Cork's superior goal-grabbing.

'Direct methods won that All-Ireland for us,' said Cork's trainer Jim Barry in Raymond Smith's The Football Immortals. 'If you ever have a football team in Cork, the nucleus of the side must come from West Cork. West Corkmen play the type of football that is best to bring success in the inter-county arena. It's better than the football played in the city – fine catchers and kickers come from the west of the county, from Clonakilty, Macroom and Beara.

'The 1945 All-Ireland was the first played after the palmed pass had been temporarily ruled out. Cavan were accustomed to the palmed pass and preferred it to the fisted pass. I remember in the training sessions allowing no kicking of the ball for a few days. I permitted them to fist it alright. I wanted to make them hungry for a kick. We finished on the Wednesday evening before the game. I always believed in finishing on the Wednesday at the latest.'

With eight representatives from Clonakilty satisfying Barry's West Cork requirement, the squad also contained an international show jumper, Mick Tubridy, and a future Taoiseach, Jack Lynch. After Tubridy's first-half goal gave Cork an interval lead of two points, Derry Beckett – whose father Jerry had played alongside Jack Young in 1911 – found the net 15 minutes after the break to set up a 2-5 to 0-7 victory. Contemporary newspaper reports all mention Young's strong running with the ball from centre-field, a feature of the triumph also commemorated in verse by Carbery.

> 'And where would you leave Eamonn Young, boys?
> He dummied and drove like his father of old,
> And showed them tricks from Dunmanway, I'm told,
> Humphrey O'Neill and Jack Lynch and Jim Cronin so bold
> Set our heroes like beagles in tongue boys...'

As the team posed for photographs on the field before the game, Jack Young stood on the right-hand side, wearing an overcoat and carrying his trilby hat in his hand. No apparent official role in the set-up, just a link with a glorious day past.

'My poor father was mad about football and he was always coaching us when we were young,' said Young. 'He was, all his life, very fond of football, He was thrilled when his son Jim [a regular with the Cork footballers too in the early forties] played in seven All-Ireland hurling finals and won five of them, and in spite of all that I was lucky to play in one All-Ireland and to win it, and I think he was more pleased about the one football All-Ireland – and Jim will hate me for saying this – than the five hurling All-Irelands!'

In 1946, the Cork footballers became the first GAA team to travel in an airplane when they flew to London for a tournament. Some of the All-Ireland winning squad hung on to bring back the county's first national football league title in 1952 but the gap between the third All-Ireland triumph and the fourth would stretch 28 years. Young trained the side that lost in 1956 and 1957 to Galway and Louth respectively. Noted for his innovative sessions and new-fangled methods of working the players, his powers didn't extend to picking the team.

'I was not a selector even though I was the trainer,' said Young. 'The selectors had total control of the team and everything connected with switches, substitutions etc. A couple of years earlier, there had been a degree of messing about by players on Cork football teams and as a result the selectors in 1956 laid down the law about their control. The rule was: "The selectors will give the instructions and nobody will do anything until he is told."'

He was a selector himself in 1967 when another Cork team came mighty close but were eventually beaten 1-9 to 0-9 by Meath. By then, Young had called time on his own playing career. After transferring back to Doheny's in 1961, he'd played on for five more years. His only concession to age was a move into the full-forward line, and he was a 45-year-old corner-forward when the club won the county junior championship in 1966. It was the perfect way to bow out.

'Every day in our jobs, there are certain things we have to do and our ability to do these things is based on normal efficiency and the ability to keep our temperament under control at the time,' said Young. 'That applies in every job, and if a man can't keep his temperament under control in Croke Park, and perform at his reasonable best, not his very best, he shouldn't be there at all. In a golf championship, in a boxing championship, in anything a person must be able to perform reasonably in the moment and if a fella can't control his temperament, he's not a performer.'

In the 1980s, another generation of Cork sports fans got to know him when he wrote an eclectic weekly column under the nom de plume of Rambler for the Evening Echo. Mostly confined to GAA matters, he would occasionally use it to point out the anomaly of Dunlop paying John McEnroe lavish sums to use their racquets while they were laying good Corkmen off down the Marina. It was during this time I came across him working as a substitute teacher at Colaiste an Spioraid Naoimh in Bishopstown.It was a dark period in Cork football history and most of us students were oblivious to this man's immense football pedigree. One particular day, I saw him marching straight-backed through the field at the back of our school, galoshes protecting his shoes from the mud. A Kerryman called Muiris McGillicuddy was trying to coach a gaggle of awkward Cork teenagers in the art of kicking points from distance. A break in training allowed Young his chance, and evincing the certitude of somebody who knew something about the game, he made his pronouncement. 'A Mhuiris,' he bellowed towards his fellow member of staff. 'That's the way we'll beat ye in years to come, that's exactly how we'll do it too, by kicking points long. We won't always be down, you know.'

And with that he was gone, squelching underfoot, enjoying the quality of his heckle, and so heartened by the prospect of a brighter future for his beloved county that his bald head shook as he went. Defiant. As ever.

Eamonn Young (right) with Tadhg Crowley during a Cork Senior Football team training session prior to the 1945 All-Ireland Football final against Cavan.

2

More than nine decades before Sonia in Sydney, a wrestler from Dunmanway, by the name of Con O'Kelly, came away with gold from the London Games. By dint of political and economic circumstance, our early Olympians had to wear the singlets of other nations. Their medal-winning feats are no less worthy of acknowledgment for that.

Olympians

Con Walsh

The writer Ulick O'Connor once posited the notion that the only truly Irish athletic event is the hammer-throw. He based his conclusion on the fact there's evidence of such a competition taking place at the Tailteann Games in Meath 300 years BC, and yet no sign of it appears in dispatches from the Ancient Greek Olympics. As good a theory as any to explain why up to 1936, every hammer gold except one was taken by a man born in Munster's Golden Vale. That the Germans subsequently inherited the mantle, only after having taken extensive photographs of the Irish training methods in the early thirties, sums up the extent of the supremacy.

That dominance may well have reached its peak at White City, London in the summer of 1908, during a Games which saw the birth of a couple of new Olympic traditions. In a welcome initiative, somebody came up with the idea of awarding gold, silver and bronze medals and the ceremony immediately became an integral part of the occasion. In a less welcome departure, international politics began to impinge upon sport for the first time.

When told they could only march beneath the Russian flag, Finnish athletes chose to march beneath no flag at all and many Irish prospects withdrew rather than obey an imperial order and compete for Great Britain. There was another way around that particular edict. This much was demonstrated most spectacularly at the completion of the hammer-throwing events when for the first and only time at any Olympics, every place on the podium was taken by somebody born in Ireland. That they were representing adopted countries was merely a by-product of the circumstances. John J. Flanagan from Kilbreedy, County Limerick and Matt McGrath from Nenagh, County Tipperary, took gold and silver in the colours of the USA, and are properly acknowledged as two giants of the sport. Less heralded, but equally fascinating, was Con Walsh.

From the mid-Cork village of Carriganima, nestling in the valley of the Foherish River, between the Derrynasaggart and the Boggeragh mountains, Walsh collected bronze wearing a Canadian singlet. Twenty-seven years old when he snagged a little piece of Olympic history, Walsh had by then already enjoyed a stellar career in another code.

He's listed in the forward line of the Nils selection (alongside Denis Irwin's grand-uncle Tom, a prominent hurler, footballer and cricketer of the time) that were defeated by Dublin Geraldines (their team bulwarked by several imports from other counties) in the 1899 All-Ireland football final on a scoreline of 1-10 to 0-6. Because of the scheduling vagaries of the time, that game wasn't played at Jones' Road until February 10th, 1901.

In the 1901 final proper - which took place in Tipperary on July 5th, 1903 - Walsh was on the losing side again as Dublin's Isles of the Sea came from behind to defeat Nils by 1-2 to 0-4. Apart from Irwin and Walsh, there were plenty of other versatile sportsmen involved in both those games. Alongside Walsh on the 1901 side was the redoubtable Billy Mackessy. A member of the Cork Celtic side that became the first civilian outfit to win the Munster Senior Cup by defeating the Leinster Regiment in the 1904 final, Mackessy also won All-Ireland hurling and football winner's medals.

Dublin had a couple of decent soccer players in their victorious 1901 line-up too. Val Harris won an Irish Cup medal with Shelbourne in 1906, was capped for Ireland and enjoyed a successful spell at Everton before the outbreak of World War I. His colleague Paddy McCann was a national sprint champion and later an excellent full-back for Glentoran and Belfast Celtic.

Walsh himself had come to national prominence via his victory at the 1901 All Ireland place-kicking championship (a big deal in that era) with an effort of 69 yards, and would retain that title in 1905 and 1906. On the latter occasion, he hit the ball over 224 feet, and reportedly landed four other titles at that year's All-Ireland athletics championships. The following year, he took the first of five consecutive Canadian national titles in the hammer, and, as a prelude to his display at White City, he also emerged triumphant in that discipline at the 1908 British AAAs.

'In May 1908 at Toronto Walsh threw the 56lb weight for a height of 15ft, 9 and a half inches setting a new record,' according to the excellent Clondrohid GAA website. 'On September 24th, 1910 at Travers Island, New York, he set a new world record in the 56lb for height with a throw of 16ft 6ins. Walsh's greatest victory came in the American championships of 1911 in Pittsburgh where he threw the hammer 179ft 6 ins. It was a world record. Later in the year he also set a new world record in the 56lb for distance with a throw of 27ft 4ins. In the same year having reached the peak of his career, Walsh retired.'

Not quite. That November, Lees defeated Nils in the Cork county senior football final. The team lists show Walsh playing in the forwards. Even still, he wasn't quite done. He crossed the Atlantic again and by the 1920s was a policeman in Seattle, Washington. Of course, the city was only too happy to have an Olympic medalist in their ranks because athletic competition between the rival forces from all over America was keen.

'Con Walsh, giant weight-tosser and one of the greatest performers on earth in the hammer throw and 56lb-weight event, will be the outstanding figure in the next National Convention which is to be held in Chicago this coming June,' went an entry in the Seattle Police Department Yearbook of 1923. 'Walsh is determined to bring home the laurels for the weight and hammer throw. In all the athletic events in which he has participated he has never failed to be the winner of the hammer throw or the 56 lb weight events.

'Mr. Walsh is a man of perfect physique. Six feet and a quarter of an inch in height, he weighs 210 pounds stripped. He is perfectly built with every muscle developed to its fullest. He is said to be one of the strongest men in the athletic world. Some years ago, Mr. Walsh picked up a quarter miler, Teevan, with his left hand and held him out at arms length. Teevan weighed 171lbs in his track togs, no wonder Walsh can toss the 56lb weight with ease. Day by day, in every way, Con is throwing the weights farther and farther and we look forward to some great achievements from him.'

'Rattle' Barrett

By the time Frederick Whitfield Barrett trained Annandale to win the 1931 Scottish Grand National, it was the sort of victory that would only merit a footnote in the story of his life. After all, he won an Olympic gold medal in polo, trained horses for three English kings, and became a major in the British Army on the back of his performance in World War I. Somewhere along the way, between Glanmire and the green fields of France, he even gained the more user-friendly nickname of 'Rattle', a colourful moniker apparently a tribute to the number of bones he broke falling from horses during a stint as a jockey.

Barrett was born in Cork city on June 20th, 1875, the same year his father, William, bought Silver Spring House. The family can trace their lineage in Ireland back to the time of Strongbow in the 12th Century and Rattle spent the first two decades of his life in the place where the hotel of the same name now stands. He joined the 15th Hussars in the spring of 1897, and by 1905 had attained the rank of captain and married Isobel Edwardes, the sister of a brother-officer, the 6th Lord Kensington.

'At the time, Barrett was well-known as a steeplechaser and took up polo seriously only in 1911 when his regiment went to India, where he served as ADC to Major General BT Mahon, then commanding the 8th Lucknow Division,' wrote Roger Chatterton-Newman in Polo Quarterly magazine in 1998. 'That was the year of the visit to India of King-Emperor George V and Barrett was among those awarded the commemorative Great Durbar Medal. On his return to England, a bad fall at Sandown put paid to his steeplechasing career and he concentrated on polo.'

It was in a sport he'd only begun playing properly in his mid-thirties that he came to leave an indelible mark. In 1914, Barrett was captain and key player on the English team that won the prestigious international Westchester Cup before a crowd of 35,000 at Meadow Brook, New York.

'The work of Major Barrett was again a display of splendid polo team play,' wrote Harry Cross in The New York Times. 'His shots were all short and accurate. He was constantly in the midst of scrimmage, ready to pass the ball back to one of his colleagues. Whenever the ball shot out of scrimmage to one of the English players for a run down the field, it was safe to assume that Barrett was behind the ball when it started.'

More than 80 years would pass before that trophy would return across the Atlantic again, and Barrett's significant role in the triumph was underlined by the fact he had also become the first player from the British Isles to gain the ranking of a 10-goal handicap.

'The best of the best is a Ten-Goal Player,' explains Jan Haddle Davis, editor of "Horse Latitudes, Journal of the Horse of the Americas". 'Few exist in the society of the game worldwide at any given time. It is an elusive title. Ten-Goal Players are men of legend - envied by other men, worshipped by young men and women entering the sport, and their names are forever printed in history. Ten-Goal men (and we say men, not because women are excluded, just because no woman has ever qualified) ride as if there were no tomorrow - calling up the fearless focus of thousands who have played before.'

In the 116 years since the rating system was introduced to the game, not even 100 players have yet earned the 10-goal standard. That Barrett did so after just three seasons seriously dabbling in the sport indicates that he must have been an exceptional horseman.

'At the beginning of 1914, Barrett had been appointed an instructor at the Cavalry School, Netheravon, and on July 5th was a member of the victorious 15th Hussars in the Inter-Regimental final at Hurlingham,' wrote Chatterton-Newman. 'A month later, England was at war with Germany and, within days, Barrett had sailed for France with the British Expeditionary Force. Mentioned in dispatches in 1917, he survived the war unscathed but a return to the polo field must have been tinged with sadness. So many of the pre-war polo masters had been killed.'

In 1919, he left the army shortly after being promoted to major. The follow-

Major Frederick Whitfield Barrett on the polo field.

ing summer, he went to the Antwerp Olympics as a member of the Great Britain polo squad. The first to be held since 1912, the Belgian Games marked the debut of now coveted traditions like the five rings flag and the taking of the Olympic oath. Despite having just turned 45, Barrett was a crucial figure on the team that won gold after a 13-11 triumph over Spain in the final. Interestingly, some record books list the victorious side as Great Britain and Ireland. Others just say Great Britain. Four years later, Barrett was again on hand to collect a bronze at the Paris Olympics before embarking on a training career that saw him saddle winners for Kings George V, Edward VIII and George VI.

Barrett had two children, a daughter Biddy who died tragically in a drowning accident in the thirties, and a son Dennis. Rattle himself passed away in 1949 and is buried in St. Bride's, Pembrokeshire. The trophy he collected for his role in the 1914 Westchester Cup was awarded to Cowdray Park Polo club in Sussex by his son back in 1972. The Barrett Cup League remains one of its most prestigious competitions. It is only fitting the name should endure in the sport it adorned.

Con O'Kelly

At the 1908 Olympic Games, a pair of policemen representing London and Hull were drawn to grapple each other in a semi-final of the freestyle wrestling. On one side of the mat stood Ned Barrett from Rahela, near Listowel; on the other was Con O'Kelly from Gloun, just outside Dunmanway. As the crow flies, less than 80 miles separated the houses that spawned them both, and here, at a tournament where Irish athletes were only allowed to compete under the Union Jack, a Corkman and a Kerryman were battling it out for a place in the final of the heavyweight class.

That O'Kelly had even got that far was remarkable. In the early hours of March 4th that year, Hull city fire brigade was battling a fierce blaze at Soulsby's Saw Mill when a gable end wall collapsed. Four firemen were buried beneath the bricks of two storeys, and after their colleagues had finally dug them out, the quartet were rushed to hospital. O'Kelly was the worst injured, the damage to his back and shoulders keeping him out of uniform for four weeks. Within a matter of months however, the 22-year-old was back tumbling around the mat in the sport quaintly described in the Olympic handbook as 'catch as catch can'.

Born in Gloun in 1886 (accounts differ about whether he was a March or October arrival), George Cornelius O'Kelly was educated at St Patrick's National School in Dunmanway. Before emigrating to England in his mid-teens, he reportedly dabbled in cycling, boxing and wrestling at a local level. Arriving in the west end of Hull, an area thick with Irish at the time, he joined the local constabulary on September 18th, 1902. An imposing figure at six foot three and 16 stone, he was quickly seconded to the fire brigade where fortuitously enough, one of his new colleagues invited him along to a grappling club to work out.

Almost immediately, he carved a reputation with Hull Amateur Wrestling club, causing a minor stir by upsetting the Northern Counties champion in a bout that took less than three minutes. Soon, he was the British Amateur heavyweight champion, and ironically, it was Ned Barrett who relieved him of that title shortly before the 1908 Olympics. Both men were ultimately selected for the Games and when their paths finally crossed at Shepherd's Bush, O'Kelly extracted revenge with an arm and crotch hold after just two minutes and 14 seconds of the contest.

Barrett would still earn his own place in folklore. An All-Ireland medal winner with the London hurlers in 1901 (they defeated Redmond's in the final), he added a gold in the team tug of war to his wrestling bronze at those games. With Barrett out of the way, only Norway's Jacob Gunderson stood between O'Kelly and his pursuit of a little piece of history. Although it took him more than 13 minutes to win his first bout with the reigning American champion, the second clincher was secured in a quarter of that time. The boy from West Cork who told people his childhood nickname was 'the clown from Gloun' had just become the first Corkman to win an Olympic gold medal.

'News of Con's victory soon reached his adopted city and when he returned to Hull the very next day together with his trainer Mr. Atkinson, over 12,000 people were waiting to greet him,' wrote Michael E. Ulyatt in "The Fighting O'Kellys". 'Con was sporting a white skull cap decorated with the Union Jack and wearing the green oak-leaf badge which Queen Alexandra had presented him with, the competitor's medal in his lapel and his gold medal was tucked away in his pocket.

'After greetings from the official welcoming party, Con was lifted and chaired by six burly colleagues from the Fire Service to cheers from the huge crowd. He was carried to a chemical fire engine, patriotically decorated with Union Jack flags and drawn by two horses to the Worship Street Fire station where he received another great reception from his work colleagues, all of whom had taken the Irishman to their hearts.'

Despite lauding him for the publicity he'd brought to the town, the authorities refused him a leave of absence to try professional wrestling, so in February, 1909 O'Kelly resigned from his job and went for it. Like so many others, he found the jump from the amateurs to the paid ranks difficult to negotiate. Incredibly, his first ever pro bout was for the world heavyweight championship and though he lost, he appears to have made a good living initially, supplementing his grappling with cabaret work in theatres.

In 1910, O'Kelly moved to Boston ostensibly to wrestle but ended up spending far more time in the boxing ring than on the mat. Although he never quite fulfilled one promoter's early billing of him as 'the future heavyweight champion of the world', he was christened 'The Harp' by the American boxing scribes, and nine wins out of 12 bouts were enough to ensure he returned to England a richer man for the experience.

Con O'Kelly

Upon retirement from the ring in 1914, he opened a pub, ran a crockery shop and dabbled in the property market. He also became heavily involved in the eventful career of his son Con Junior, who boxed for Britain at the 1924 Olympics in Paris, fought professionally at Madison Square Garden and was eventually ordained a Catholic priest. For a time in the 1930s, O'Kelly returned to Cork to run a poultry-farm at Elm Park near Macroom, and though he was living in Stockport when he died in 1947, he, his wife and his children are all buried at St Joseph's Cemetery, Ballyphehane.

Back when he coached young boxers in a specially-constructed gym at the back of his house on Freehold Street in Hull, O'Kelly had a simple mantra he repeated often.

"Come on lads, train hard and learn, it's good for the soul. Use your energy and make yourself into a man."

The creed he lived by.

Denis Horgan

The scene was a sports meeting in New York in the early years of the last century. A rivalry had been brewing for some time between a pair of well-known Irish shot putters, Mayo's Martin Sheridan and Denis Horgan from Banteer. Just off the boat from Ireland the day before, Horgan was sitting in the crowd, his friends having advised him not to compete after such a long, arduous journey. Eventually, the jeers of Sheridan's supporters became too much to bear.

Horgan leapt into the field, stood next to his great nemesis and announced: 'Here I am, and it's not my ghost that is here either!' He stripped down and beat Sheridan's best throw that day by two and a half feet. A tall tale? Well, we tend towards believing this kind of yarn about Horgan merely because the record books do not lie. Instead, they offer a map on which we can trace the breadth of his achievements.

Born in Fermoyle, two miles south of Banteer, on May 18th, 1871, he broke the world record for the first time at Cobh Sports on October 9th, 1897 when he flung the shot put over 48 feet. By that stage, he was more than halfway through a run of seven British AAA titles in a row and already becoming a legend in the sport.

'A man of very genial nature, he never put in much time practicing but depended on his strength and physical power for his prowess,' wrote Con Tarrant in “Seanchas Duthalla, 1986”. 'On one occasion at a meeting in Tralee, he turned up very late having missed his train. This delighted the others entered in the weight-throwing. At the last moment, a whisper went round: "Denis is here", and immediately, the jubilant ones became silent. Their chances of victory had gone. The invincible Horgan was an unbeatable proposition.'

To a tally of 13 UK championships (a record which still stands), he would add a silver (representing Great Britain) at the 1908 Olympics, and two years shy of his fortieth birthday, he even managed to take the American amateur crown for the first time.

'Cork hosted the All-Ireland Athletic Championships for the second time in 1905,' writes Jim Cronin in his superb chronicle "Cork GAA: A History 1886-1986". 'A very successful meeting was carried out, the feature of which was a world record created by the genial giant from Banteer, Denis Horgan, in the weight-throwing events. He won three Irish titles that afternoon."

The tragedy of Horgan's career is that he was 37 when he travelled to his first Olympic Games in 1908. In Athens 12 years earlier, America's Robert Garrett won gold with a throw that was seven feet shorter than Horgan's best effort that season. It was a similar story at the following two Games. At both, the Olympic title was won by a throw inferior to the sort of distances the Corkman had been routinely making in competition elsewhere at the same time.

There is no one explanation why he didn't enter the competition until he was too old to do no better than silver. The obvious theory is he couldn't afford the travel expenses involved. This falls down a little considering that, for a time, he worked as a New York cop and competed extensively in America. Whatever the exact reason, that he was the best shot putter of his generation appears without question, especially given the circumstances behind him finally annexing his own little slice of Olympic glory.

One year before competing in London, Horgan was on the beat in New York when he was set upon by a gang of Italian hoodlums. According to reports, they struck him several times on the head with a fire shovel and left him for dead in the street. The doctors saved his life, put a silver plate in his head and then marvelled at the way he returned to competition within a matter of months. The quality of his comeback may have had something to do with his unorthodox approach. He reputedly liked to warm up by consuming a dozen eggs broken into a pint of sherry.

Denis Horgan

'He did not believe in working on an empty stomach and once proceeded to consume half a dozen buns whilst a few friends hurriedly undressed him and got him into his togs,' wrote Con Tarrant. 'He had a peculiar habit of tapping the ground with a sort of convulsive movement of one foot whilst he gripped the shot and balanced on the other leg.'

Horgan lived the last years of his life in Crookstown, where he ran a pub with his wife, but he is buried nearer home in the churchyard at Lyre. This is a short distance from the Banteer sportsfield where a six year old boy once watched him throwing. Although he was by then a veteran of 40, the sight of Horgan in full flight left quite an impression on the youngster. His name was Pat O'Callaghan. In time, the world would come to know him as Dr. Pat.

Patrick J. Flynn

In the annual international fixture against Scotland held in Belfast on July 19th, 1913 Patrick Flynn won the four-mile race as Ireland defeated the visitors by seven points to four. From Ballinadee near Bandon, he was listed as representing Kinsale. Seven years later, the same man, now wearing the singlet of America's Paulist Athletic Club, stormed to victory in the 3,000m steeplechase at the US national championships at Travers Island, New York. His winning time was nine minutes 58.2 seconds. Between those two events, he had moved countries, fought and was injured in World War I, but never relinquished his Olympic dream.

Patrick Flynn in action at the Olympic Games in Antwerp, 1920.

The 1920 US championships doubled as the team trials for the Antwerp Games, and although more renowned at that point in his career as a long distance runner, Flynn had finished second to Michael Devaney in the steeplechase at the previous year's nationals in Newark. Although there are some reports that suggest he was initially entered for the shorter course in error, and would have preferred the lengthier contests, others contend he actually was the pre-race favourite in Belgium. In any case, it was in this event which - along with the five-ringed Olympic Flag and Athletes' Oath - was making its debut at the Games, that Flynn would make his mark.

Born in Ballinadee, between Bandon and Kinsale, in 1895, Flynn grew up in an era when burgeoning Cork athletes had no shortage of esteemed predecessors, the exploits of whom would have fired their adolescent imaginations. Timothy O'Mahony, nicknamed "The Rosscarbery Steam Engine" for his big-hearted running, was three-times Irish champion at the quarter-mile in the mid-1880s. O'Mahony once defeated the American title-holder in a contest at Madison Square Garden, New York. At the storied venue, the "Steam Engine" ran 440 yards in 52-and-a-half seconds in 1888. Other Cork runners of note in the era preceding Flynn were the Phibbs brothers, Con and Bill, from Glenville. They also figured prominently alongside O'Mahony in the so-called 'American Invasion' by Irish athletes in 1888.

At the age of just 18, Flynn made his own imprint on the national consciousness when he won the 1913 IAAA championship in a time of 21 minutes, 59 and two-fifths seconds.

'He was soon a champion athlete, becoming a national and international four-mile champion in 1913, before his 19th birthday,' wrote Diarmuid O'Flynn in the Irish Examiner. 'In September of that same year, he emigrated to the USA. There, he continued his exploits, but now competing in the 5,000 and 10,000 metre events. While still a teenager, he came within a yard of Olympic champion Hannes Kolehmainen, when the latter set a new world record for the 5,000 metres. He was a certainty for the US team for the 1916 Olympics in Berlin. Unfortunately, that part of Europe was otherwise occupied at the time and Patsy played his own part in that bloodiest of wars, being wounded in 1918.'

He recovered from that setback to earn his trip to Antwerp and the Sixth Olympiad just two years later. In a country that had been ravaged by the conflict, the Olympic stadium wasn't finished in time, athletes were ferried to and from events on the back of lorries and the American team's accommodation was in an abandoned school building. Many of the visitors complained. As a former soldier who'd just coped with much worse travails than that, the conditions probably didn't bother Flynn unduly.

His hopes of gold, however, were dashed by ill-fortune. On a track turned to near mud by constant rain, a fall at the water jump put paid to his chances of winning the race. He still dug deep enough to finish a very creditable second behind Great Britain's Percy Hodge. Some say Flynn was 100 yards back when the man from Surrey AC crossed the line, more figure it to have been just half that distance. What isn't in dispute is that he took home a particularly hard-earned silver.

In 1998, a statue was unveiled to Flynn in his home town. Dave Guiney, another great Cork athlete who was Irish shot put champion from 1944 to 1956, conducted the ceremony. That Guiney did the honours was only fitting. He had spent much of his journalistic career researching and then highlighting the Olympic achievements of Irish athletes running for adopted countries in the first decades of the 20th century. Guiney always felt their feats were being forgotten. For too long, Flynn certainly fell into that category.

Since 1932 when Dr. Pat O'Callaghan won his second gold medal, many Cork men and women have tried to capture Olympic glory. A few seconds can ruin the Olympic dream as can be seen by the disappointment expressed by Gearóid Towey and Sam Lynch at the 2004 Athens Olympics.

3

From an endless catalogue, here is a diverse selection, some cameos of brilliance that punctuate our history. These are episodes of excellence in which individuals make their mark on the sports landscape or teams forge national reputations that have endured for decades after. Some of the protagonists are Cork-born, others are merely visitors to these parts. All contribute greatly to our heritage.

Moments

Larry points the way forward

Growing up in Cork in the 1970s and early 1980s, the annual Munster football final defeat by Kerry was so much part of summer's ritual that it became difficult for my generation not to invest our oppressors with near mythical powers. Before adulthood bestowed the gift of perspective and allowed us to acknowledge the sheer greatness of Mick O'Dwyer's team, we could not quite understand their superiority. Even allowing for that one magical victory in 1983, it was an era of unrelenting gloom but thankfully, a character by the name of Sweeney wrote an Evening Echo column which leavened our depression with wit.

On Saturday evenings in the summer, we found solace in his relentless lampooning of the Kerry manager's annual post-Munster final comments about Cork always giving his side their most difficult game in the championship. One article culminated in O'Dwyer, unable to finish a speech about Cork being the second best team in the country due to the onset of manical laughter, being carried away, howling, by men in white coats. No journalist ever captured the angst of his audience better than Gerard Sweeney.

This was the down-at-heel county then that Billy Morgan took over in 1986. His very presence and impeccable pedigree immediately beaconed hope that the suffering might soon be at an end. By the time Morgan's first championship in charge came around, he had invited on board a former Kildare footballer called Larry Tompkins. Most people had never even heard of the guy before, and the only concrete information about him was that he'd played for a couple of years alongside the Collins brothers from Castlehaven out in New York.

Larry Tompkins raises the Sam Maguire Cup in victory after Cork defeated Meath in the 1990 decider.

Larry Tompkins swerves past Meath corner back Robbie O'Malley during the 1990 All-Ireland final.

Upon returning to Ireland, Tompkins threw his lot in with the West Cork club because, following a row about the price of a transatlantic air ticket in 1985, he wasn't interested in returning to play for Kildare. So quickly did he answer the call from Morgan to join the Cork panel that he ended up making his debut in red and white before ever donning the 'Haven's blue and white. According to most reports, Cork had picked up a useful footballer who could probably help their cause. Nobody ever thought he would become the talisman for the most successful decade in the history of Cork football. Of course, it probably helped that he was joining a squad under the baton of a kindred spirit.

'Larry and Morgan are the same kind of animal,' says one former Cork player. 'You don't find too many as mad in what they're prepared to do for football. If Morgan had burst his two knees he would have done the exact same thing as Larry has. I mean, you take someone like Niall Cahalane, who has cycled the 50 miles from Skibbereen to Cork for training sessions when he was coming back from his knee injury. He's a raving lunatic, but he's not in the same class as Morgan and Larry.'

From the moment he arrived, his fitness set a new benchmark for every one playing alongside him. There's a story told about a Castlehaven player taking up an invitation to join Tompkins for a spot of extra-curricular fitness work one afternoon. The poor soul signed up for some training with a club colleague, he ended up catching a glimpse of a living hell. The venue for their work-out was Vernon Mount, the severely undulating motocross track on the outskirts of the city. Anybody with an imagination and a basic knowledge of Tompkins' attitude to physical extremes should be able to visualise what transpired.

Pain was a four-letter word usually marked absent from his vocabulary. This is a man who snapped the cruciate ligament in his right knee in the second half of the 1990 All-Ireland final, played on regardless, scored two more points, and didn't bother to even mention it to team-mates until the following day.

'It was an accidental tackle and I nearly severed the ligament in my knee. My medial ligament was totally severed. Playing against Meath and being captain was the motivation to continue. It was very painful and my knee was totally unstable. I was barely able to jog on it. It was going from underneath me. I knew well I was in serious trouble but I couldn't let go. At the time, I didn't care if it was my last game once we won.'

A couple of years later, he was suffering from severe sunburn when he came off the bench in a vain effort to save a championship game against Kerry. Nobody else would have even considered attempting to play. Nobody else would have been asked.

A native of Eadestown, Tompkins was educated across the county bounds in Wicklow. At Blessington Vocational School, he used to gather the other kids during lunch breaks and after school for extra training if there was a big match coming up. The work ethic was its own reward. He was on the Kildare under-21 team from the age of 16. A decade or so later, one of his many rehabilitations from injury brought him to Lilleshall in Shropshire where several professional footballers - including Rangers' striker Ally McCoist - were absolutely flabbergasted by his fitness levels and stunned he wasn't paid to maintain his body in such condition.

'He was arguably the most dedicated footballer in Ireland in the second half of the eighties, and if dedication breeds success, then Larry deserved it,' wrote Pat Spillane in Shooting From The Hip. 'He was the closest thing Ireland ever had to a professional Gaelic footballer. His whole life revolved around training and games. He was unbelievably fit. He brought a whole new dimension to the Cork team, particularly in the scoring area as he was an accurate free-taker and he could also kick long-range points from play.'

His impact on Cork was immediate and resounding. Fourteen seconds into his first Munster final against Kerry at Pairc Ui Chaoimh, he kicked the opening point. Just over seventy minutes later, he converted a long-range free to salvage a draw after Mikey Sheehy's miraculous injury-time goal appeared to win the match for the holders. It was a scored that demonstrated Tompkins was made for the big stage and it garnered more than just a replay. Many feel it finally punctured that Kerry team's air of invincibility. Later that summer, Tompkins performed a similar last-ditch act of heroism against Galway in the All-Ireland semi-final. Before the 1987 final, his rise to prominence had him firmly in Meath's sights.

'Larry Tompkins was just another player, although another very good player when he played for Kildare,' wrote Liam Hayes in his memoir "Out of Our Skins". 'Not too many people gave him the credit he possibly deserved because Kildare were never around long enough in the Championship to attract a great deal of attention. Now he's back just three months and everybody is talking about him. He has captured the imagination of the entire country, but I still think he's the same player I've known for the last eight years.'His free-taking is superb, it always was, and if anything he's even more accurate now. He's probably practising a lot more, and he's getting more games than ever before, so he probably has improved. But Larry is still Larry. We've played against him too many times to think of him as anything else. Anytime anyone is fouled in training, in match-type situations, the guilty party is christened "Larry". Throughout the field this evening lads were shouting "Well done, Larry!" to make sure that we all get the message. Any free given away to Cork within fifty yards of our goals will be as good as chalking up another point for Larry Tompkins.'

There was far more to his game than just accuracy from placed-balls. This much is reflected in his subsequent selection on both the Cork and Kildare football teams of the millennium. His stamina allowed him roam the field and he was such a fantastic ball-winner and distributor that at various intervals over the next five summers, Morgan would move Tompkins from centre-forward to centre-field if Cork needed a spark. There, he often partnered Shea Fahy, another Kildare exile whose transfer of allegiance had been precipitated by an Army posting to Collins' Barracks. Apart from his physical size and wonderful fielding, Fahy was also a key contributor in his first four championships with Cork.

After the defeats by Meath in 1987 and 1988, Cork and Tompkins returned to the All-Ireland final in 1989 and won a classic encounter over Mayo, after which both sides were praised for the open nature of the contest and the lack of niggling. Mayo manager John O'Mahony later admitted he'd warned his defenders not to foul any Cork forward within 50 yards of the posts because to do so was to offer Tompkins a free shot at goal.

Castlehaven won the county championship that season to crown a remarkable year and when Cork returned to face Meath in the 1990 decider, Tompkins was captain. In three and a half years he'd played his way into a county's hearts and it was somehow appropriate that he lifted Sam Maguire as the second half of the double was completed.

Putting it all on the line. Larry Tompkins in action on the side line during his term as Coach of the Cork senior team.

'I think we should have won three All-Irelands in a row,' said Tompkins in Eamonn Rafferty's Talking Gaelic. 'We threw it away against Meath in 1988. A level of frustration had set in among the supporters but it came good in the final of 1989 against Mayo and we proved our worth by beating Meath the following year. Regarding my contribution to the Cork team, I think that a sense of dedication came through and maybe lifted others. I was totally dedicated to training and very often trained on my own. I know I worked harder than anybody else, practicing the skills, free-taking, building up a high level of fitness and strength. I never looked on myself as a Messiah. It was sheer commitment. I think my whole approach to the game helped to motivate Cork.'

In the first half of the nineties, Tompkins' body suffered so many crippling injuries, another cruciate, a disc removed from his back, that one school of thought blamed the damage on his own tendency to over-work it in training. Had he been fully fit and available, there's every chance Cork would have won the 1993 All-Ireland final, and perhaps that sense of unfinished business informed his unlikely inter-county comeback in the summer of 1998. By then, he'd succeeded Morgan as manager but was in such stellar form for Castlehaven that his fellow selectors pressed him to rejoin the panel as a player.

He faced Kerry in Fitzgerald Stadium with what Sean Moran described in The Irish Times as 'a body so patched-up and repaired that it could have been released from the dungeons of a castle during an electrical storm.' There was no miracle. Cork were beaten. Tompkins looked old and battered and for the first time since his arrival from New York, his reputation shipped flak locally. The criticism was misguided and failed to realise that the outsized determination that persuaded him to try for one last hurrah was the same madness that helped Cork win four consecutive Munster titles when he was in his prime.

Turning down the chance to play any game wasn't in his nature. In hindsight, it looked like an over-ambitious gamble but what else could they have done? Had Cork lost, they'd have been asked why one of the best forwards in the county (which he still was) hadn't been considered? Not to mention that Tompkins' entire career had been about pushing back boundaries and attempting the impossible. This just happened to be an instant when it didn't come off.

After a disastrous start -185 training sessions culminating in defeat by a last-minute Martin Daly goal against Clare - in 1997, Tompkins' managerial reign might have had a storybook ending if his well-drilled and disciplined side overcame Meath in the 1999 All-Ireland final. Ironically, the lack of a reliable free-taker was one of the factors in their defeat. Instead of in glory, his stint in charge ended ignominiously in a bad-tempered defeat by Roscommon in an All-Ireland qualifier at Hyde Park in the summer of 2003. Insult was added to injury when a Cork supporter (although calling him that demeans the word) invaded the pitch to remonstrate with Tompkins. Twenty-four years earlier, Hyde Park was where his intercounty playing career had begun, at a time when Kildare regarded him as the great lilywhite hope.

'You can't beat a guy that wants to do it, that wants to succeed and wants to win an All-Ireland medal,' said Tompkins once in an interview. 'You can't beat that guy. Give me that guy any day. He will out-battle the guy that maybe is that bit better at doing things. You can't beat the guy who is totally and utterly focused on one thing in life and that's to win. To find out if they have it, it might be hard, difficult or ruthless - sick in ways, however you want to describe it.

'But there is no point in finding out in May or June. Acceptance can gather momentum when you're successful - when you're winning Munster championships. It's easy then to get the momentum but I'm looking back to December or February and the winter nights and the dark and cold, wet and wind and snow. You're battling through the muck and the gutter. There's no shortcuts to All-Irelands.'

Perfect practice. Larry Tompkins gets in some shooting practice during a training session with his club Castlehaven.

Eight years after Tompkins lifted Sam Maguire, Kildare defeated Meath to win their first Leinster football title for 42 years. The winning goal that afternoon at Croke Park was scored by Brian Murphy, a native of Bishopstown who had starred with Cork minor and under-21 teams before work took him up the country. That a Corkman would billow the Meath net and end the Kildare famine. Well, some people would call that karma.

A dual star is born

Halfway through the replay of the 1982 All-Ireland camogie semi-final at Ballinlough. Kilkenny had taken full advantage of the wind to lead 3-6 to 1-2. Goals from Marion Sweeney, Mary O'Leary (Seanie's sister) and Mary Geaney subsequently brought Cork back into the game and the sides were level at the final whistle. In a potent gesture, the home players sprinted down the hill and back on to the field for extra-time where they finally pulled clear of the side that had beaten them in the previous year's final. Amid so much drama, 18-year-old Sandie Fitzgibbon's cameo as a substitute in that memorable encounter was merely a footnote.

Her arrival into the game late on was dwarfed by the contributions of giants of Cork camogie like O'Leary, Pat Lenihan and Marion McCarthy (winner of eight All-Ireland medals). The subsequent final victory over Dublin – where O'Leary and Lenihan scored the entire 2-7 between them – earned Fitzgibbon the first of her six O'Duffy Cups and half of her sporting claim to fame. Elsewhere on her CV, under the heading of basketball, there are four National Leagues, three National Cups, six Cork Senior Leagues, and six Cork Senior Championships.

Born on March 16th, 1964, the greatest female dual star of her generation started playing camogie with Glen Rovers at the age of nine. More than quarter of a century later, she'd retire having done enough to merit a place on the sport's Team of the Century. A Cork minor for the first time as a 14-year-old, her arrival on the scene heralded a run of success, with the county winning four All-Irelands in a row at that grade. As a student in North Pres she took up basketball and featured on a school team that won the All-Ireland cadet title in 1978.

Left picture: Sandie Fitzgibbon clears the ball while playing camogie for Cork against Kilkenny. Right picture: She races clear of the Granagh-Ballingarry defence during Glen Rover's victory in the Munster Senior Club Camogie Final.

After her cameo appearances for Cork in the 1982 campaign, Fitzgibbon won a starting spot on the left-wing in the following championship which culminated in her second medal. A few months short of her 20th birthday, she looked to be having one of those blessed careers. Unfortunately, the rest of the decade was to yield Cork camogie one hard-luck story after another. Fitzgibbon ended up on the losing team in 1984, 1987, 1988 (when the team was captained by Mary Ring, daughter of Christy), 1989, 1991. Three more times in that span, Cork fell at the semi-final hurdle.

Fittingly for one who suffered so much, Fitzgibbon was captain when Wexford were beaten 1-20 to 2-6 in the 1992 final, a game she also dominated from centre-field. Twelve months later, the O'Duffy Cup was retained and this time, Linda Mellerick, her Glen Rovers' clubmate and future colleague on the Team of the Century, took possession of the trophy.

All the while, she had developed into a good enough basketball player – at just five-foot six-inches – to captain Blarney to one of their National Cup triumphs and to be picked to play for Ireland. Remarkable as it may be for somebody excelling in two sports to enjoy an international hoops career that yielded 64 caps, in many ways, Fitzgibbon is just typical of a strain of camogie players who have always been multi-talented. Among the women she won All-Irelands alongside were Liz Towler, who eventually cut short a highly-promising camogie career to become a soccer international, and Mary Geaney, who missed the 1982 final because she had to keep goal for the Irish hockey team in a World Cup qualifier.

On occasion, the juggling can prove difficult. One weekend in October, 1990, Fitzgibbon played an All-Ireland club semi-final in Derry on a Sunday, then flew to Boston, Massachusetts. There, she starred in three games with

Sandie Fitzgibbon in action for Blarney against Killester of Dublin during a National League game at the Parochial Hall, Gurranabraher.

the Irish basketball team before flying home to figure prominently in Glen Rovers' defeat of St. Paul's of Antrim at Nowlan Park that weekend. Her inter-continental heroics were recognised with the Jury's Sports Star of the Month award and nobody would have been surprised by the intensity of her commitment to the club. When she finally retired from the Glen, she had four All-Ireland clubs, and ten county championships, including a six-in-a-row.

Her departure from the inter-county scene in 1997 was inevitably tinged with glory. Immediately after the shock defeat by Galway in 1996, she'd talked of retirement but had been persuaded back for one more campaign. The cajoling proved vital as she was a key player in the 1997 triumph over the same opposition. At the luncheon held in the Burlington Hotel the following day, the Cork players were presented with their winners' medals. The loudest cheer rang out when Fitzgibbon's name was called. Everybody present knew that the player who came off the bench without fanfare at Ballinlough 15 years earlier was taking her leave and deserved to be trumpeted.

'Sandie was one of the finest exponents of the game,' wrote Mary Moran in "Cork's Camogie Story". 'She was a master of her craft and gave special pleasure to those who love pure skill. She won every honour in the game in a remarkable career. Sandie was extremely fast to cover ground and had an exceptional work-rate. She always went for the ball and controlled it expertly."

Exactly how basketball people remember her too.

Burgerland and Britvic serve up final feast

With thirty-three seconds remaining and Team Britvic's point guard John Cooney taking the ball down court, the scoreboard had his side and Burgerland level at 91 points each. Nearly 4,000 people were crammed into the three-week old Neptune Stadium on North Monastery Road, and an epic weekend's basketball had come down to the last half-minute. Cooney played the ball around for 20 seconds or so, then, as he flung a pass to Timmy McCarthy, Terry Strickland pounced to intercept, stole down the court and just beat the buzzer with a lay-up. The venue erupted. Burgerland hadn't led since the first quarter and yet now, improbably, were the 1985 Calor Kosangas National Cup champions.

The celebrations only marked the beginning of the drama. An announcement over the public address pointed out that for the record, the winning scoreline was actually 92-91 not 93-91 as previously thought. Due to an official's error which saw an earlier Ray Smith two-pointer credited as a three, both teams had played the last three and a half minutes with an incorrect scoreboard as their guide. Britvic's Jasper McElroy, a six-foot five-inch graduate of Western Michigan, had kicked the plastic off one of the chairs after Strickland's lay-up went in but now that disappointment turned to anger. As Burgerland captain Tom Wilkinson was being presented with the trophy, Britvic coach Barry Deasy was besieging game commissioner Brian Nesbitt, banging his hand in frustration on the scorer's table.

Deasy's complaint was obvious and legitimate. With 33 seconds left on the clock, he'd called a time-out thinking his team were all-square. Britvic would surely have ran that last play differently had he known they were leading by

Ray Smith of Burgerland trying to get past Team Britvic's Timmy McCarthy during the 1985 National Cup Final at the Neptune Stadium in January.

a point instead of drawing. The denouement of a classic encounter had been affected by the faulty scorekeeping. That was a pity, yet in a sense the post-match controversy surrounding the error merely added another layer of emotion to an evening of sporting theatre. It turned one great cup final into a historic event. January 20th, 1985 became Irish basketball's own version of the 1972 Olympic final debacle between America and the Soviet Union. The comparison is apposite; the Burgerland (Neptune)-Britvic (Blue Demons) rivalry was often of Cold-War proportions.

'I'm pretty passionate about this,' says Kieran Shannon, now a Sunday Tribune sportswriter, then teenage basketball zealot. 'I can honestly say, in all my time following a lot of sport, the only thing that can rival the Neptune-Demons rivalry, and in fact, Irish men's basketball itself from, say, '84 to '88, in terms of consistent quality and drama, is Munster hurling. Nothing else compares. People talk about the Dublin-Kerry football rivalry of the '70s but apart from the '77 semi-final, did they serve up a decent game between them? Neptune and Demons was always even better than the hype. From October 1982 to October 1989, they played each other 17 times between league, cup and Top Four and only once was there more than nine points between them. The '85 game was only a taste of what those two served up.'

It was the sort of local conflict outsiders couldn't quite understand, yet immediately bought into.

'I think it was the amount of hate between them that was so incredible,' said Terry Strickland who grew up in the tobacco-growing country of North Carolina, and arrived in Cork from the University of South Carolina in 1983. 'I hated Demons and I didn't know why. You arrive at the airport and they tell you you have to hate Demons.'

Strickland, McElroy and a host of others (not all of whom matched up to that pair) had been imported following the visionary decision by Killarney and then the Irish Basketball Association to allow two American professionals per team. They came across the ocean and revolutionised the way the sport was played in Ireland. They brought colour to a country that was still one of the whitest in the world, added a touch of glamour, a higher level of skill, and offered a first glimpse of the aerial game then coming into vogue in the States. Up to that point, the joke was that everybody in Irish basketball thought dunking was something done best with a biscuit. Not anymore.

'It was a strange thing,' says Tom O'Sullivan who played in the 1985 final for Burgerland at the age of just 19, 'that in the middle of a recession in the 1980s, so many Irish clubs could afford to pay two Americans maybe three or four hundred quid a week. But they managed it somehow.'

It helped that when the Americans came along, they were surrounded by genuine quality. There was such a base of local talent in Cork alone that the three clubs from the northside reached the 1985 cup semi-finals, the presence of Team Harp Lager (North Monastery) confirmed the city's brazen claim to be the capital of the sport in Ireland. Apart from an up-and-comer like O'Sullivan (top Irish-born scorer in the final with 14), Wilkinson was a seasoned international. On the other side, Timmy McCarthy and Gerry Wheeler had also played for Ireland, as did Cooney, a former teenage prodigy who'd started his first senior basketball match at 15.

As often happens in sport, a number of different factors melded together at just the right time and created something special. A generation of home-grown stars came of age in an era when American imports improved the standard of play, sponsors became aware of the sport's potential, and the Cork public got swept up in the phenomenon. Four thousand shoehorned in for that first cup final at Neptune Stadium. Very often, players made inbound passes sandwiched between spectators kneeling courtside. At the first game played there - the cup quarter-final against St. Vincent's three weeks earlier on New Year's Day, 1985 - Pat Boylan went to the free-throw line for the Dublin team in the final seconds and the noise from the foot-stomping and chanting of Burgerland supporters actually shook the basket he was aiming for.

How far the sport had travelled in so short a time. There were a few men watching Strickland lay-up for victory on the day the arena came of age who had played their first games of indoor basketball up in Collins Barracks. That was a venue where the soldiers boots had coarsened the floor so badly every fall was an open cut, and the referee often had to look out the window for Shandon to work out how much time was left on the clock. The new stadium was a monument to the ambition of those men, the financing of its £500,000 construction in a depressed economy was as unlikely an achievement as Burgerland's snatched triumph. It also allowed their supporters to endlessly boast about its superiority to Demons' less-salubrious home at the Parochial Hall in Gurranabraher

Neptune had renamed their team after the fast-food franchise when its owner Jackie Solan generously pumped £300,000 into the club, a deal that both sides did very well out of. The club even splashed out on an American coach, bringing in Ken Black on the recommendation of Strickland in 1984. Their second import, Ray Smith, was a huge talent who later finished top-scorer in the Spanish league. Britvic's American tandem that season consisted of the flamboyant McElroy and Dale Roberts, a six-foot nine-inch giant out of Appalachian State University.

As was normally the case in games of that era, the Americans dominated the scoring for both teams. Still, the first half of the final was a tactical affair where Britvic's tough, aggressive defence slowed down Burgerland's fast-paced running game. Roberts worked especially hard preventing the post-entry passes reaching Strickland and Smith, and although there were never more than five points in it before the interval, this was mostly down to Strickland popping up with key baskets and Jim Nugent making some brilliant drives late on.

After the break, Britvic emphasised their superiority, quickly extending a four-point half-time lead to nine. McElroy was on his way to 41 points and there were even press reports of some of their supporters prematurely celebrating what at that stage looked like a certain win. Burgerland didn't launch a comeback as such, more of a sustained effort at staying in touch that culminated in the dramatic last-gasp basket.

Their cause was helped in that second half by Black's canny use of the strength-in-depth on his bench. By contrast, only six Britvic players got playing time and they were definitely wilting towards the end. Throughout the second half, Smith improved inside against Roberts and McElroy went to four fouls with just over 11 minutes to play. Despite all that, and Roberts missing a succession of free-throws, Britvic retained the upper hand and were 89-82 up when Strickland fed Smith for the shot that the scorer incorrectly put down as a three. The score that at least one half of the northside felt changed everything.

'The post-game feelings of the Britvic camp, disgusted at literally throwing the game away, and then realising the seriousness of the scoresheet error, were based on understandable frustration,' went the match report in Basketball Ireland magazine. 'Anyone watching the game, with the exception of the ardent Burgerland/Neptune people, must have considered Britvic, led by Americans Jasper McElroy and Dale Roberts, a superior team in most facets of the game. Britvic should, realistically, have wrapped up the game, midway through the second period.'

Britvic lodged an objection afterwards. Nothing much came of that apart from a further ratcheting up of the rivalry. When the two teams met again in the Top Four final on St. Patrick's Day that year, Micheál Ó Muircheartaigh could be heard on radio bemoaning the fact that there were more people at a basketball game in Cork than at the Railway Cup finals. RTE television had taped the semis and final of the National Cup and broadcast it over the ensuing weeks on Sports Stadium. The knock-on effect from the final was that the station always showed the cup decider live from then on. They never got another final quite like that one. How could they have?

Murphy's law endures through generations

On January 20th, 1990, Ireland was on the receiving end of a 23-0 hammering from England at Twickenham. The sort of result that was depressingly commonplace at that time, the game is not one that many Irish fans would care to remember. It also happened to be the day a little piece of history was made. When Kenny Murphy ran on to the field to win his first senior cap, he was tracing the footsteps of his father and grandfather before him. The Murphys thus became the first family to have three generations play international rugby at the highest level for the country.

Six decades earlier, the sequence had begun in similar circumstances. Noel Francis Murphy also took his international bow against the English but his debut came at Lansdowne Road on a February afternoon. The 25-year-old had better luck too, his first game ending in a 4-3 victory for Ireland. A back-row forward from Cork Constitution, he won 10 more caps over the following four seasons, and played every game in the 1932 campaign in which Ireland won a share of the international championship.

A former captain of his club, Noel Murphy Senior then embarked on an administrative career that culminated in him becoming president of the IRFU in 1960. The following year, he managed the Irish team that toured South Africa. By that point, his 24-year-old son and namesake was an established international who in 1959 had been the youngest member of the Lions squad on an epic tour of Australia, New Zealand and Canada. In what may have been a case of reverse nepotism, Noel Arthur Augustine Murphy - having figured in 17 of the previous 18 internationals - failed to make it onto the back-row of the Irish team for any of the Test matches in Africa.

Three generations of international rugby players. Noel Murphy Senior (left) Noel Junior (centre) and Kenny (right) .

Despite that curious omission, Noel Junior, or Noisy as the rugby community came to know him, enjoyed the most stellar career of the three. Four of his 41 caps came as captain, many were won in the company of his cousin Tom Kiernan, and he featured in two tours and eight Test matches for the Lions. Parallel to his international exploits, there were eight Munster senior cup wins as part of what was arguably Cork Constitution's greatest ever side. Noel Senior had won two cups in 1929 and 1933, and Kenny, along with another son, Charlie, played for the Con team that won the inaugural All-Ireland League in 1991.

Murphy's final appearance for Ireland came in unfortunate circumstances in 1969. Having defeated France, England and Scotland, he was part of a side that went to Cardiff Arms Park with a shot at the Grand Slam. They left after being destroyed by the Welsh in a game marred by Brian Price flooring Murphy with a first-half punch, a blow that caused a scandal because it occurred with the 21-year-old Prince of Wales watching from the royal box.

Ten years later, Murphy enjoyed perhaps his finest run as a coach. Under his stewardship, Ireland went to Australia and beat the hosts in both Test matches. At that point in the game's history, no team from Ireland, Scotland, England or Wales had ever won a Test series in the southern hemisphere. Better yet, the victories were a vindication for a controversial selection policy by the coach. His decision to opt for Ollie Campbell over Tony Ward divided the Irish rugby community, garnered huge media coverage but paid off handsomely. A year later, Murphy joined the select band who've played for and coached the Lions when he took charge for the controversial tour of apartheid-era South Africa. Under the captaincy of Bill Beaumont they won 15 out of 18 games but crucially, lost three of the four Tests.

Previous page: Noel Murp Junior (extreme right) lend his support to Ireland's Ronnie Dawson as he heac for the French line during the 1964 International at Lansdowne Road.

Murphy was appointed Irish Under-21 manager in 1989, served as senior team manager from 1992-1995, and also did a stint as chairman of the selectors in that most difficult decade for Irish rugby. As the game struggled with the pressing need to go professional, Ireland was often off the pace against the best teams, and although the manager was arguably less culpable than the coach, the flak was distributed equally.'He has coached his club, province and country and played for and coached the Lions,' wrote Edmund Van Esbeck in a trenchant defence of Murphy in The Irish Times in March, 1994. 'He has been president of his club and of the Munster Branch. Notwithstanding that immense contribution, he answered the call five years ago to manage the Irish under-21 team, to bring his vast experience and expertise to an important area of development in the game.

'Then, when asked, he took over as manager of the Ireland side at the start of last season. From the outset of his tenure of office, Murphy has been subjected to criticism and innuendo without parallel in the game in this country from some quarters. He is bone of the bone a rugby man whose family roots are deeply embedded in the game and its tradition in this country. He has made an immense contribution to the game and could stand aside now content on that score.' During that problematic era, nothing seemed to go right for Ireland. Even the little things. It fell to Murphy to introduce 'Ireland's Call', Irish rugby's replacement for the national anthem at a press conference in Johannesburg's Sunnyside Hotel before the start of the 1995 World Cup. A tape recorder was provided, the cassette was put in, and Murphy duly called everybody assembled to order. Of course, when he pressed the button, 'A Rainy Night in Georgia' was the song that started playing.

Noel Murphy Senior shake the hand of the Viceroy of Ireland before an international game at Lansdowne Road.

Kenny Murphy (with ball) in action for Munster.

Thirty-eight years after his father had held the office, Murphy became president of the IRFU in 1998, the final accolade for a life spent in service to the sport. Contrary to the caustic media portraits of him in the nineties, he is known throughout the game for his genial good humour.

'I told him (Murphy) that my only ambition in life was not to win an Oscar but to run on to the field in a green jersey on international day at Lansdowne Road,' said Richard Harris one time. 'I am going to do it before I die and I said to Noel: "I want your co-operation." "How?" says he and I told him I'd be waiting outside the dressing room in an old coat and then when the 15th Irish player comes out, I'd take the coat off and run out in the Irish jersey to the middle of the pitch and pretend I'm on the team. I'd probably be arrested by the gardai but so what? Anyway Murphy says: "Look, you don't have to hang around in an old coat. Give me £50,000 and I'll get you into the team!"

As a boy, Murphy had hurled with Grenagh and played soccer with Victoria Rangers before mainlining rugby in his time at Christian Brothers College. An ecumenical approach to sport though was a feature of his life. When based for a time in Limerick, he was asked to train the Limerick soccer team in order to improve their fitness. The side he worked with won the League of Ireland in 1960. This surely makes him the only good friend of Christy Ring able to boast of having played a part in the winning of that title. The rugby international and the hurling legend bonded initially through their work raising money for the Cork Polio Shelter, which says a lot about the character of both men.

'In Ireland, rugby is a small game in a small country,' said Murphy after a defeat to France in March, 1995. Small game. But a big impact for one family to have.

Athletic get rich beyond their wildest dreams

Early in 1953, Cork Athletic were desperate for a run in the FAI cup to salvage a very disappointing season. Out of contention for the League of Ireland title by Christmas, they were casting about for a signing that might simultaneously ignite interest and spark the team when word filtered through that Raich Carter was ready to come out of retirement. Having just turned 39 years old, one of the great English inside-forwards was looking to restart a career, the prime of which had been seriously truncated by World War II.

In the Manchester Hotel in Hull on February 1st, Carter inked a deal with an Athletic delegation of secretary Donie Forde and director Dan Fitzgibbon. At a time when the maximum wage in English football was £14, they agreed a fee of £50 per game plus expenses. An extravagant contract for which the silver-haired former English international would eternally be dubbed "Rich" Carter by the Cork public, it turns out he was value for money. So much so he's generally acknowledged as the most successful short-term import ever in the domestic game.

It helped that the Athletic side he hooked up with were no slouches themselves. Sure, they'd failed to punch their weight prior to his arrival but this squad wanted for neither talent or experience. Half of them had won FAI Cup medals just two seasons previous, almost all had gained representative honours with the League of Ireland XI. From Ned Courtney in goal to Paddy O'Leary up front, the team contained names – like Jackie Lennox, Dave Noonan, "Small Seanie" McCarthy and Willie Cotter – that are writ large across the history of the sport in the city. Carter was merely the catalyst required to set them off. 'Carter was

Facing Page: Action from the all Cork F.A.I. Cup Final at Dalymount Park, Dublin between Evergreer United and Cork Athletic Evergreen goalkeeper Der Barrett watches Raich Carter's (right) effort sail just past the post.

In the Manchester Hotel in Hull on February 1st, Carter inked a deal with an Athletic delegation of secretary Donie Forde and director Dan Fitzgibbon.

that rare being, a magnificent maker and taker of goals, and were he playing today his transfer valuation would surely be astronomical,' wrote Ivan Ponting in a1994 obituary for The Independent newspaper in London. 'He shot thunderously with either foot, especially his left; his ball control was impeccable and his body-swerve little short of sublime. Crucially, he possessed the intelligence to put these natural gifts to maximum use. He could roll immaculate passes through the tiniest of gaps, sometimes seeming to shred defences at will, and much of his work alongside Stanley Matthews, when the two formed a right-wing pair for England was breathtaking.'

Born in Sunderland on December 21st, 1913, Horatio Stratton Carter was rejected by Leicester City as a teenager because he was too small. Sunderland thought his physique less of an issue, and in 1936, he skippered his home town to the English league title, becoming the youngest captain ever to do so. A year later, he scored one and laid on two more as Sunderland won the FA Cup. When World War II broke out, he joined the RAF, and worked rehabilitating injured airmen at Loughborough while often guesting for Derby County at the nearby Baseball Ground.

With Northern Ireland's Peter Doherty as his foil, Derby won the first post-war cup final in 1946, and alongside Tommy Lawton and Matthews, Carter is one of only three players to have represented England either side of that conflict. Prior to the visit from Messrs. Forde and Fitzgibbon, he had been player-manager of Hull City. Having led them to the Third Division North title in 1951, he retired in April of the following year with an impressive record of 58 goals in 136 appearances for the club.

Although he later confessed that his chief worry on the way to Ireland was the cumulative effect of 10 months out of the game, Carter's concerns were unfounded. He did exactly what he had been signed to do and that he was subsequently voted man of the match in a representative game for the League of Ireland against their English counterparts offered telling proof how much he still had to contribute.

In the first round of the FAI Cup at Tolka Park, he scored the only goal in a taut encounter against Drumcondra. He followed that up with a brace in the 3-2 victory at Waterford in the next round, an infamous match during which play was held up when a spectator knocked out a few of Carter's team-mate John Moloney's front teeth.

'The Victoria Hotel was my headquarters in Cork and there I enjoyed good service, good food and every assistance from a very pleasant staff,' wrote

Carter in an evocative piece for the 1953 Hollybough. 'I used to travel from Dublin to Cork by motor car and at first, I sat alongside the driver Alec Crean, who was the Cork representative in Dublin. Alec then found out that I could drive and I was detailed as chauffeur with Alec as navigator. We had some wonderful trips in rain, fog and snow but we always arrived back in Dublin in the early hours of the morning after the match. I enjoyed Cork very much, meeting the other directors of the club and making new friends. People were most kind and I was invited to several homes where I had some very happy times.'

At a windswept Dalymount Park, the semi-final against Limerick was a dour affair with a pair of Lennox goals eventually securing Athletic passage's to meet fellow Corkonians Evergreen in the final. A bizarre FAI judgment ruled that the all-Cork decider should be played in Dublin. After a less than scintillating 2-2 draw – Carter and Noonan were on the mark for Athletic – both teams were brought back to the capital the following Wednesday for the replay. Lennox opened the scoring on 17 minutes, the Englishman added a second nine minutes after the interval and although Liam O'Neill pegged one back for Evergreen, Athletic held on for the win.

'I thought that afterwards I would be able to return home but I found this impossible because the Cork officials and players had to attend a reception upon their return to Cork the following evening,' wrote Carter. 'I shall always remember the welcome we received both inside and outside the cinema where the reception was held. It was a great sight to see all those people and to know they were thrilled that Cork had won the cup, and they had enjoyed our efforts on the field.'

The FAI cup ensured Carter kept up his record of winning at least one medal with every club he played for. This statistic gained some poignancy four years after his death when it emerged his entire collection of memorabilia – including his FAI Cup memento – were set to be auctioned off. At the last minute, Sunderland City Council stumped up to purchase the collection before the sale, and placed it on permanent display in their Civic Centre, his career ending where it began.

Ashes to ashes, Midleton to Melbourne

On the first day of the first ever test cricket match, Tom Horan was the third batsman in. Twenty-three years after being born in Midleton, he strode to the crease at the Melbourne Cricket Ground to do his bit for Australia versus England. It was March 15th, 1877, and the rivalry that would launch the international dimension of the sport had just begun. As a player and journalist, Horan would be centrally involved in its first four decades.

His dexterity, both at the crease and with the pen, earned Horan the unique privilege of both playing in and later writing about the legendary Test at the Kennington Oval in August, 1882 which set up the Ashes Series. This was the game that inspired The Sporting Times in London to carry a mock obituary for English cricket, the body of which it said would be cremated before the ashes were taken to Australia. The following sample of Horan's account of the event offers a flavour of his style:

'The strain, even for the spectators, was so severe, that one onlooker dropped down dead, and another, with his teeth, gnawed out pieces from his umbrella handle. For the final half-hour you could have heard a pin drop, while the celebrated batsmen A.P. Lucas and Alfred Lyttleton were together, and (Fred) Spofforth and (Harry) Boyle bowling at them as they never bowled before. That was the match in which the last English batsman had to screw his courage to the sticking place by the aid of champagne, when one man's lips were ashen grey and his throat so parched that he could hardly speak as he strode by me to the crease; when the scorer's hand shook so that he wrote Peate's name like "Geese", and when in the wild tumult at the fall of the last wicket, the crowd in one tremendous roar cried "Bravo Australia! Bravo Australia!"....'

Horan didn't have a particularly good time of it in the game that gave birth to the legend of the Ashes, managing just two runs both times he was in. To be fair, this was well below his average. In that first match between the countries five years earlier, he'd followed up a 12 in the first innings with a 20 that was Australia's highest second innings score as they hung on to win by 45 runs.

'Tom Horan was in his time the crack batsman of Victoria,' went his obituary in "Wisden Cricketer's Almanack", the cricketing bible. 'He formed his method and earned high distinction as a batsman before enjoying the advantage of a trip to England. He had no special grace of style, but his defence was very strong, and he excelled against fast bowling. Even after an interval of nearly thirty-five years one recalls the masterly way in which he played John Crossland (in a touring match against Liverpool and District) at Liverpool in 1882, getting him away again and again on the leg side.'

Born on March 8th, 1854, the right-handed Horan played fifteen tests in all for Australia, his finest hour coming against England in a game that began on New Year's Eve, 1881. Batting number five, he hit six fours on his way to his highest test score of 124 before being run out. The biggest innings of his first-class career was 250 not out for East Melbourne v. Tasmania at East Melbourne in December, 1879. Over ten hours at the wicket, he never came close to getting out. He was capable of assisting with the ball in hand too, managing to take 11 test wickets in all. A round-arm, right-arm, fast-medium bowler, he managed to snag six for 40 in the first innings against England at Sydney Cricket Ground in February, 1885. A month later, he was bowled out for 20 in the fifth test of that series in Melbourne, and though he soldiered on with Victoria (for whom his two sons later played) until December, 1891, that was to be his last appearance for Australia.

'The period between the years 1879 and 1916 saw the birth and early development of Australian cricket and the start of the wonderful Ashes Test series versus England,' wrote Brian Crowley who co-edited an anthology of Horan's journalism. 'It was also the period during which Australia's first great cricket writer, the Irish-born immigrant Thomas Patrick Horan, journalist and Test cricketer (he captained Australia versus England in 1884), wrote about three million words on the noble game for The Australasian newspaper in an unbroken sequence covering 37 years.

Tom Horan (second left, middle row) was born in Midleton, Co Cork and played cricket for Australia during their 1878 tour of England.

'And he was as adept a writer on cricket as he was a player and Test captain. According to a contemporary Australian Test player, the great all-rounder George Giffen, Horan's writings did much to "cultivate a true, genuine interest in our beloved game". The late Ray Robinson, acknowledged doyen of Australian cricket journalists (bar perhaps the legendary Bill O'Reilly), wrote that "wise editors provided generous space for articles by Felix (Horan's pen name)", while O'Reilly has called the legacy left by his Irish-born counterpart "a gold mine of imperishable memories".'

Bringing to bear the perspective and contacts that only somebody who participated in the genesis of the sport possibly could, Horan's weekly column entitled "Cricket Chatter" was beloved of fans. The Australasian's annual publication of his "Round the Ground" article was considered the official closing ceremony of the cricket season. In his last such piece before he died in April, 1916, he lamented the fact that, with the world at war, the chances of an England team touring any time soon were slim.

'I do not think they will be here, but if they should come, I hope you and I may be here to see,' wrote Horan, 'and that I shall have the pleasure once more of going round the ground to tell you all about the goodliest company of famous cricketers, whereof the world holds record.'

Racing in the streets

On April 23rd, 1938, eight cars lined up on the grid for the start of the first and only grand prix race to be held in Ireland. They were primed for 33 laps of a circuit that began and ended on the Carrigrohane Straight. In between, they went around Victoria Cross to Dennehy's Cross and out along Model Farm Road as far as the Poulavone Hairpin. There they veered right by Hellhole Bend under the shadow of Carrigrohane Castle and back into the home straight.

More than a decade before Formula One as we know it today was established, Alfa Romeo, Delahaye, Maserati and Bugatti had entered a race to be run to the International Formula, then the highest grade in the sport. First prize was £1,000.

Pole position was taken by Rene Dreyfus, a Frenchman in a Delahaye with a Monaco Grand Prix win on his CV. Alongside him in the front row were 23 year old Prince Bira – a member of the royal family of Siam – in the Maserati, and another Delahaye driver Franco Comotti.

The notion that Cork could host a Grand Prix had been born just three years earlier. Although a motorcycle race was held on the Carrigrohane Straight in 1929, it was following the success of a motor race in Limerick that a group of enthusiasts in Cork – among them Lord Mayor Sean French - came together in 1935 with the aim of putting together a similar event.. They realised the city had one remarkable natural asset that lent itself to just such a contest. With the two and a half miles of the Carrigrohane Straight as the centrepiece, there was an impressive, pre-existing road circuit of six miles within walking distance of town.

RALLY
V8
30

ANOTHER
24

Previous page: The Start and finish line of the Grand Prix circuit at the Victoria Cross end of the Carrigrohane Straight.

The inaugural Cork Car Race of 1936 went so well that the County Council decided to widen the Carrigrohane Straight by nine feet. Once they'd further enhanced that stretch of the circuit, the Royal Irish Automobile Club (RIAC) were able to appeal to the international governing body of the sport to grant the event an elevated status for its next running. Despite inclement weather conditions, the 1937 Cork International Motor Race went off without a hitch too. The foundations for a Grand Prix proper had been laid.

'In January, 1938, it was announced that the Irish Motor Racing Club, in co-operation with the Cork and District Motor Club, would promote the Cork International Car Races meeting on Saturday April 23rd,' wrote Wilford J. Fitzsimmon in his evocative pamphlet about that brief golden era. 'It was further announced that thanks to the generous sponsorship of Mr. Joseph McGrath of the Irish Hospitals Trust, who would present the entire prize fund together with a substantial contribution towards the organisation (the balance being locally subscribed in Cork), the 1938 event would take on an increased significance.'

Once the time came for the teams to arrive, Fords cleared an entire bay at their plant on the Marina to give the teams and their mechanics a proper facility in which they could work on their cars. Despite the late arrival of the Bugatti car and a troublesome Friday practice that required mechanics to pull an all-nighter to get her ready, great things were still expected from France's Jean Pierre Wimille on the back row of the grid.

Wimille never figured. The race belonged to Dreyfus. Although he had to give best at the start to the bold driving of Prince Bira, the Frenchman only needed one lap to regain the lead. When winning the Grand Prix de Pau two weeks earlier he'd finished over two minutes clear of the nearest challenger, and although Bira gave bold chase in his old Maserati and fully deserved second place, Dreyfus was a comfortable winner again.

The extant photographs convey the wonder of the day. One shows Dreyfus, goggles strapped to his head, straining to guide his number 14 car around the hairpin from the straight into Victoria Cross. In another, it looks like his front wheels are buckling as he negotiates Inchigaggin Bridge. At the finish, there are splashes of oil from a cracked gearbox all over his jumpsuit.

'Dreyfus and the Delahaye won Ireland's first formula Grand Prix with great ease, and in the most convincing manner, at the new record speed of 92.95

mph, making a new lap record of 95.71 mph in the process,' wrote Athol Harrison in The Irish Motor News. 'It seems probable he could have gone even faster if he had been pressed. Dreyfus is one of France's two best drivers and a good fellow too; Laury Schell who entered the cars and is of Irish descent, has a charming personality, and altogether the victory was a most popular one.'

There would be no reprise of the event. Joe McGrath withdrew his crucial funding, and the local racing fraternity was always going to struggle to find financial backing on that scale. In any case, within eighteen months, the world was at war and Dreyfus enlisted in the French army. Dispatched on a goodwill mission to drive in the Indianapolis 500, he was stranded there when Paris was over-run, and gained fame later in life as the owner of Le Chanteclair, a restaurant in New York.

Prince Bira Bongse from Siam, now Thailand, at the starting line of the Grand Prix held at the Carrigrohane Road circuit.

Davey boy makes Bayern see red

It's apparently not true that Dave Barry fixed a plumbing problem at Musgrave Park a matter of hours before scoring there for Cork City against Bayern Munich in a UEFA Cup tie. He was working on the morning of the match all right, putting in a back-boiler in a house up in Ballyphehane. The legend grew later that he had been tinkering with the stadium pipes at the rugby ground before togging out to face the Germans because that is what happens with folk heroes. We think them so extraordinary that we figure nothing is beyond them.

The afternoon he humbled Bayern in front of a crowd of 4,000 in September, 1991, Barry was just two days past his 30th birthday but his prematurely receding hairline had given the visitors a certain impression about the dual star and his colleagues. It doesn't matter now what exactly Stefan Effenberg said in reference to the age of the City squad, a few of whom were farther into their thirties than Barry. The gist of the story is the supercilious German obviously said something to annoy the home side.

Whether he specifically described Barry as 'looking old enough to be my father', merely made a more general inquiry asking 'who are these old men?' or warned them that he expected a facile six-goal victory, may have been lost in translation.

'We didn't need motivation to play Bayern Munich,' said Dave Barry. 'Effenberg certainly provided us with an extra incentive to go out and do something. He was an arrogant type and slagging us off before the game only served to fire us up.'

Dave Barry in action for Cork City.

adidas
GUINNESS

As the Germans slumped off disgusted, a grou

The differences between the German aristocrats and Cork's latest League of Ireland incarnation were so stark that The Guardian of London dispatched Matthew Engel, one of its best sportswriters, to cover the game.

'Bayern fielded five internationals - three German, two Brazilian - and had five more on the bench or injured,' wrote Engel. 'Cork did not. Cork were 5/1 in the local bookmakers to score a goal - something they had not managed against Derry City or Shamrock Rovers in their last two games. Bayern were about the same price to win the competition. Bayern hold one of the proudest footballing traditions in Europe; City are only seven years old, six different Cork clubs having collapsed in the past 15 years. Hibernians, Athletic, United and so on have all come and gone, and the place is starting to run out of serviceable names.'

Engel wasn't to know then that the 19-year-old Christian Ziege was going to blossom into a full international or that the Bayern coach Jupp Heynckes would later win a Champions League with Read Madrid. The historical context only made what followed more amazing. Twenty-six minutes in, Mick Conroy dispossessed the Brazilian Bernardo in the middle of the park and found Pat Morley. His through ball put Barry in the clear and his right-foot shot on the run was parried to the net by Gerald Hillringhaus in the Bayern goal. On his way back for the kick-off, Barry asked Effenberg when he was planning on scoring the six goals mentioned earlier.

Typically, the lead invigorated the home side and for a time unnerved the Germans. Between their struggles with the not exactly baize-like surface and Noel O'Mahony's instructions to his players to close down the full-backs early, it took the visitors until two minutes before the break to equalise through an Effenberg shot. The goal inevitably had him dubbed 'Effin' Effenberg by some in the crowd. 'Against teams like that we knew that we would have to work like never before,' said Barry. 'That went without saying. If we slacked off we knew we would get a hiding. So we of kids were chanting 'We're going to win the cup'

charged at them from the start and worked at closing them down and confining any space they had. Going forward we were conservative. Our main aim was to avoid getting caught for numbers on the counter attack.'

In his second stint as manager following sterling service as a player with Cork Hibs and Albert Rovers, O'Mahony had put together a nice blend of local talent and imports. The bulk of this team would make up the side that finally won the league in 1993. Conroy, McCabe and Paul Bannon lent crucial experience for a few seasons but the likes of Barry, future manager Liam Murphy, John Caulfield, Declan Daly and Morley became intertwined with the club's history. The latter trio stand first, second and third in terms of appearances for City, with Caulfield leading the way on 455.

Although Phil Harrington made a vital stop from Mazinho, another Brazilian early in the second and Berthold – a World Cup winner the previous summer – missed one simple chance, City were well worth the draw on the day. They might even have snatched a victory in the final minute when Barry forced a good save from Hillringhaus. As the Germans slumped off disgusted, a group of kids were chanting 'We're going to win the cup' and everybody present was glad they'd forked out for tickets that started at a steep £8.

'I felt as fulfilled as the afternoon I won the first of my two All-Ireland medals with Cork,' said Barry afterwards.

With an illustrious soccer bloodline – great-grandfather Harry Buckle and grandfather Bobby Buckle had won FAI Cup medals with Fordsons and Cork FC – Barry's debut for City had been an unfortunate affair. He'd broken his leg against Dundalk in Oriel Park, four weeks before he was due to play for St. Finbarr's in the 1984 county final against Imokilly. They lost that game and for the rest of the decade Barry had constant problems juggling the two codes. When Cork lost to Meath in 1987, he was playing against

Bray Wanderers at the Carlisle Grounds the same afternoon. He was back in the team for the 1988 defeat and in the 1989 All-Ireland final showcased all the talents that had seen him make his senior inter-county debut at just 18.

'The superior application of Cork's experience was shown more than anyone by Dave Barry,' wrote Val Dorgan in The Cork Examiner about a Barry performance that included three points from play. 'Cork had other heroes, notably Teddy McCarthy, Niall Cahalane and Paul McGrath, but throughout, Barry created the right climate for a Cork win, at times holding the ball until it seemed he must lose possession. But his willingness to accept responsibility for the good pass was the kind of steadying influence his side needed when the chance of a third All-Ireland defeat was very real. This was a combination of the best of the modern and the traditional game.'

City emerged from the second leg at the Olympic Stadium in Munich in 1991 with a highly creditable 2-0 defeat, only conceding the second goal in the final minute. Having retired from Gaelic football in 1991, Barry's City playing career eventually evolved into him becoming manager during a troubled time in 1996. His first task was to avoid relegation and he built on that achievement with consecutive fourth, third and second place finishes in the league. In 1998, a Derek Coughlan goal against Shelbourne gave City its first FAI Cup win at Dalymount Park. That was the only trophy to have eluded Barry as a player. Not much else did.

No longer playing but still on the ball. Manager Dave Barry takes control of the ball while watching his Cork City charges against Waterford United at Turners Cross.

Rebels at the Double

After coaching Cork to victory in the 1990 All-Ireland hurling final, Father Michael O'Brien put the hype building as the county footballers prepared for their own decider against Meath a fortnight later into some context.'The double isn't won,' said O'Brien, then parish priest of Carrigaline. 'It happens. The footballers will be trying to win an All-Ireland. If they do,the double happens.'

It happens. Once a century, it happens. The previous winter, county secretary Frank Murphy made reference in his annual report to how Cork, represented by the hurlers of Aghabullogue and the Midleton footballers, had won the All-Ireland double in 1890. No matter how fittingly symmetrical the notion, any talk of a prospective repeat of that feat a century later would have been deemed ridiculously far-fetched then. The footballers had won Sam Maguire in 1989 but any resurgence from the hurlers appeared to be somewhere off in the distance.

How quickly the incoming coach O'Brien, and his chosen trainer Gerald McCarthy changed that mindset. After an unimpressive first-round dismissal of Kerry, the initial signs of the revival were glimpsed on the first Sunday in June. Waterford, victors over Cork after a replay the previous year, were thoroughly beaten by 16 points. A promising result, yet no measure of greatness. Tipperary remained the benchmark and the opposition for the Munster final. With Teddy McCarthy and Tomás Mulcahy unavailable through injury, the reigning provincial champions were hot favourites, a status epitomised by their coach Babs Keating's infamous comment about Cork during the build-up that 'donkeys don't win derbies'.

Marching into history. Larry Tompkins leads the Cork team in the parade of the teams before the 1990 All-Ireland Football Final at Croke Park.

Whether or not Keating's remarks were taken out of context, they certainly provoked Cork's ire. Seven of the team were playing in their first Munster final, and in the absence of Mulcahy, his fellow Glenman Kieran McGuckan, one of the rookies, captained the side ably from wing-back. The return of Tony O'Sullivan, bringing with him so much experience and class, was also a huge boost for Cork. On a balmy afternoon at Semple Stadium, O'Sullivan opened the scoring with his first possession shortly after the throw-in with a typically delightful point.

It was a newcomer, however, who would put his own individual stamp on this match.

On the way to a historic personal tally of 2-7 – only Mick Mackey had ever equalled it in a final – Mark Foley's deftly-taken goal just before half-time was crucial. Having been rattled by two Tipperary goals, Foley's riposte sent Cork in just two points down. The second half was close for long spells until John Fitzgibbon's second goal two minutes from time finally finished

Tipperary. A precocious and enigmatic talent, the 23-year-old had spent portions of his youth practicing Jimmy Barry Murphy's moves up in the Glen Field, and greeted each goal with a jump reminiscent of Ring's trademark celebration. His strike-rate in this championship would have him christened Schillaci, after the Italian predator who had just played a starring role in that summer's World Cup.

The wonderful performance against Tipperary, and the obligatory canter past Antrim, still weren't enough to convince most pundits that Cork were capable of beating a Galway team which had won back-to-back titles in 1987 and 1988. The final was another topsy-turvy affair. Kevin Hennessy goaled after 48 seconds, yet Cork trailed by five points at the break. Worse was to follow when Galway had extended that lead to seven by the 43rd minute. Given the greater experience in their team, Cyril Farrell's outfit looked in prime position to gain revenge for Cork's triumph of four years earlier.

That was the juncture however when O'Brien and his selectors turned the course of the match. Apart from carving out a wonderful solo goal for himself, the switch of Mulcahy to centre-forward also negated the previously influential Tony Keady. At the other end, Jim Cashman finally started to subdue Joe Cooney and suddenly Cork were on the way back. In many ways, however, the resurgence was only still viable because of the goalkeeping heroics of Ger Cunningham. He'd made a couple of blinding stops,

Teddy McCarthy leaps highest to win possession agains Galway during the All-Ireland Hurling final. He ensured his own place in th history of Cork sport by becoming the only player ever to win All-Ireland senior hurling and football medals in the same year.

preventing a certain Michael Naughton goal with his face, and as the game wore on, his puck-outs seemed to go longer and longer too.

Another of the older heads, Hennessy, (who hadn't even been on the panel in 1989), created the opening for a Foley goal that put Cork in front with less than quarter of an hour remaining. Galway got back level before Foley turned provider, setting up Fitzgibbon for a goal in the 61st minute. Barely sixty seconds later, Hennessy put the Glen Rover through for his second. A Brendan Lynskey goal immediately after that appeared to preface a potential comeback but when John Moore blew the final whistle, Cork remained three points to the good.

'To win the All-Ireland is one thing, but to come from several points down speaks volumes for the character of our lads,' said Gerald McCarthy. 'Tomás was an inspiring captain. He led by example when the need was greatest and the goal put us on the way back, while John Fitzgibbon's two beauties sped us on the path. With ten minutes to go we were flying.'

That they were flying with the cup on the line in the last minutes of the championship was of course a tribute to McCarthy's own training methods. The bold selection policy was vindicated too. Nowhere was this more evident than in the decision to start Teddy McCarthy at centre-field in the final. Although he was one of those sportsmen who seem genetically

Action from the football final. Cork's Shay Fahy contests a high ball with Meath's Liam Hayes while Teddy McCarthy (No 11), Kevin Foley (Meath) and Danny Culloty (background) await the outcome.

Double Champions. John O'Driscoll wearing a Meath jersey (left), Danny Culloty (centre) and Tony Nation (No 2) celebrate after the final whistle.

programmed for the big occasion – he'd made his debut for Cork in the 1986 All-Ireland win over Galway – his selection after a long injury lay-off was a big gamble. Though obviously not fully fit, McCarthy contributed three points and set himself up for a place in the history books.

His path to double glory had begun inauspiciously. An ankle injury picked up in a football challenge match against Mayo looked to have put paid to McCarthy's summer. Although he played no part in the Munster final wins of either team, and only resumed training three weeks before the Galway clash, he may have clinched his place on the football team during the comprehensive win over Kerry back in July. At one point in the second half, Cork were well ahead and cruising when Billy Morgan noticed the voice beside him on the bench urging the players forward in search of another goal was McCarthy's. With his leg in plaster, he was still showing the sort of commitment that Morgan loves in his footballers.

McCarthy had never lacked for commitment or passion. More than a decade earlier, he'd tried to fight Kevin Hennessy after an Under-12 match in Midleton. He reckoned that Hennessy had refereed a game involving McCarthy and Sarsfields unfairly, and the then 12-year-old sought retribution, even though his punches couldn't reach his future (and much taller) team-mate's face. Feted for his spectacular fielding ability as a footballer, his selection at left-half-forward in the starting XV to face Meath meant he

Canon Michael O'Brien (right) congratulates Sean O'Gorman (extreme left) after Cork's victory over Galway in the All-Ireland Hurling final, while in between them, Ger Cunning-ham, Brendan O'Sullivan and Denis Walsh (Galway jersey) admire the view from the winner's podium.

stood 70 minutes from being the only man to win All-Irelands in both codes in the same year.

Denis Walsh had made his own bit of history when winning Munster football and hurling medals within weeks of each other back in July, but despite a great display against Kerry, he'd lost his place for the semi-final win over Roscommon. That sort of summed up the strength in depth available to Morgan and his selectors, who named a different team for every match. Indeed, the quality of the substitutes for the final said much about the standard of that squad. Apart from Walsh, there was Mick Maguire, Colman Corrigan, John O'Driscoll, Tony Davis, John Cleary, Jimmy Kerrigan, Paddy Hayes and Mark O'Connor.

Thirty-one minutes had gone against Meath when Colm O'Neill was sent-off after an altercation. A late call-up to the squad before the Kerry match, he'd kicked 11 points in that game, three more against Roscommon in the semi, and had rattled the Meath crossbar early on. A huge loss, yet, as so often is the case, the team reduced to fourteen men simply dug deeper. A point clear at the break, they were two points up when the final whistle sounded. That the 0-11 to 0-9 game was hardly a classic mattered not a jot. More important by far were the circumstances of the win. Questions had been asked about the mettle of the Cork footballers in previous encounters with Meath and aspersions cast about their triumph over Mayo 12 months earlier. Before this final, one Meath selector even asserted that Cork didn't have the bottle to beat his team. Niall Toibín, speaking obviously on behalf of the People's Republic, retorted: 'You can take the cork out of the bottle but you can't take the bottle out of Cork'. The wisdom of that was demonstrated by a team that overcame a sending-off and the added pressure heaped upon them by the success of the hurlers a fortnight earlier.

'It was sheer character that won it for us,' said Morgan. 'We played our best football in the Munster final but it was tense out there today, and good football went out the door. The lads were determined to beat Meath and nothing was going to stop them. The two points by Shea Fahy and Paul McGrath after half-time put us motoring and I knew there was no way Meath would pull us back. I am proud of every one of them.'

That Meath had been restricted to just one clear shot at goal summed up the efficacy of the Cork defending, and that second-half Brian Stafford effort was brilliantly turned away by John Kerins at the expense of a 45. It was one of those days when different players made cogent contributions at different times and everything appeared to be done for the good of the team. The double-winning McCarthy felt later he'd had a poor game but his manager thought otherwise.

'Teddy made a very decent contribution to our win, winning a fair amount of ball and giving it on quickly,' said Morgan. 'He was playing wing-forward and didn't get the chance to make spectacular catches and so people didn't notice him. I was very happy with the way he played.'

For all the ill-feeling that had festered between the two counties, the premature and tragic deaths of Kerins and Mick McCarthy (scorer of two first-half points) some years later produced a poignant post-script to the enmity. Many of those Meath players travelled to Cork for the funerals to pay their respects to former rivals in a touching gesture.

At Sam Maguire's homecoming to his own county on the Monday night, the footballers on the platform down Patrick Street were joined by Mulcahy and the Liam McCarthy Cup. That was about the point when the cheering reached a crescendo. Those two trophies had never been in the same county in the same year before. The double was won. It happened.

Miah the Magnificent

Over an hour of the 1972 FAI Cup final had passed without a goal when Waterford's Alfie Hale tried an audacious back-heel to a colleague who wasn't there. Cork Hibernians' player-manager Dave Bacuzzi took possession inside his own half and steered the ball to Miah Dennehy down the inside-right channel. He outpaced Vinny Maguire and Tony Cottle, and was almost on the end-line when he somehow found the gap between goalkeeper Peter Thomas and the near post. At last, the deadlock was broken.

Five minutes later, John Herrick won a solid tackle then cannily lifted the ball over Maguire and released Dennehy again. Despite the best efforts of his pursuers, Maguire and Cottle again, he ran 20 yards before superbly flicking it beyond the advancing Thomas. The ball struck a post and was rolling across the line when Dennehy followed it up and joyously billowed the net for his second. Hibs had one hand on the trophy even if their fans at Dalymount Park weren't taking anything for granted.

One week earlier, Waterford had scored three times in the last 12 minutes to defeat Hibs, their nearest rivals, 3-2 and so clinched the league title before a crowd of 26,000 at Flower Lodge. Two days after that loss, the squad had arrived for training to discover Bacuzzi had a unique rehabilitation programme in mind. He took them to the nearby quarry, the traditional venue for his most sapping work-outs and tried to erase the game from their memory banks by running them into the ground.

The drama at Dalymount hadn't ended yet. With ten minutes remaining, a frantic goalmouth scramble culminated in Joe O'Grady palming a John

Action from a Cork League of Ireland game between Cork Hibs and Shamrock Rovers at Flower Lodge. Miah Dennehy is on the right behind Dave Wiggington as "Wiggy" heads the ball.

O'Neill effort straight into the air, and Bacuzzi clearing a subsequent Johnny Matthews' header off the line. That was to be the final scare. In the 83rd minute, Tony Marsden chased a long ball downfield and when Thomas attempted to be too clever with his clearance, the Hibs' striker stole the ball and fired it across the box. Dennehy had time to take it down before scoring his third.

In 1969, Dennehy, who had cut his teeth with Northvilla, had gone to watch Cork Hibs' reserves playing and was invited to tog out when they found themselves short-handed. Three years on, he took 18 minutes to complete the first hat-trick in FAI Cup final history. Inevitably, the goalscorer grabs the headlines but the rest of the Hibs team that April Sunday contained names that evoke an era in the history of the city, not just the game: O'Grady, Bacuzzi, O'Mahony, Sheehan, Herrick, Finnegan, Sweeney, Lawson, Marsden, Wiggington and unused sub, Dreaper.

'It was a proud day for Cork football, a great one in the history of the club and a memorable one for Miah Dennehy,' wrote Billy George in Monday morning's Cork Examiner. 'The slim, blonde 22-year-old carved his name in history with a second-half hat-trick of goals. He personified Hibs' courage and professionalism with an aggressive, imaginative performance to set the seal on a magnificent season for him personally and for Dave Bacuzzi's entire squad. Hibs took the glamour prize of Irish football in the grand manner.'

Much to the chagrin of Cork viewers, RTE's live broadcast of the match ended before Neil Blaney T.D, then president of the FAI, presented the cup to Bacuzzi. For a chance to glimpse the silverware, the majority had to wait until an open-topped bus took the victors from Kent Station down to the Grand Parade on Monday night. The front page of the Evening Echo that hit the streets hours before the procession contained a caricature of Dennehy, beneath the headline 'Miah the Magnificent' and he became the city's pin-up. It would be seventeen months before a crew-cutted Jimmy Barry Murphy would take that mantle from him for his exploits in a different code.

By then, Dennehy was ensconced at the City Ground following his February, 1973 £20,000 transfer to Nottingham Forest. In a photograph of the Forest team at the start of the 1973-74 season, Dennehy is sitting on the far left of the front row. Martin O'Neill is standing directly behind him. The former Celtic manager's assistant at Parkhead, John Robertson, is a few

Cork Hibs celebrate their 3 - 0 victory over Waterford in the 1973 F.A.I. Cup Final. John Lawson (left) and Miah Dennehy have the cup on their heads.

places to his right. Over the course of the three seasons, Miah played less than 50 first-team games. Originally signed by Dave Mackay, he had finally established himself as a regular during the first half of the 1974-75 season and was in possession of the number 7 shirt when Brian Clough's arrival spelt the end of his tenure.

That summer, he departed for Walsall where he scored 22 goals in 128 appearances over three years. Following a season with Bristol Rovers and a short flirtation with Cardiff City, Dennehy was playing with non-league Trowbridge Town when Cork United brought him back and briefly made him club captain in the early '80s. There was a stint with Waterford United too after that but his time at the highest level was winding down.

His exploits in the FAI Cup final had earned Dennehy a call-up to Liam Tuohy's Irish squad that travelled to the Brazilian Independence Cup in June, 1972. He made his debut in a 3-2 victory against Ecuador on that trip, and although seven of his subsequent 11 international caps came as a substitute, he scored twice for Ireland, against Norway and Poland. He also figured in the memorable game between Brazil and a Shamrock Rovers' All-Ireland XI at Lansdowne Road in 1973. Having kept to himself the fact he was struggling with a broken toe, Dennehy came off the bench for a bit part role in the 4-3 defeat by a side containing Jairzinho and Rivelino.

'You couldn't coach Miah Dennehy,' said Paddy Mulligan in the 1975 edition of the Bass Sports Book of Irish Soccer. 'This fellow has complete natural ability and you shouldn't even try to stifle it. You should just tell Miah to go out and play. He'll probably end up scoring some miraculous goal, like taking a shot from forty yards and doing a Pele on some poor goalkeeper! He's great for taking on people – he's got great pace and there's no question mark about his heart – he'll run till he drops.'

Vindicating a commonly held belief in his home city, that for Dennehy it was always about the love of the game, he was still togging out for Mayfield-based Village United in the Cork AUL at the age of 51. Once he crossed the white lines, everything else was incidental. Having hurled with St Vincent's, he used to play Gaelic football for a club in Leicester at the height of his professional soccer career. In 1976, he even won a British inter-provincial title on a Warwickshire team that defeated a London side containing Tony Grealish in the final.

'When you are successful in any sport in Cork, the people show you so much respect,' said Dennehy. 'And I will never forget the respect that was shown to me over the years."

Fans chair Miah Dennehy from the field after Hibs won the League of Ireland play-off decider against Shamrock Rovers at Dalymount Park, Dublin in April 1971. Also in the picture is Hibs centre forward, Tony Marsden

Fast Eddie's Triple Crown

At the finish, Brian O'Driscoll and Eddie O'Sullivan led the Irish squad on a lap of honour around a gleeful Lansdowne Road. Nineteen years had passed since the last Triple Crown win and to the appropriate soundtrack of U2's *Beautiful Day*, the captain and the coach did a circuit of the old ground. The victory over Scotland that clinched it wasn't pretty but that wouldn't have bothered O'Sullivan unduly. Upon taking charge of the team, he'd declared a wish to be respected rather than liked. On March 27th, 2004, the Corkman saw his players ensure he'd get plenty of both.

'At 16-16, the question was whether we had the composure and mental strength to come through and we proved we did.' said O'Sullivan of the 37-16 win. 'We didn't talk during the week about the Triple Crown, which was going to be the outcome of winning the game. It was all about what we needed to do to beat Scotland, but now that we've done that, it's starting to sink in. It's very good to win a Triple Crown. It was good on a number of fronts. Two of the tries in the first half came right off the training ground, and that was very satisfying.'

As his second full season at the helm yielded Ireland's seventh Triple Crown, it was fitting O'Sullivan would make reference to the training ground because that is where he has spent so much of his sporting life, the furnace in which he has forged his reputation.The 45-year-old in the sharp business suit taking the plaudits that Saturday afternoon in Dublin 4 had spent his thirties travelling half-way around the world from America's west coast to east Galway, establishing his coaching credentials. The only constant was that everywhere he went, he deepened his store of knowledge and improved himself.

Eddie O'Sullivan keeps a studious eye on the kicking practice before Ireland's Six Nations game against France at Lansdowne Road, Dublin in March 2005.

Before the 1991 World Cup, O'Sullivan had been retained as a fitness adviser to the Irish team. When his own work was done, he'd hang around afterwards picking up knowledge of the parts of the game traditionally beyond the ken of former wings. He'd sit atop the scrummaging machines during training sessions, pestering the coach Ciarán Fitzgerald with questions about the finer points of scrums and line-outs. To those in the inner sanctum it was obvious then that here was a guy desperate to know everything he could about every aspect of the sport.

Shortly after being promoted from assistant to Ireland boss more than a decade later – the manner of his succeeding Warren Gatland prompted several comments about O'Sullivan's Machiavellian streak – he turned up at Trinity College for a seminar being given by the legendary Scottish coach Ian McGeehan. O'Sullivan took lengthy notes from a seat in the back of the hall and six months later, his team embarrassed McGeehan's 36-6 to become the first Irish outfit to win at Murrayfield in 18 years. Wherever he goes, whatever he does, there is always something to be gleaned.

'Eddie is some bloody operator, I can assure you,' says Ireland's much respected manager Brian O'Brien. 'He's the best we've ever had, that's for sure. His work ethic is unbelievable. Yes, he drives the boys hard, but he's also a sensitive man manager. If you make the big commitment, he'll be there for you every time.'

The leader of the pack. Eddie O'Sullivan leads his team on to the field for thei warm up routine before the Six Nations game against England in February 2005.

The players who won the Triple Crown for him had experienced first-hand his holistic approach to their welfare. With training camps held in environments as diverse as Poland and Tenerife, they'd been introduced to the joys of ice baths and cold therapy for injuries. More than once the squad turned up for team meetings to discover a guest speaker. Before their trip to the 2003 World Cup, the former middleweight champion, Marvin Hagler and the intrepid English explorer Ranulph Fiennes were among those brought in to help the players understand mental toughness. It may not have paid off at the World Cup, but a few months later, it did.

'O'Sullivan is a professional coach and is the first in Irish rugby,' said George Hook, fellow Corkonian and O'Sullivan's boss at a number of stops along the way. 'He is educated for it and he is genetically built for it. Gatty (Warren Gatland) was not a professional coach, he just sort of fell in to certain jobs when he stopped playing. Technically, I would think that O'Sullivan is one of the best coaches in the world. The problem is that, being Irish, we automatically assume he isn't. Some of the stuff he did in Connacht was extraordinary and some of the stuff he did in America with a very poor team was extraordinary too.'

Born on November 21st, 1958, his first steps on a rugby field were taken at Youghal RFC and after secondary school at the CBS in the town, he enrolled at Thomond College, from which he graduated with a degree in physical education, maths and science. His professional teaching career began at Holy Rosary College, Mountbellew, and his further rugby studies were conducted at Garryowen. When he joined the Dooradoyle club, he weighed ten-stone and was potentially competing for an out-half job with Tony Ward. He began pumping iron until he'd gained three stone, earned the nickname 'The Beach Boy' and became a decent enough winger to play for Munster and Ireland 'B'.

The decision to give up his ambitions at one position for another that would require an overhaul of his physique reeks of the pragmatism that would later hallmark his career. Although Garryowen's coach PJ Smyth was the first to suggest to O'Sullivan he should consider coaching, his initial success came when leading the Holy Rosary Under-16 girls basketball team to an All Ireland in 1983. Five years later, he became a development officer with the IRFU and began coaching Galway junior outfit Monivea. The first training session he took culminated in several of their players vomiting. Though near the bottom of the coaching food chain, O'Sullivan was already looking up.

From there, his peripatetic journey to the top of the sport took him all over the map. Hook employed him as an assistant-coach at Connacht, but it was when he graduated from assistant to the top job at Blackrock that O'Sullivan began making his impact on the national consciousness. Early in the 1993 season, Blackrock were briefly leading the All-Ireland League, a position made all the more remarkable since most pundits had tipped them for relegation. The stint at the top earned their coach a Philips manager of the month award that influenced the direction of Irish rugby.

'The award at that time was a great boost to my confidence,' said O'Sullivan. 'I was deciding whether or not to stay in professional sport or go back to teaching - so at the time it was the thing I needed. I always liked the idea of being a professional rugby coach, but it's a big decision to make. There's not much security in professional sport. But I remember winning the Philips award and it was a huge shot in the arm for me, it was confirmation that maybe I had a future in this game. For that reason it played a big part in making my mind up.'

Not everybody was persuaded of his talents. Although his Irish Under-21s won the country's first-ever Triple Crown at the grade in 1996, he failed to land a provincial coaching contract from the IRFU. For a married father of two, the lack of faith had financial implications beyond just affecting his morale. Dismayed, he took up an offer to become director of American rugby in 1996. Although he juggled that role with looking after Buccaneers in the AIL, the decision to go to the United States looked a curious one for such an ambitious coach.

Yet, his two and a half years in that job were as productive as any because he was working in the nation where coaching science has always been ahead of the curve. He studied grid-iron, saw the immense and detailed structures put in place to support the players off the field in the NFL, marvelled at the umpteen specialist assistant-coaches retained by every club, and realised there was so much about their methods that could be applied to rugby. Like every other aspect of his life, that interlude seems one more instructive step preparing him for the job of ending Ireland's wait for a Triple Crown.

The 2004 Six Nations began inauspiciously with a 35-17 defeat by France in Paris. Wales were disposed of quite easily in Dublin before a trip to Twickenham loomed. The English team that had won the 2003 World Cup was reputedly the best-organised, most-prepared outfit in the history of the sport. O'Sullivan's side wasn't quite at that level yet but were ready to beat the champions in their first home fixture since the tournament. Ten minutes into the second half, Girvan Dempsey slid in near the corner flag for what proved to be the winning try. It came at the end of a thrilling phase of attacking play, specifically planned and designed by O'Sullivan.

'I think a national side should be coached by one of its own,' said O'Sullivan. 'I am not saying that a non-Irishman cannot be successful with Ireland or a non-Englishman with England, but they start with a disadvantage because they do not know the little ways of the country they have moved to. You understand your own players better when you are one of them.'

Kitty hits Dublin for six

Kitty Buckley scored six goals for Cork in their facile 7-5 to 1-2 victory over Dublin in the 1941 All-Ireland camogie final. Her individual tally nabbed in a forty-minute game set a record, but that's really only the half of it. As captain that day, Buckley became the sixth Cork woman to lift the O'Duffy Cup and she could claim some act or part in every one of them. A teenage substitute on the 1934 side that took the county's first, she had carved her reputation as a lethal goalscoring forward over the rest of the decade.

'She was in a class of her own and was a real artist of the game,' wrote Mary Moran in her encyclopedic "Cork's Camogie Story". 'She possessed superb ball skills. Kitty played on the right-hand side of the field, right-centre or right-forward where she displayed great anticipation and always took the right option.'

In 1935, in the first camogie decider to be played outside Dublin, Buckley, while still a student at St. Aloysius school, goaled in Cork's 3-4 to 4-0 defeat of Dublin at the Athletic Grounds. She subsequently found the net against Louth in 1936, and against Galway in the 1939 and 1940 triumphs. Of course, she was not alone in her prowess. In '39, Renee Fitzgerald had scored four goals in the final as Cork dominated the first ten years of inter-county camogie.

Like so many other sports, Cork can make unique claims on this one. When the Keating Branch of the Gaelic League in Dublin resolved to devise an Irish game for its distaff members, Tadhg O'Donoghue from Carrignavar

Cork Camogie team of 1941. Kitty Buckley, front row centre.

christened it camoguidheacht. O'Donoghue's sister Cait – in Dublin to work as his housekeeper - later led out the Keating Branch team that took on a selection called Cuchullains in the first public camogie match, held in Navan on July 17, 1904. Half a century later, Nell McCarthy from Carrigtwohill would coach Dublin to ten All-Irelands in a row between 1957 and 1966.

Cork didn't participate in the first or the second All-Ireland camogie championships, but in 1934, their inaugural appearance was a winning one. The history-makers were a unique bunch. Monica 'Girlie' Cotter would later become a regular on the Irish Ladies' international golf team, and president of the Irish Ladies' Golf Union. Kate Dunlea would cycle 22 miles each way to training sessions. Josie McGrath would captain Cork the following year while still a student at St. Aloysius.

Buckley had first come to prominence when St. Aloysius entered the county championship because they were so dominant at schools level that it was felt the challenge of taking on senior teams would be good for them. In their first venture into the grade they won the 1932 championship (which was played in 1933). Between them, Buckley, McGrath, Sheila Brennan, Maura Cronin and Lil Kirby, the spine of that teenage side, would win 21 All-

Ireland medals. Kirby would also serve as president of the Camogie Association, and chairwoman of the Cork Camogie Board, and McGrath played an integral part in establishing the Old Als' club in 1937.

Having started as a schools' player, Buckley had moved on to UCC and then played out the later stages of her career with the alumni outfit. The real achievement of women like Buckley, McGrath and the rest of this generation was keeping Cork at the top in an era when the lack of financial support was embarrassing. It once almost cost the county a title. After coming out of Munster in 1939, they couldn't afford to travel to Louth for the All-Ireland semi-final and had to offer their opponents a walkover. In a wonderfully sporting gesture, Louth reacted to this news by sending money to fund the trip. Many of the travelling contingent did a day's work on Saturday before driving north to beat their generous hosts by four goals the following afternoon.

These were remarkably resourceful and talented sportswomen. Of the '39 team alone, Buckley, Mary Fitzgerald, Mona Hobbs and goalkeeper Peggy Hogg, were all top-class tennis players. In the thirties, camogie clubs formed in locations as contrasting as factories - Lee Hosiery and Dunlops – and church choirs; the ladies from the Sacred Heart went under the moniker of Cecilians. The Cork three-in-a-row team was dominated by the Old Als' connection, and in the '41 win, two of their representatives, Maureen and Patti Hegarty, also became the first twins to win medals. In more ways than one, that year was a special vintage

'The Cork line-out contained some of the most outstanding players ever to wear the red and white,' wrote Mary Moran. 'The statistics of the matches played speak for themselves. Cork scored 22-9 in three games and only conceded 2-7. The team were a very united group who loved to play camogie. They got on very well with one another. They considered it an honour to play for the county. Often they had to pay their own fares when travelling. To put this into context, the weekly wage at the time was about 12 shillings and six pence. The weekend trip to Dublin used to cost between two pounds ten shillings and three pounds. They won cups but got no medals but did not mind as long as they were playing the game.'

Although the split of 1944, which saw Cork exiled from the championship for eight years prematurely ended the intercounty career of Kitty Buckley and many of her peers, nobody has yet broken her record of six goals.

Gold glistens on Blackwater

The impressive manner in which Gearóid Towey and Tony O'Connor qualified for the final of the lightweight pairs at the 2001 World Rowing Championships in Switzerland had earned them the tag of pre-race favourites. Perhaps motivated by that, the Dutch and Italian pairs pushed off the hardest at the start and 500m in, Towey and O'Connor were trailing in fourth place. By the halfway mark they'd only improved to third by cruising past the English, but that was about when their form finally began to tell.

After 1,500m, the Irish boat had finally edged into the narrowest of leads. Their rivals from the Netherlands were straining hard to pull level and then the Italians threatened with a late surge of their own. Towey and O'Connor remained steadfast. This close to the finish, they would not be overhauled and held on to win by a length from the Dutch. The 24-year-old Corkman and the 32-year-old Dubliner took Ireland's third gold at the end of a historic week for the country's rowing fraternity.

'It hasn't really sunk in yet. It was a bloody hard race', said Towey on the banks of Rotsee Lake in Lucerne.

For the veteran O'Connor, the gold was the culmination of a career during which he'd medalled four times at the Worlds without ever winning a final. For Towey, it was confirmation that he was now an elite rower with the ability to mix it with the best on the planet. Both had been part of a highly-rated lightweight four that had failed to perform at the Sydney Olympics less than a year earlier.

Gearóid Towey (left) and S.
Lynch in training.

Although Towey and O'Connor had been the beneficiaries of government grants that allowed them to train more or less full-time, there is no money to be made from rowing. Thus, the victory itself was their only reward for an insane commitment and dedication beyond even athletic norms.

Towey's journey to that picturesque body of water that lies between two mountains in central Switzerland had begun at the family home in Kilworth seventeen years earlier. He'd watched his first Olympics, the Los Angeles Games, on television and been smitten.

At the age of ten, he started on his way in the sport, taking his first strokes at the nearby Fermoy club on the River Blackwater. His older sister Janette was already involved in rowing and she was talented enough to win a silver at the World Under-23 championships in 1990.

The size of his own potential first became apparent in 1995. On a July afternoon at Inniscarra Lake, the then 18-year-old defeated Niall O'Toole, the pre-eminent Irish rower of the time, in the final of the men's senior sculls. Having narrowly missed out on a place in the lightweight sculls for the Atlanta Olympics the following year, he travelled as a substitute. He subsequently made up for the disappointment at the World Under-23 championships. There, he went one better than his sister with a blistering performance to annex gold in the lightweight single sculls final.

Listing off the exotic venues and the various stand-out performances doesn't quite paint a full picture of what Towey had to sacrifice to reach that level. In rowing, the amount of intense training is somewhere between amazing and sadistic. To reach the highest level, each competitor has to row around 5,000km a year in training for about a decade. The racing season lasts just 10 weeks and the other 42 are given over to the brutality of preparation. A light evening work-out for Towey and his partner might have involved a 16km spin where they worked purely on technique.

'The technical end is the hardest,' said Towey. 'Like when we are really tired, in the death-throes of a race, last 250 metres, that's the stage where you can technically fall apart. I can start doing my own thing, he can start doing his own thing, because you end up going into self-survival mode. The more together you are there, when you are absolutely dead, the better obviously, because races can be won and lost by inches.'Two years after Lucerne, Towey and his new partner Sam Lynch became the first Irish rowers to medal in an Olympic class event when they took bronze in the lightweight double sculls at the World Championships in Milan. That result made them look a viable prospect for the Athens Games but their hopes subsequently unravelled in Greece. At the time of writing, Towey is preparing to row across the Atlantic Ocean as part of a busman's holiday from the competitive scene before beginning his countdown to the Beijing Olympics.

The pursuit goes on.

Lofting the Viaduct

Before 6,000 eyewitnesses on St. Patrick's Day, 1955, Mick Barry hurled a 16oz. bowl clean over the Chetwynd Viaduct. Although a subsequent effort to loft a 28-ouncer hit the metalwork up top, he had still done enough to enter Cork sports lore. There is perhaps no other place in the county as inextricably linked to a single individual as the Viaduct is to Barry. People who have never seen a score in their lives could still name one road bowler and list one feat: Mick Barry and the Viaduct. If that span first built in 1849 is bowling's Everest, Barry is our own Edmund Hillary.

Barry also won 11 All-Ireland titles for road bowling and is generally regarded as the finest-ever exponent of the sport. For the casual fans, however, these are minor details next to his most famous achievement. Other people have lofted iron balls of various weights over the 21-feet wide rail bridge that stands 90 feet above the Cork-Bandon road since then, but Barry was the first to do so. Bill Bennett – a famous athlete and bowler from Killeady - is supposed to have managed it in the 1930s, yarns about Bandon's Dan Hurley succeeding before that are common too. In the absence of tangible evidence backing up those claims, the honour remains Barry's.

Born in Barryroe on January 10th, 1919, this little piece of history belongs to somebody who actually grew up in Waterfall, not too far from the structure that would become the monument to his own greatness. Fourteen years old when he began working at UCC for the head gardener Harry Glavin, he held that position himself for over two decades before he retired in 1985. Half a century of physical toil on campus can only have enhanced the power of a man reputed to have been born with preternatural arm strength.

Mick Barry (second from right with short sleeves) and Denis Donovan (Centre) see before a score in Dublin Hill in 1954. Mick Barry won 1 All-Ireland titles for road bowling.

Half a century of physical toil on campus can only have enhanced the power of a man reputed to have been born with preternatural arm strength.

'A familiar sight on summer evenings during his years at U.C.C. was that of Mick Barry taking a short run at the College Road end of the old Quarry and hurling a 28 oz. iron bowl over the bar onto the embankment at the opposite or quadrangle end; insurance companies or claimants do not seem to have been quite as rapacious in those days!' wrote Professor Seán Ó Coileáin in his citation at the college's conferring of an honorary degree on Barry in December, 2003.

'Before he could be made permanent, he was required to pass an oral examination in Irish.The then Professor of Irish, Tadhg Ó Donnchadha (or 'Torna') and his brother Éamonn were gentle souls, and the task was accomplished without too much difficulty. Confirmed in his gardening duties, his workmate Jerry Murphy commented that from now on he could say 'tá go maith' to the jennet, then the only official form of College transport.'

Although he began bowling in his teens in the 1930s, the sport's first national senior championships were not held until 1954 when his brother Ned was beaten in the final at Cloghroe by Liam O'Keeffe, another Waterfall man. Barry himself didn't win his first formal title until the following year. Following the introduction of Armagh to the competition in 1963 (when it was reconstituted as an All-Ireland), he began a rivalry with Danny McParland who went by the nickname of 'The Gun from Armagh Town'. McParland beat him in the 1964 showdown but a year later the Corkman won a thrilling encounter on his opponent's home turf when the stake was £1,700. Some money for 1965.

Barry would later claim that score against McParland was his finest bowling hour but his supporters could gorge themselves on the memories of so many different days. Second only to the Viaduct is perhaps the episode in which he lofted Mary-Ann's pub up in Dublin Hill during a score. Once every customer had been evacuated from the building, Barry let fly, sending the ball over the roof, and more importantly and impressively still, landing it back on the road to keep it in play.

Like most sports, the origins of road bowling are nebulous. By one account, Dutch soldiers brought it with them when they arrived under the banner of William of Orange in the 17th Century. Another reckons it may have been imported from Yorkshire by linen workers during the Industrial Revolution. Whatever the genesis, it put down firmest roots in Cork and Armagh, the two strongholds of the sport. Representatives of the two counties first met in competition in 1928 when Fairhill's Timmy Delaney travelled north and got the better of Peter 'The Hammerman' Donnelly on the Knappagh Road. Twenty years before Barry was even born, Blackpool's John 'Buck' McGrath was vying for the title of the best in Cork against Sonny O'Leary, James Barrett, and Waterfall's own pair, Ger O'Driscoll and John Buckley. The prevalence of the game can be gauged from the fact Michael Collins played it as a boy, and some of his fellow Corkonians going to work at Ford's in Dagenham would later bring the game with them to England as a little slice of home to be savoured on Sundays.

The Dutch still play a version called Moors Bowling and having participated in the first international meet in 1969, involving teams from Ireland, West Germany and the Netherlands, Barry excelled at this variation in the 1974 event. He took silver in the road bowling that same year. Ironically, it was a foreigner then who finally conquered the only part of the Viaduct challenge that had proved beyond Barry back in his prime. In September, 1985, a crowd of over 10,000 gathered to watch Germany's Hans Bohllen loft a 28oz. bowl over the parapet.

Although he cleared the top by a good ten feet, Bohllen's feat was performed by running up a ramp – a feature of the game in Germany – to give himself a platform to throw from. That same day, three other Corkmen, Eamon Bowen, Dan O'Halloran and Bill Daly emulated Barry's feat by succeeding with a 16oz. bowl. Originally from Leap, Garda Daly was perhaps the finest Irish player of that generation, winning the first two World Road-Bowling Championships in 1985 and 1987.

As for Barry, he brought the curtain down on six decades of bowlplaying in the summer of 1997. Two years shy of his 80th birthday, he defeated his good friend Liam O'Keeffe in the veterans' final held at Dublin Hill. It was fitting that his last score was there, the scene of some of his greatest triumphs.

Billy Daly lofting a 16oz bowl over the Chetwynd Viaduct in 1985.

Stormin' Norman's Cheltenham double

On the first circuit of the 1995 Gold Cup, Norman Williamson and Master Oats made several jumping mistakes and were not looking good. Trapped on the inside, the 100-30 pre-race favourite wasn't getting enough daylight at the fences, so going down the back second time around, Williamson knew he had to make some sort of move. After hitting the fence before the water particularly hard, it briefly crossed the jockey's mind that he might not even reach the finish.

'I switched him to the outside going to the water, gave him a slap down the shoulder and he grabbed hold of the bridle,' said Williamson. 'After that he jumped super. At the top of the hill, Graham Bradley on Merry Gale said we were 10 lengths clear, but I didn't reply - I just concentrated on the next jump.'

Master Oats broke clear of Merry Gale and the only threat then came from Dubacilla, making an audacious run from way back. At the second last, Dubacilla was just six lengths behind but had no more to give. On the way up the hill towards the finish, Williamson had 15 lengths to spare and his whip hand in the air as he crossed the line for his fourth winner, a tally that earned him the Ritz Club Trophy for leading rider at that year's festival.

Two days earlier, he'd partnered Alderbrook to victory in the Champion Hurdle. The Gold Cup win meant he and Kim Bailey became the first jockey-trainer combination to land that double since Vincent O'Brien and Aubrey Brabazon 45 years earlier. By the time Williamson started riding in his home town of Mallow, O'Brien had long since moved from Churchtown to Ballydoyle, but the teenage jockey didn't want for a local hero to emulate. There was never a time in his formative years that he didn't dream of being Jonjo O'Neill.

'He was from the next village, and we all idolised him,' said Williamson. 'When he came back home, people would run into the street to see him. It was like the Pope himself had come to visit.'

Before 1995, Williamson had never rode a winner at Cheltenham. When he steered Alderbrook past the post on the Tuesday, he punched the air in a manner redolent of O'Neill atop Dawn Run nine years previously. Indeed, one British journalist wrote that the 26-year-old punched so vigorously he looked like he might fall off. Williamson was entitled to the animated celebration. Twelve months earlier, a suspension robbed him of victory on Flakey Dove, and after cruising for most of the race, coming to the last hurdle on Alderbrook, he knew this jump was crucial. That leap brought him alongside Large Action and from there his ride had the speed to prevail.

'This is the day I've dreamt of all my life,' said Williamson at the end of the festival. 'Tuesday was unbelievable with my first winner in the Champion Hurdle, but it wore off a bit quick thinking about today. Thank God it all happened."

Norman Williamson rides Nick Dundee to victory at the Buttevant to Doneraile Steeplechase at Cork Racecourse, Mallow, Co Cork.

After starting out on ponies, the farmer's son began his Turf career as an amateur riding for Dermot Weld out of The Curragh. There, he found himself working alongside, amongst others, Mick Kinane, and benefiting hugely from the experience. He then began riding point-to-pointers for P.P. Hogan – his first win coming on a horse called Give Me A Break – and soon began to dominate that scene. Far removed from the glamour of Cheltenham, it was a time when his favourite saying at a point-to-point meet was 'five score makes a hundred', meaning a Sunday with five rides at £20 a go was a profitable afternoon's work.

In 1989 he got an offer from John Edwards to move to Hertfordshire. He rode his first winner for the trainer at Windsor but was so homesick that immediately afterwards, he went straight back to Cork. At which juncture Edwards called him up to put him straight on the way the professional game operated.

'He phoned me up, told me it was a man's job and said I had better be manly about it,' said Williamson. 'I went straight back the following weekend and in 1990 rode my first major winner for John on Multum In Parvo in the Mackeson. A guy like me coming over from Ireland simply doesn't have a clue. I had no idea how to talk to important owners or anything like that. I had a hell of a lot to learn and John Edwards taught me it all. He is a tremendous trainer and when the yard was going through a period of decline he was the one who advised me to look elsewhere.'

A subsequent link-up with Kim Bailey was to bring the Cheltenham success that had eluded them both up to that point in their careers. It was also to spark the most profitable years of Williamson's career, a time when he was briefly right up there with the best in the sport and known to his fans as "Stormin' Norman".

'Part of his secret is that he settles them so very well,' said Gerald Delamere of The Sporting Life. 'He is strong but never a butcher - not that they're allowed to be butchers any more. There are a lot of similarities between Williamson and (Richard) Dunwoody, although you might argue that Dunwoody is still fractionally better at having a horse naturally on a stride. But, to be fair, Williamson is very good indeed all round these days.'

The Gold Cup-Champion Hurdle double would be the highlight but there were 1,266 other National Hunt winners (including nine more Cheltenham triumphs) before a succession of neck injuries sustained in falls forced him

Joy all around as Norman Williamson leads Lady Rebecca into the winner's enclosure after winning the Cleeve Hurdle at Cheltenham for the third year in-a-row in January 2001.

to retire at the age of 34. Fortunately, a new life mixing a farm he bought in Meath with television commentary beckoned for a man who always had an exemplary work ethic. Williamson left the party to celebrate his Gold Cup win at half past four in the morning. By seven, he was back at Bailey's stables in Upper Lambourn to work.

Kohler caps illustrious career

On October 8th, 2003, the most-capped Irish women's hockey international of all time announced her retirement from the squad. Only 29, Rachael Kohler had played 166 games for her country over the previous decade, and she called it a career after captaining the side to a creditable sixth place at the European Nations' Cup the previous month. A veteran of two World Cups, and umpteen international tournaments, she'd started out playing five-a-side games in Rockboro primary school, got serious about hockey under the aegis of Ivan Leopold and Mary Power at Midleton College, and along the way became one of the players of her generation.

'I'll miss it, it's been a fantastic few years, the people I met, the countries I visited, I loved it all, but all that travel away from home and work is a huge demand on any amateur player, and those demands have been increasing so much in recent years,' said Kohler who'd been juggling a full-time career as a hotel marketing manager with her commitments to Harlequins and her country.'International hockey now is unrecognizable compared to when I started, although the demands were tough then too. I can remember, as an 18- or 19-year-old, travelling on the 5.30 train from Cork to Dublin, and then getting a bus to Belfast for training. It is harder now though, but it needs to be, such are the rising standards in international hockey. We have to be this professional if we're going to keep up.'

As an 18-year-old, she made her debut against England in a five-nil defeat at Bisham Abbey. A precocious teenage talent, she joined a squad bulwarked by two older Corkonians and UCC alumni. Mary Logue would go on to become the first Irish woman to win 100 caps, Sarah Kelleher (who later won an English Premiership title with Slough) was the second to pass that milestone, and the pair of them also served terms as captain of the national team. Kelleher led the Irish team into the 1994 World Cup finals in Dublin, and when Kohler wore the captain's armband for the same competition in Australia eight years later – a privilege she described as 'the proudest moment of my life' – she had succeeded Logue in that role.

'Nobody expects too much, certainly not at this level," said Kohler before that tournament by way of explaining that Ireland's real achievement was simply qualifying. 'We know we're up against it, we're in with the elite of world hockey and every team we play will expect to beat us. The only pressure on us is the pressure we put on ourselves.'

Despite Ireland's obvious disadvantages against the game's traditional powers, Kohler never looked out of place against the finest international exponents of the sport.

'I am very sad to lose such a fine hockey player, but understand her decision,' said Riet Kuper, the national coach, of Kohler's decision to retire. 'She has been an outstanding athlete to work with both as a player, a captain and as a person.'

After graduating from UCC, Kohler returned to Harlequins' senior team and figured prominently in May, 2000 when the club reached their first Irish Senior Cup final. Kohler scored the second in their 2-0 victory over Ballymoney at Farmer's Cross in the semi-finals. In the decider itself, Harlequins trailed Hermes by a goal with 16 minutes remaining but following goalkeeping heroics from Sharon Hutchinson, Jean Logue equalised and Ciara McGrath struck for the winner 34 seconds from time. Fittingly, Kohler became the first Harlequin to collect a trophy which had last been inside the province when Cork Hockey club won it back in 1934. The following year, Kohler was voted player of the tournament as Harlequins captured the European Cup Winners' Cup (B Division) in Vienna.

'Rachael has been an outstanding ambassador for Ireland both on and off the pitch and will be missed by all her international colleagues,' said John Smyth, president of the Irish Hockey Association when Kohler announced her retirement. 'Her dedication and enormous contribution over the past ten years has won the admiration of all involved in Irish hockey and she will always be an outstanding role model for the aspiring Internationals of the future.'

Clonakilty and Dromtariffe's five-card trick

In the week of Jack Lynch's death in October, 1999, Professor John A. Murphy recounted the story of a flight to America in the seventies during which he, Lynch and a host of politicians from Belfast and Dublin were standing at the back of a jumbo jet discussing the issues of the day. As a Northerner in the company began to fulminate at length on the intractability of the Ulster question, Lynch turned to Murphy and asked: 'John A, I don't suppose you remember the great Clonakilty-Dromtariffe games back in 1941?'

That anecdote revealed as much about Lynch's enduring passion for the sport as it did about the impact the matches he referred to had on that generation of Cork people. Paired together in the first round of the county football championship, it took five matches to prise them apart. The sort of epic that inspires grandiose claims. Many of those present claimed afterwards that in one encounter Miah Murphy, a blacksmith from Dromtarriffe kicked a ball off the ground that flew 63 yards straight to the Clonakilty net. Who are we to quibble?

'Miah Murphy was a tall, lean long-legged white-skinned chap with curly black hair,' wrote Eamonn Young in "Cork 78". 'The middle of the field was his natural place. He had a tremendous leap in the high-jumper's fashion, for he strode in, gathered himself and went up. Very determined and cross enough when needed, on his day, he was impossible to beat, and for years, both he and Dick Harnedy were the heroes of North Cork and the despair of opponents.'

As they prepared for the first game, Dromtarriffe's hopes of upsetting the more fancied Clon side were largely founded on Murphy and Harnedy, their inter-county duo who would later figure on the Cork team that won the 1943 Munster Championship. Clonakilty came into that summer with high hopes. They'd lost six county finals during the 1930s before finally making the breakthrough in 1939 and were determined to make another go at bringing the cup west.

The first match in Dunmanway on July 27th was, as suggested by the score-line of 1-3 to 0-6, a dour affair. Dromtarriffe had scored four points to Clonakilty's one during the second half to earn another chance. A fortnight on they met again at the Castle Grounds in Macroom. Weakened by the absence through injury of their Cork stalwart Mick Finn, Clon nicked an early goal through Jim Aherne. Four years later Aherne would come on as a sub for Cork in the 1945 All-Ireland final, but under an assumed name, because as a clerical student he wasn't supposed to be playing.

The quality of the fare on offer was greatly improved but the result was the same. The game ebbed and flowed throughout the second half and with five minutes remaining, Dromtarriffe had edged two points clear. A couple of late points from Seamie O'Donovan and Sean Ahern brought Clonakilty level though and when Andy Scannell blew for full-time, both teams had managed 1-7. One week later, they returned to Macroom to try and finally resolve matters but after a Miah Murphy point in the last minute pushed this meeting into extra-time, they were still level at the end of that.

'The third replay took place on August 31st at Macroom,' wrote Diarmuid O'Donovan in the Irish Examiner. 'By now the games had caught the imagination of the entire county with the result that 1,000 people travelled to see it. A goal by William Smith gave Clon a 1-3 to 0-3 lead at half-time. However, Dromtarriffe refused to yield, and in fact, led by a point with time almost up. It was left to Thady O'Regan to kick the equalising point and to finish another magnificent encounter in deadlock. No extra-time was played. It was back to Macroom on September 7th.'

Before the fifth match between the sides, word was out that the county board had issued firm instructions that this match was to be played on until one side emerged. There could be no more replays. An ominous enough warning that wasn't necessary because Clonakilty finally got the upper hand. Bolstered significantly by the return of Mick Finn, recovered from the broken hand sustained way back in July, and the introduction of Derry

Burke, a Kerryman studying at Darrara Agricultural College, their superior goal-getting was the difference between the teams.

It finished, finally, 3-5 to 0-5, and Clonakilty went on to meet Bantry in the second round. That fixture begat a saga of its own and culminated, after two controversial matches, in both sides being thrown out of the championship. Clonakilty became the only team to play seven times and never get beyond the second round of the county.

Clonakilty goalkeeper Humphrey Duggan saves a shot during the fourth repla between Clonakilty and Dromtariffe at Macroom in September 1941

Yuri hammers Mardyke into history

They stopped taking money at the stiles shortly after 7.30 pm. By then, the few desperate souls who had clambered on to the roof of the Sacred Heart Church and hung from trees down by the riverbank had already caught a glimpse of history. In the space of an incredible hour, the world record in the hammer had been bettered six times by a pair of Soviet athletes at the Quinnsworth Cork City Sports.

The evening of July 3rd, 1984 began inauspiciously enough. Shortly before six o'clock, Sergei Litvinov, world record holder and reigning world champion, stepped into the circle. Still wearing his tracksuit bottoms, he fouled off his opening throw. A few minutes later, his compatriot Yuri Sedykh, gold medallist at the 1976 and 1980 Olympics, picked up his hammer and launched his first effort 86.34 metres. The 29-year-old had gone seven feet past the mark of 84.14 set by Litvinov 13 months previously, and set the craziness in motion.

'I thought they would be dour blokes,' said Gary Halpin, the future Irish rugby international who finished fifth in the event with a personal best of 58.08m. 'This is the impression created by the media, but they were very approachable, particularly Sedykh who speaks good English. At first I thought they would be two huge men but they looked fairly average. However, their speed and strength were something else altogether.'

Since 1980, the Soviet pair had dominated the event and swapped ownership of the world record four times in that spell. Taking full advantage of the perfect throwing conditions on a glorious summer's evening, Litvinov's second throw of 85.14m was a remarkable response to his comrade. A personal best, it would have been a new world record itself half an hour earlier.

This was to be Sedykh's night however. A graduate of the Central Sports Academy in Moscow, his second attempt was another monster, lingering in the air for 85.98m. A less impressive third still went through the 85m mark and even his last legal throw was 84.16. In reply, the best of Litvinov's remaining throws was 84.64m. He'd twice thrown better than ever before in his life, yet his travelling partner had four times gone better than the old world record.

A scientist once calculated that Sedykh flinging the hammer over 86 metres required him to build up enough momentum so that at the release point, the 16lb ball effectively weighed 900lbs. For this performance, he was inevitably judged the best athlete at the meet, an accolade for which he was awarded the US Ambassador's Cup. The irony wasn't lost on anybody. This was a Cold War summer when the Soviet bloc countries were getting ready to boycott the Los Angeles Olympics. Rather embarrassingly, the Soviet ambassador to Ireland, Mr Alexei Nesterenko, had arrived too late to witness Sedykh's historic throw.

'I feel very good but it doesn't compensate for not going to the Olympics,' said Sedykh afterwards. 'It's difficult to speak about that. It's not compensation because there is no compensation. But now I think there is no limit to man's ability. I always believe that and I think this proves it. It's good to be back in the land where the hammer event was started and I would like to come back next year. The warmth of the spectators is something I will always remember from my visit to Cork.'

Having submitted to dope testing and, for the first time in Ireland, sex tests, Sedykh and Litvinov ran a joint lap of honour on the track and received a joyous reception. Many of the other events were dotted with world-class competitors too. Eamon Coghlan was surprisingly defeated in the 5,000m; Daley Thompson ran the 200m in preparation for Los Angeles; Peter Elliot was second in the 800m; and local favourite Marcus O'Sullivan returned from Villanova University to finish fourth in the 1500m. Predictably though, it was the throwers who hogged the following day's headlines.

'We were delighted,' said Owen O'Callaghan, whose company, O'Callaghan Properties, had sponsored the hammer event. 'And we brought Sedykh out on the town that night. And he loved his pints, but he'd no money. We fed him.' The next morning, Sedykh paid a courtesy visit to Topps chewing gum factory in Ballincollig, and the hammer he used was taken under Garda escort to the Department of Weights and Measures in White Street. After being weighed and measured, a certificate of verification was issued to Finbarr O'Brien of the Cork City Sports committee.

When reporters asked Sedykh whether his record was likely to be broken at the Olympics, he answered with an emphatic 'No'. He was correct on that score. It stood for almost two years until he broke it again by going 86.66 metres at an international athletics meeting between the Soviets and East Germany in Tallinn, Estonia. A silver medallist in Seoul in 1988, he moved to Paris following the break-up of the Soviet Union. Still the owner of the world record, he now travels the world giving throwing clinics.

His Mardyke effort remains the third furthest ever.

Twice Olympic champion Yuri Sedykh in action at the Cork City Sports at the Mardyke. During the course of the hammer competition, Sedykh and fellow Russian Sergei Litvinov broke the world record six times. Sedykh won the competition with a best throw of 86.34 metres.

Ralph's boot the key to Con triumph

The inaugural All-Ireland League wasn't especially programmed so the top two clubs would meet on the last Saturday of the season to decide the destiny of the trophy. It just happened to work out that way. A campaign designed to sort out the best team over a series of games came down to just one. Cork Constitution and Garryowen were level at the top of the table, and, as the calendar had dictated, were scheduled to meet in Dooradoyle on January 26th, 1991.

Home advantage and a superior scoring record meant the Limerick side only had to draw to be the first club in the country to lay claim to the title. At a time when the European Cup was years away from even being dreamt up, this was the most sought-after piece of silverware in the country and the mood around the game was captured best by Con Houlihan.

'Such a decider would have been lost in the vastness of Belfast or Dublin; in the intimacy of Limerick you couldn't go for a pint or a hamburger or even a bag of crisps without being aware of the impending duel,' wrote Houlihan in the Evening Press. 'The game had taken over the old city; at half past eleven in the bar of the Railway Hotel I might have been in Thurles on the morning of a Munster hurling final; all that was missing was the meat tea. This was a Munster final with a difference – it was also an All-Ireland final; it was great to have a ringside seat at the making of history.'

Cork Con and Garryowen had some serious history. Almost 90 years had passed since they'd first clashed in a Munster Senior Cup match at Turner's Cross. There was nothing between them that day and it took a replay up in the Market's Field for the Cork side to prevail. A rivalry baking almost a century then came out of the oven on a cold winter's day on the southside of Limerick. Led onto the field by captain Michael Bradley, Cork Con refused the invitation to pose for the pre-match photograph. The symbolism was obvious. They had business to attend to.

Ten thousand people – including Jack Lynch – had filled the ground, and a smattering more clung to well-placed trees that offered some view of the action. It was the kind of day when any vantage point would do.

'When I got out on the pitch, there was this wonderful feeling of being involved in something really big,' said Con full-back Kenny Murphy. 'I said to Ralphie Keyes this reminds me of the Munster-All Blacks game last season with all the temporary stands and the crowd so close early on. And what a noise they made. On one occasion, I shouted something to Brian Walsh a few yards away but he never heard a thing. I had to go right over to him before he could hear me.'

The early going was predictably more tough than glamorous. Con had the better of things and for nearly 15 minutes were camped in the Garryowen half. Eventually the home side conceded a penalty for offside. Ralph Keyes – whose father Mick had won a Munster Senior Cup with the club in 1957 stroked that over to quiet the crowd.

The lead was short-lived. In the 25th minute, Con were caught offside 35 yards out from their own line on the right-hand side. The angle was tight enough but Kenny Smith's left-footed effort sailed between the posts to draw Garryowen level. That was how it stayed until half-time and beyond. A game where running rugby was at a premium, the play was being dominated by the hard working packs and afterwards the contributions of Packie Derham, Paul McCarthy and Philip Soden in the front row would be toasted. It was, inevitably, up front where the game was eventually won and lost.

The Cork Constitution pack smothers another attack during their 1990/91 All-Ireland League campaign.

'Michael Bradley had found touch near the Garryowen line on their left,' wrote Edmund Van Esbeck in The Irish Times. 'That started a siege that will be remembered by all who saw the match as long as memory holds. It lasted for seven minutes. Eight scrums took place, seven times Constitution had the put in. But the Garryowen pack held the drive by the Constitution pack, if only just. From the fourth scrum (Victor) Donnelly almost made it, but the scrum was awarded to Garryowen. They won the ball under pressure, but Nicky Barry, their young outside half, was unable to clear as the Constitution back row closed in and he was forced to concede a five-yard scrum. Three times too, Garryowen were penalised by the referee for collapsing the scrum and Constitution opted for scrums instead of kicking at goal, until the third offence when referee Derek Templeton from Ulster awarded a penalty try.'

There were ten minutes remaining when Keyes converted to put Con 9-3 clear. Plenty of time left for drama. From 32 yards, Smith's first attempt to reduce the deficit came back off the upright, but when Con failed to clear, another penalty was awarded. Again, Smith's effort cannoned off the timber and back into play. Garryowen laid siege but could not break through the cover. Finally, another penalty afforded Keyes the chance to find touch and move his side out of danger. They had done enough. The country's first All-Ireland rugby league had come down to a game played in the sort of knock-out atmosphere which had brought them 22 Munster Senior Cups down the decades. Con relished it and were deserving champions. Uniquely, the county then housed the All-Ireland champions in rugby, gaelic football and hurling.

Ralph Keyes sets up an att for Cork Constitution agai Shannon during the 1990/ All-Ireland League campai

Kiernan drops England at Lansdowne

When Rob Andrew missed a penalty that would have put England 13-10 ahead, there was really only time for a couple of more plays before the whistle would finally sound and a draw would put an end to Ireland's hopes of a Triple Crown. For the subsequent drop-out, Paul Dean's job was to try to find Brian Spillane and allow him to charge infield with the ball. That tactic yielded a line-out inside the English 22 and the Lansdowne Road crowd sensed this would be the last shot at glory.

'In those final despairing minutes,' went the report in The Times, 'when it seemed the lungs of half Dublin must burst, so much breath was being held.'

Spillane lined up opposite Bob Hesford, realised how tired he looked, and then signalled Ciaran Fitzgerald to try a quick throw. The captain delivered, Spillane gathered, and Donal Lenihan grabbed it from his team-mate to begin the drive forward. Lenihan laid it back for Michael Bradley and a nation held its breath again. On March 30th, 1985, the Triple Crown would come down to this final moment. The scrum-half turned to fling out a pass to where his fellow Corkman Michael Kiernan was poised.

In a moment like that, with history on the line, it's best to place the responsibility on somebody with a pedigree. Kiernan certainly had that. He was a 24-year-old centre whose first three international caps coincided with the 1982 Triple Crown. From the richest of Cork sporting bloodlines, his mother Angela Lane had been a camogie star, his father Jim had made it as far as the final trial as a player and later became a selector on the Irish team. Two of his uncles, Mick Lane and Tom Kiernan, were British Lions, and he'd worn that red jersey in a Test himself for the first time at just 22. This was the guy upon whom the destiny of the season now rested. Exactly where you'd want it to rest.

Born on January 17th, 1961, Kiernan learned the game at Dolphin and Presentation Brothers' College. Outside of rugby, he was fast enough to become the national 200m champion in 1981, clocking a winning time of 21.48 seconds. His Uncle Mick had been a renowned champion sprinter back in the forties and speed was regarded as a family heirloom.

'Angela Lane was a great opportunist who notched dozens of vital scores in her career,' wrote Mary Moran in Cork's Camogie Story. 'She possessed the natural speed of the Lane family and developed a very accurate shot that made her an automatic choice for Cork and Munster.'

Athletics might have been his sport except for somebody with his genes, there was another path already set. Uncle Mick had cut a dash as a pacey wing three-quarter for UCC, Dolphin, and Ireland in the late forties and early fifties; Uncle Tom was the calm, collected full-back with the unerring boot in front of goal for UCC, Cork Con, and Ireland between 1960 and 1973. The nephew's game seemed to incorporate the best elements of each of them.

When Ollie Campbell departed the scene, Kiernan took over the kicking job. Replacing somebody who'd become a byword for reliability looked like a thankless task because every wide would invite inevitable talk of how much Campbell was missed. The thing was there weren't too many wides as the Dolphin man kicked his way into history, surpassing his predecessor as Ireland's top international points scorer, and setting a record tally that wouldn't be beaten until 11 years after he retired.

Of course, he wasn't just there for his boot either; Kiernan was one of only six players to have featured in all six games of the '82 and '85 triumphs. Although nine of his 43 caps were won on the wing, he formed an impressive pairing in the centre with Brendan Mullin and for a time they were the world's most capped combination in those positions. For everything he achieved in general play however, it's his kicking that is remembered most from that season.

On the way to the England clash, he'd kicked well. Two conversions and three penalties in the 21-9 win over Wales; two conversions, one drop goal and a penalty in the scintillating 18-15 thriller in Edinburgh, and five penalties in the 15-15 draw with the French. This day had started badly however. After Mullin charged down an attempted clearance and ran it in for a try, Kiernan missed the conversion. The conditions were wet and drizzly but he atoned for that miss with a penalty that gave Ireland a 7-3 lead at the interval.

An unconverted Rory Underwood try and another Andrew penalty had England in front as the clock started to tick down. Kiernan brought them level with a penalty to set up the final dramatic denouement.

'There was a try on but Mick had made his mind up,' said Brian Spillane of the moment the ball was in the centre's hands and the winning or losing of the Triple Crown depended on what happened next. More than one pundit labelled the shot on goal the wibbly-wobbly wonder as it careered through the posts at the Havelock Square end. There have been more aesthetically-pleasing drop goals but none that mattered quite as much. In the treacherous conditions, it was an achievement to get it over at all.

'That drop-goal has been replayed more often than the Angelus,' said Kiernan once.

Why wouldn't it be?

Michael Kiernan clears Ireland's lines during the Ireland V Scotland International at Murrayfield, Edinburgh in February 1985.

Three glorious All-Irelands in a row

Nine minutes before half-time in the 1976 Munster hurling semi-final, Jimmy Barry Murphy was sprung from the bench. With their defence dominating, Tipperary had controlled proceedings to that point and the Cork selectors, among them Christy Ring, felt his introduction might liven up the forwards. It did so to such effect that Barry Murphy ended the year with his first hurling All-Star. A Cork side laden with talent was struggling to impose itself until that juncture but every great conflagration needs an initial spark to set it ablaze. As a starting-off point for the epic journey that would be known as the three-in-a-row, that moment may have been as pivotal as any.

There were plenty more significant cameos that day in the Gaelic Grounds. A Charlie McCarthy goal had brought Cork to within three points at the interval, John Fenton found the net with a free from forty yards early in the second half, and Martin Coleman prevented two certain goals with dramatic stops. With three minutes left, Coleman was beaten by Seamus Power but saved by the post. The rebound broke fortuitously for Cork and when the ball reached the other end of the field, Seanie O'Leary scored what was to prove to be the winning point. It finished 4-10 to 2-15.The game could have gone either way. As it happened, Cork went on to greater glory and Tipperary didn't reach their next All-Ireland decider until 1988. Despite Eamonn Cregan notching four goals and a point, Limerick were disposed of quite handily

1978 captain Charlie McCarthy of St Finbarrs.

in the first Munster final to be played at Páirc Uí Chaoimh. Nothing better illustrates the quality available to coach Fr. Bertie Troy at that time than the presence among the Cork subs for the All-Ireland final against Wexford of John Horgan, Fenton, Eamonn O'Donoghue and Bertie Óg Murphy.
In the first six minutes, Wexford reeled off two goals and two points without reply and looked worth the favourite's tag given them following their 17-point Leinster final destruction of Kilkenny. The bleeding was eventually tamped by some long-range shooting from centre-fielder Pat Moylan that helped the rest of the team find their range. By half-time, Cork were level. A Tony Doran goal early in the second half invigorated Wexford but was soon cancelled out by a picturesque Charlie McCarthy goal, the sort of strike that won him his reputation as one of the most aesthetically pleasing of all hurlers.

It was nip and tuck after that and the championship ended for Cork as it begun with a canny switch making all the difference. The hitherto anonymous Jimmy Barry-Murphy was moved from wing-forward to centre-forward where Mick Jacob had been imperious throughout. Barry Murphy duly rattled over three points to put Cork clear before Moylan added an insurance score to ensure Ray Cummins became the first Blackrock hurler since Eudie Coughlan back in 1931 to captain the county to an All-Ireland.

With only slight changes to the line-up, the same squad would win him the 23rd and 24th titles over the following two years. What an outfit, it was. The names alone evoke a special era in Cork hurling. Alongside Barry-Murphy, Denis Coughlan and Brian Murphy, Cummins was one of four dual stars in the side. He was the first player to win All-Stars in hurling and football, but each of the other three could make a legitimate claim to have been among the best dual players of all time.

From the redoubtable Coleman in goal - where he played the last 15 minutes of the 1976 decider with one of his contact lenses gone and the other in his mouth for safekeeping – this was a remarkable collection. Nearly the entire squad later served Cork hurling as manager, trainer or selector. Brian Murphy was the first man to win All-Ireland medals in both codes at minor, Under-21 and senior, and at one point in the 1978 campaign, his corner-back partner John Horgan had been Cork's joint top-scorer

1976 captain Ray Cummins of Blackrock.

due to his prowess from long-range frees. Between them, Martin O'Doherty's performances in the 1977 final (when the Galway-born full-back became the first non-native to captain the county to victory) and, in particular, the following year, set a new standard for full-back play.

A decade after captaining Cork to one of the special All-Irelands, the 1966 win that ended the famine since '54, Gerald McCarthy belied his status as one of the oldest players on the team. The only difference between the callow fresh-faced youth who'd become the only man to captain a senior and Under-21 team to titles in the same year was the droopy moustache he'd grown along the way. In an unfamiliar centre-forward role, his performance against Mick Jacob in the 1977 final was one of the key factors in Cork again beating Wexford.

Although Wexford had put together a late rally in that game - they were killed off by a spectacular Coleman save three minutes from the end - Cork's toughest match of that campaign had come against Waterford who led them by nine points in the 43rd minute of the Munster semi-final. With Tom Cashman and Tim Crowley making their debuts as a new centre-field pairing that day, Cork eventually pulled level through the (almost obligatory) Charlie McCarthy and Seanie O'Leary goals, and won by five. Crowley's first touch in the subsequent Munster final against Clare was the conversion of a penalty after 75 seconds. Dermot McCurtain also came through to cement a place in the starting line-up during that campaign.

Apart from the three consecutive Liam McCarthys, Blackrock (three times), Glen Rovers and St. Finbarr's (twice each) won the All-Ireland club championships every year except 1976 between 1972 and 1979. In its own way, this demonstrates how much talent was in the county during this time and how difficult it must have been to break into the team. Little wonder O'Leary started the 1977 final despite breaking his nose in a collision with a sliotar during the pre-match puckaround. He still managed to snag 1-2.

Their path to the third title had again almost been blocked by Clare in Munster. Having failed to capitalise on the wind advantage in the first half, some Herculean defending was necessary before Cork eventually prevailed by two points. As they prepared to face down Kilkenny for the third leg of the three-in-a-row, Cork were conscious of the fact that an All-Ireland won against the old enemy had more cachet than all others. In the final, Johnny Crowley at centre-back and O'Doherty behind him again distinguished themselves. Tim Crowley was man of the match, Charlie McCarthy played a captain's part with seven points, and appropriately, the deciding goal in the second half was scored by Barry Murphy. The three-in-a-row had been completed.

Facing page: 1977 captain Martin O'Doherty raises the Liam McCarthy Cup. On the right is President of the GAA Mr Con Murphy of Cork. He had the unique honour of presenting the Liam McCarthy Cup to a Cork captain in each of his three years in office.

The Greatest Cork soccer team of all

On February 6th, 1940, Cork Association Football Club was founded. Following the January demise of the short-lived Cork City, a public meeting at the City Hall had elicited a slew of financial donations from fans towards quickly establishing a replacement outfit. By the time the new side played its first game in green and white, its name had been changed to Cork United. From such unlikely origins then was born the most successful soccer team ever to represent the city. In seven full seasons, they won five League of Ireland titles, two FAI Cups, and one double, dominating the domestic scene like no other side before or since.

Their march into history began quietly. Having acquitted themselves well in their initial foray into the league in the spring of 1940, they'd started their first campaign proper with just five wins from 17 games prior to Christmas. Eventually, they settled on a winning combination, won 12 matches in a row (nine of them league fixtures) and placed themselves in contention for the league and cup double. From the veteran Fox Foley in goal to teenage wunderkind Seanie McCarthy up front, the first XI was star-studded; half of them would win caps for either the Free State or Northern Ireland at different stages.

The quality of the players was matched by the attitude of the supporting cast. When United reached the 1941 FAI Cup semi-final, the squad were brought to Bray for a week by coach Billy Little for collective training. After duly disposing of Dundalk, they drew 2-2 with Waterford in the final at Dalymount Park before clinching the trophy with a 3-1 victory in the replay. Owen Madden, the captain, had opened the scoring for United but then got

Action from a League of Ireland Shield game between Cork United and Limerick at the Mardyke.

sent off following an incident with Jackie O'Driscoll (one of four Corkmen in the Waterford team), but future international winger Jackie O'Reilly followed up his brace in the first game with two more.

Although that second encounter between the clubs is regarded as a classic, a planned sequel to decide the destination of the league title in a play-off never took place. Seven Waterford players – including three of the Corkonians: Tawser Myers, Tol'Ol Daly and Timothy Jim O'Keefe – were sacked in a row over bonus payments. In an effort to save the day, United directors offered to pay the money due to their opponents but their charity was declined; Cork were awarded the championship and Waterford left football for four years.

Despite the unfortunate circumstances in which they'd been crowned, United's double was still a remarkable achievement at the end of their first full season. In a bold move, they re-signed the entire squad and deepened it considerably by picking up Richie Noonan from St. James' Gate and Ballincollig-born Billy Hayes from Huddersfield Town, a 25-year-old who would be acclaimed as the finest full-back of the era. Mirroring the previous campaign, they embarked on a 20-game unbeaten run in November that established their challenge to retain the title, and although Shamrock Rovers kept pace until the end, they couldn't unseat the holders.

Although Dundalk got the better of them in the FAI Cup final, winning two successive titles was quite a feat, made more so by the entertaining manner of it. United averaged three goals per game during their unbeaten spell.

Christy (Sheriff) Curtin (Waterford) and Owen Madden (Cork United) at the Mardyke, prior to a League game in the 1940's.

Madden managed fifteen despite missing a huge chunk of the season through his post-Cup final six-month suspension, and McCarthy was developing into a feared striker. On his way to finishing top-scorer in the country for three years running, he scored 19, many of them classics. After a wondrous solo effort against St. James' Gate in Dublin, it was reported that the opposing defenders actually congratulated him. Among the four he bagged in the 1942 FAI Cup semi against Drumcondra was an overhead kick hit so sweetly that the legend is he didn't even have to turn around to check whether it had found the net.

'He wasn't far-off six feet and in the later years of his career, he filled out in the firm build of a man – but when he first began knocking in goals in the League of Ireland, he was about as skinny as Lester Piggott in his prime,' wrote Con Houlihan of McCarthy in the Evening Press. 'Sean wasn't particularly fast and he certainly wasn't aggressive; he depended on a sweet fusion of skill and intelligence. It helped too that he was brave to a fault.'

The team that made history by becoming the first to win three league titles in a row in 1943 differed slightly from its predecessors. Liam O'Neill, Jerry Riordan, Jimmy Hooks and Brendan McFarlane (his son Bik was the leader of the Republican prisoners during the Maze Hunger Strike four decades later) all moved to the Irish League. Those gaps were filled by Jackie

O'Driscoll and Timothy Jim O'Keefe, returning from their stints in exile, and local talent like Christy Curtin, who were promoted from the reserves.

The faces may have changed but the destination of the trophy remained the same. Well, just about. Needing three points from their last two games to clinch the title, United drew both fixtures. Dundalk failed to take advantage of the slip-up, conceding a last-minute goal against St. James' Gate to draw a game they should have won. Thirty-nine years later, Dundalk would wreak revenge with their 1-0 defeat of Cork City on the final day of the 1991 season.

Before a crowd in excess of 30,000, Drumcondra shocked the league champions 2-1 in the Cup final but that defeat paled next to the significance of the three-in-a-row. What made it all the more special is it was achieved at a time when the quality of Irish football had been improved by the presence of so many players who but for the war would have been plying their trade in Britain. There is an argument that the standard of play was perhaps never better.'The boys were conscientious about their training,' said United trainer Timmy 'Beckett' Murphy. 'They knew that an extra little bit spent on the training ground was a prerequisite to success.'

After a lack-lustre 1943-44 season, United reached new heights the following season. On their way to a fourth title in five years, they averaged 4.2 goals per game. The pivotal moment in the campaign was the six goals they scored against previously unbeaten Shamrock Rovers at The Mardyke on January 22nd. Billy Harrington had taken over from Foley in goal, Small Seanie McCarthy joined the squad alongside his namesake, and Willie Cotter, who'd gain equal fame later as a soccer journalist, arrived on the scene.

This was the campaign too where Tommy Moroney became a first-choice player. A superb wing-half, he would eventually leave for West Ham United, win 12 international caps, and leave a lot of people wondering about whether he'd have played rugby for Ireland too had he stayed at home. Moroney won two Munster Senior Cups with Cork Con, and played out-half for Munster. The second of those medals came against Garryowen at The Mardyke in 1946, a game that he started just 24 hours after losing an FAI Cup semi-final to Shamrock Rovers at Dalymount Park.

United's defeat in the 1946 cup semi-final put paid to another potential double because they had dominated the league again on their way to a fifth

In seven full seasons, they won five League of Ireland titles, two FAI Cups, and one double.

triumph in six seasons. After Seanie McCarthy had been lured to Belfast Celtic, Paddy O'Leary, who had played with Limerick while stationed there with the Irish Army, came back to replace him. He did so with some aplomb, finishing top-scorer and scoring six in a 9-1 demolition of Drumcondra at The Mardyke. O'Leary's aerial power was such that it was said he scored more goals with his head than his feet.

'The sight of Cork United at the top of the table became one of the familiar signs of spring, like blossoms on the trees or the sound of the cuck-oo,' wrote Plunkett Carter in "A Century of Cork Soccer Memories". 'So great was their reputation that when they met Drums in their away fixture, the biggest crowd ever to watch a league game in this country (31,000) turned up at Dalymount Park.'

The 1946 edition of Cork United often put out a first XI containing ten locals and Ned Courtney in goal. A Dubliner stationed in the city by the Irish Army, Courtney had won a Munster championship as custodian with the Cork footballers in 1943. In 1947, United, who contended for a long time before eventually relinquishing their grip on the league to Shelbourne, won the FAI Cup with a team made up of 11 Corkonians. The side that defeated Bohemians after a replay was Fox Foley, Johnny McGowan, Florrie Burke, Davey Noonan, Jackie O'Reilly, Paddy Noonan, Jackie O'Driscoll, Seanie McCarthy, Paddy O'Leary, Tommy Moroney, Owen Madden.

Between retirements and transfers to cross-channel clubs now competing seriously again in peacetime, United found the going tough the following season. Frank O'Farrell, an impressive new signing from Western Rovers, the type of player perfect for rebuilding the side, was sold to West Ham United against the wishes of many. After a mediocre campaign, the club began preparing for the 1948/49 season.

On October 2nd, 1948, an experimental Cork United line-up (including my grandfather Tommy Morrissey) defeated Shamrock Rovers 3-1 in their first Shield fixture of the season at The Mardyke. It was to be United's last appearance at the venue they'd bestrode for eight years. The following week, the club was disbanded after a match against Limerick at the Markets Field. United had been making a loss every year of their existence, and their finan-cial woes were partly blamed on the fact a paltry 100 people in the city owned season tickets.

Facing page: Johnny McGowan (Cork United) leads Jackie O' Driscoll and Willie Cotter to the pitch for a clash against Shamrock Rovers at the Mardyke.

Two weeks later, Cork Athletic was formed to fill the gap. The pattern had an unfortunate way of repeating itself.

Jamesy's wearing of the green

Roughly 150 years after the first steeplechase had been run from Buttevant to Doneraile, in a location about 12 miles down the road in North-East Cork, another race took its place in the local folk memory. At Ceim, just outside Rathcormac, an annual event was held where the divide between spectators and participants was very pronounced. The gentry raced their horses over fences, the working-class watched them battle it out by the banks of the River Bride.

That was the way it always was and that was the way it would be until the day came when one farmer decided to jump rank and enter the featured contest of the afternoon. As they lined up at the start of a six-mile point to point, it was easy to distinguish Jamesy Kelleher on his mare Home Chat from his fellow competitors. They were kitted out in the finest riding gear; he was wearing the green jersey of the Dungourney hurlers. The difference only emphasised the gap he was trying to bridge.

'Tension mounted as the minutes passed and the spectators kept a look-out for the field to re-appear in the distance,' wrote Tim Horgan in "Cork's Hurling Story". 'Then a loud shout of encouragement went up as the horsemen came in sight again, and led by Kelleher and his mount, headed for the final fence. Over they went amid wild cheering that grew even wilder as Kelleher's horse cleared the jump and sprinted for home. Within seconds, the horse was over the line and Jamesy was the new champion. It was a great moment for him and for every working-class man and woman at the race. It was more than a cup victory in their eyes. It was a triumph for the common folk over the aristocracy.'

Kelleher was lifted off Home Chat by the crowd and shouldered around the field in triumph. That exultant position was one he knew well from his exploits in a different sporting arena. He had quite a reputation as a horseman but it hardly compared to his standing as a hurler.

'For all-round merit among backs, he is the king of them all' wrote Carbery of his performance in the 1907 All-Ireland defeat by Kilkenny, a game traditionally acknowledged as the first great final. 'On ground or overhead, out of his hand or a flying drop, a doubler or an incoming ball, he commands them all with equal skill.'

Though only 5ft 9in, he played full-back and was peerless. This much can be deduced from the fact so many of his contemporaries from other counties have been quoted describing him as the greatest player they had ever seen. Renowned for never being blocked when striking clearances, he was fast, skilful and yet, able for the physical contest too. The most fantastic part of his legend was the story of the day he took a puck-out and drove it over the opposing bar for a point. It bounced once on the way through.

He first came to national prominence when invited aboard the Redmonds team that represented Cork in the 1901 championship. Having won the home final against Wexford, they were later caught on the hop by London in the final proper, a match that didn't take place until 1903. Cork made amends the following year. Although the logistical problems of the time again meant the 1903 final was staged on September 11th, 1904, it was a unique fixture.

Jamesy Kelleher

Following Dungourney's first county championship success – defeating Shanballymore in a final played at Turner's Cross – they were representing the county. So, Kelleher led a selection bolstered by guests from Blackrock, Carrigtwohill, Sarsfields, and Redmonds out on to the Cork Athletic Grounds for the decider against London. He won the toss, elected to play with the slight breeze and immediately ended what hope the visitors might have nurtured of causing an upset. They didn't raise a single flag as Cork cantered to a 3-13 to 0-0 win.

With Blackrock pulling the strings, Cork retained the title in impressive fashion too. Waterford were destroyed in the 1903 Munster final and Kilkenny were beaten by eight goals in the game that decided who would take on the English representatives for the title proper. Hibernians of London were subsequently put to the sword by 3-16 to 1-1. Having contested three finals in a row, Kelleher looked set to amass plenty more All-Ireland medals but Cork's fortunes changed over the rest of the decade. He was on teams that lost to Kilkenny in the 1904, 1905, 1907 and 1912 deciders. Kelleher also led a Cork squad on a tour of Belgium in 1910 during which they were greeted on arrival in the village of Malines, north of Brussels by a chorus of local kids singing 'God Save Ireland.'

'All the Mahers, Leahys, Gleesons, Ryans – all the great and noble hurlers from Thurles to Toomevara, Tom Semple, Hughie Shalley and Mick D'Arcey,' wrote John Power in "The Cork Book of Champions". 'Go through Kilkenny from "Fox" Maher out, remembering the brilliance of this grand hurler, of the Doyles and Graces, of "Drug" Walsh and Matt Gargan. Consider all their merits, then have a look at Limerick and Dublin and Galway, not forgetting Bob Mockler or Seán Óg Hanley or Mick Gill or Mick Mackey. Compare them all, I say, with Jamesy Kelleher and if you are an honest man you'll agree with me that the like of the old Dungourney captain never trod the green fields of old Ireland.'

Golden Boy leads Celtic revival

Cork Celtic's second last game of the 1974 season was a home tie against St. Patrick's Athletic. The task was a simple one. A victory would clinch the club's first League of Ireland championship and make liars of all those who questioned their ability to sustain a title challenge. They dismissed any lingering doubts with a 3-0 win so emphatic that long before the final whistle, dozens of the 5,000 present had made their way inside to the touchline to be best-placed to begin the celebration. That the goals in the deciding fixture had come from Alfie Hale, John Carroll and Bobby Tambling told the story of the only Cork Celtic team to win the domestic game's premier trophy.

Carroll was a local boy who'd learned his trade with Glasheen and had been at Celtic since the late sixties while Hale, one of Waterford's finest, and Tambling, a former England international, were signed at a time when talk of winning the league would have still been deemed ludicrous by the club's critics. The arrival of that duo, along with the prolific Shamrock Rover Ben Hannigan, Paddy Shortt (the man from the Middle Parish had been plying his trade with Waterford) and Carl Davenport (returning for his third spell) turned the side into genuine title contenders. Those astute pick-ups for combined fees of just £8,000 were a credit to the ambition of the chairman Pierce Moore and the judgment of the manager Paul O'Donovan.

Paul O'Donovan in his playing days.

When somebody's nickname is 'The Golden Boy', they have a lot to live up to, and O'Donovan had spent his life doing just that. There is surely no other manager on the planet who can claim to have signed both Jimmy Barry-Murphy (briefly as a teenager) and George Best. After cutting his teeth with Tower Rovers, O'Donovan went straight from their minor side to playing League of Ireland with Evergreen United, kicking off a thirteen-year professional playing career. Evergreen eventually became Cork Celtic and through sojourns at Cork Hibs, Swansea City and Drumcondra, he earned a reputation as a clever dribbler with an eye for the flamboyant trick.

That day in 1974, O'Donovan became the first Corkman to manage a Cork team to the League of Ireland championship. The eclectic make-up of the side – not to mention his use of 21 players during the season - was a tribute to his man-management skills. Few others would have had the ability to accommodate veterans like Tambling, Hale and Hannigan, or to appoint Keith Edwards, a 21-year-old Welsh defender who'd fetched up at Turner's Cross the previous season via one appearance in the Leeds United first team and a spell at Swansea City, as captain. The wisdom of that decision could be gauged by the sight of Edwards being fervently chaired off the field by Celtic supporters after collecting the trophy.

While Edwards played his part, the clean sheet in that historic victory over St. Pat's was kept by Alec Ludzic. Five years earlier, the Derby-born custodian had been signed by Amby Fogarty, and at 19, made his debut for Celtic against their fiercest rivals Hibs at Flower Lodge. In a 1-0 defeat, he was still exceptional. Clad all in black, the newcomer made a series of athletic saves and even after Dave Wiggington finally beat him in the 70th minute, he stopped a Davenport penalty near the end to further endear himself to the Celtic fans. After starting the 1973-74 season in an experimental and quite successful role as centre-forward, Ludzic was so consistent thereafter that Brighton and Hove Albion were on his trail.

Celtic scuppered the move by asking for too much money and the goalkeeper vowed never to play for the club again. Despite that, he would go on to become the only footballer to play in the League of Ireland in four different decades with Albert Rovers, Cork Alberts, Cobh Ramblers, Limerick, Cork United and finally Cork City, where at the age of 44 he stood in for Phil Harrington. His premature passing in December 2002 would cast a pall over the city and thieve it of one of its great characters. Truly, the Englishman of Polish extraction had wound his way into the fabric of the game in Cork, entertaining the different generations with his brilliance on the field and warm personality off it.

Of all the different parts of the jigsaw that O'Donovan pieced together - Barry Notley and Richard Brooks were two other former Derby players initially bought by Fogarty - the most bizarre had to be Tambling. Notwithstanding Ludzic juggling groundsman duties with shot-stopping, Tambling was the only full-time pro on the staff. At the age of 33, Chelsea's all-time record goalscorer with 202 had moved to Ireland as part of his missionary work as a Jehovah's Witness. In Cork, he encountered a different type of holy trinity – Messrs. O'Donovan, Moore and Donie Forde - who persuaded him to throw his lot in with Celtic.

It was an audacious swoop for a player of real pedigree that greatly irked Hibs whose fans traditionally regarded their near-neighbours as inferior. If that was a good omen, the surest sign that Celtic's name was on the trophy came in their annual trip down the road to Flower Lodge. Hibs had led the table into the New Year and with both teams chasing the title, 18,000 (among them the Fianna Fail leader Jack Lynch) flocked to Flower Lodge for one of those epochal games that everybody present holds up as an example of just why this was the golden era for soccer in the city.

With goals from Carroll in the 27th minute and Shortt on the hour, Celtic set themselves up for their first derby win in six years. Carl Humphries pulled one back to set up a potentially explosive last 25 minutes but-itors never looked like conceding another. Although there were some hairy moments in the run-in - dropped points against Limerick and Sligo Rovers looked ominous - there was too much class throughout the side for them to let the lead slip. Celtic crowned the season with a victory over Bohemians in the now defunct Top Four cup, and fittingly, O'Donovan was voted Soccer Writers' Personality of the year.

Cork Celtic captain Keith Edwards holding the league trophy after beating St. Pats.

Choppy waters tear apart Fastnet

On August 11th, 1979, 303 vessels sailed out of the Isle of Wight to take part in the Fastnet Race. From Cowes, their course took them down the south-west coast of England beyond Land's End and across the Western Approaches towards Fastnet Rock. Once that lighthouse four and a half miles off the tip of the County Cork had been rounded, they were to head for the finish at Plymouth where the Royal Ocean Racing club had its offices on the dock. The race within the race included 54 elite yachts competing in the fifth leg of the Admiral's Cup.

Among the fleet that set off that beautiful, sunny Saturday were former British prime minister Edward Heath aboard Morning Cloud, Ted Turner, the American media mogul and future founder of CNN on Tenacious, Hugh Coveney, TD for Cork South Central on Golden Apple of the Sun, and the legendary America's Cup yachtsman Dennis Conner at the helm of Williwaw. They sailed out into calm seas and for the first two days, those were the prevailing conditions as they made towards the rock that rises nearly 100 feet out of the water off Cape Clear.

One local legend explaining the origin of the Fastnet Rock contends that Satan himself picked it out of the nearby Mount Gabriel and flung it into the sea. Hardly a good omen for sailors about to come face to face with a storm so fierce it would cause the worst disaster in the history of the sport. A weather system that originated on the great plains of Minnesota the day before the race began reached the Irish coast late on Monday afternoon and started to wreak terrible havoc. Gales began to reach force 10 and Mayday calls went out with increased rapidity.

The storm brews as the first competitors reach the Fastnet Rock.

'Rounding the rock was an awesome sight, the noise of the wind and the sound of the foam,' said Neil Kenefick who sailed on Golden Apple of the Sun. 'We were still very much in the racing mode doing 17 knots. When dawn broke we were looking at seas as high as multi-storey car parks.'

Kenefick, Coveney and the rest of their crew were among the lucky ones, winched to safety by a Royal Navy helicopter and taken to Culdrose. Another Irish yacht, Regardless, skippered by Cork businessman Ken Rohan, was towed out of harm's way by the Baltimore lifeboat under Christy Collins, and a crew that included 70-year-old Paul O'Regan.

Apart from the heroics performed by the members of the various Irish and British air-sea emergency services, every other ship in the region got involved. The Irish Continental Line ferry, St. Killian, with 600 passengers on board, stood by and sheltered a British yacht in difficulty until it could be towed to safety. A Dutch destroyer, The Overijssel, saved the lives of several sailors, as did French trawlers. Over the course of 24 hours, the race had spawned the largest rescue operation in peace-time as 20,000 square miles of sea were desperately searched for more survivors.

'From first light we began coming across yachts, all under bare poles, battened down and riding it out,' said Commodore John Kavanagh, then captain of the LE Deirdre, the Irish naval vessel, in an interview with The Irish Times. 'Later in the day, down towards the Scilly Isles, we found one abandoned yacht with no life raft. It turned out that the crew's bodies were

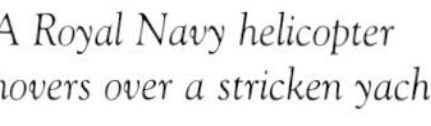
A Royal Navy helicopter hovers over a stricken yacht

picked up. The life raft wasn't storm-proof, and many of the boats found themselves in that position. We continued searching, but it was hard work when there were no sails up. Just looking for masts was like looking for twigs against the horizon.'

Of the 303 boats that started, 85 finished the race, 195 retired, 18 were abandoned, and five sunk to the bottom of the sea. Fifteen sailors were killed, six had been thrown overboard and lost when their safety harnesses failed, the other nine died of hypothermia. One of those, Hal Ferris, was lying in the water, his hands clasped together on his chest, still breathing, when airmen lifted him into their helicopter. He never regained consciousness and the widely-published photograph of his rescue perfectly captured the horror of what had happened.

'It's an experience that I do not think anybody would want to go through again willingly,' said Edward Heath. 'It was a raging sea with enormous waves and one of them picked us."

During the rescue, officials of the Royal Ocean Club had handed the champagne being chilled for the celebrations out to those who came to Plymouth to learn whether their loved ones were safe, hoping to calm their nerves. Yet, most bizarrely of all, despite the tragedy in their midst, it was still a race to some. The chief concern of Ted Turner was whether his 61-foot

A survivor is wrenched on board the Royal Navy helicopter.

Tenacious had actually won the Fastnet Cup awarded to the boat with the best corrected time.

'If we hit one of those lightly constructed fibreglass boats, Tenacious would crush it, smash it in two and everybody would be killed,' wrote Turner in an article about the race for Motor Boating and Sailing magazine. 'Of all the things that happened that night, that was my greatest fear, and that is the only thing that had me scared – that, and the fear that something aboard Tenacious might break, causing us to lose the race. You're supposed to have a strong vessel with crew and equipment for any condition. I felt a little like Noah. I knew that the flood was coming and I had a boat ready that would get me through it.'

During a subsequent debate in the House of Commons, a Labour MP asked whether the "well-heeled, well-to-do people" who indulged in the sport might be asked to pay the bills incurred in the rescue operations. An official inquiry after the race led to stricter entry conditions, governing yacht design and safety but absolved organisers from all blame. On the 25th anniversary of the race, a ceremony was held outside Cape Clear Harbour to remember the fifteen who perished. A lone piper sounded the lament 'Going Home', a wreath was laid in the water and fifteen bells tolled in their memory.

Give it to Gah

It was a Sunday morning in Thurles. The Cork hurlers had travelled up to take on Tipperary and in the team hotel, Father Eddie Fitzgerald – whose father was a former Lord Mayor of Cork and first president of Blackrock hurling club - presided over a private mass for the players and officials. As was customary at such affairs, the curate rounded off proceedings by good-naturedly requesting that the Man upstairs might look kindly on the players knelt before him and bring joy to them that day.

Michael "Gah" Aherne

At a subsequent breakfast, Fr. Fitzgerald repeated that blessing while saying grace and it was about midway through the repast, some of those gathered noticed that Michael 'Gah' Aherne was being especially quiet. After a couple of attempts failed to bring him into the conversation, one of his colleagues pulled him up.'What's wrong with you this morning?' According to reports, Aherne lifted his head, turned his gaze upon the priest nearby and then back to his friend, before replying.'Ah I don't know about all this. To tell you the truth, I'd rather beat them fair and square.'

The exact date and time of the story aren't as important as the tenor of it. Aherne was a goal machine on the Cork team that emerged in the second half of the 1920s. With his brother Paddy or 'Balty' as he was known usually alongside him in the full-forward line, the Blackrock man wreaked havoc.

'Between them, they formed the greatest combination ever seen in a forward line,' wrote John Power in his "Cork Book of Champions". 'And into their house in Ballintemple brought no fewer than ten All-Irelands, nine senior and a junior.'

Having won a junior title in 1925, Aherne was a member of the Cork team that won the first national hurling league the following year. He retained his place for a championship campaign that culminated in an All-Ireland final against Kilkenny. On the train to that game, copies of a ballad containing the following verse were distributed to supporters.

'Our forward line is swift and sure and Dr. Kearney there,
With Balty and with Gah beside him, boys we need not fear,
Though there may be steel in Balty's eye, he'll forget his eye is sore
And Balty, Doc and Gah will keep piling up the score...'

With a side containing three sets of brothers, the Ahernes, Eudie and John Coughlan, and Maree and Eugene O'Connell, Cork won by 4-6 to 2-0. Two years later, Seán Óg Murphy captained a star-studded Cork outfit – Eudie Coughlan, Tom Barry, Jim O'Regan et al - to a facile All-Ireland final victory over Galway. The scoreline of 6-12 to 1-0 tells its own story but omits a couple of crucial details. All but one point of Cork's tally was scored by Blackrock stalwarts, and a whopping 5-4 came from the stick of 'Gah' Aherne, the first two goals and two points coming significantly when the game was still a contest.

It's a record unlikely to be beaten. However, one of his predecessors at Blackrock, Andy Buckley, is credited with seven goals and four points in Cork's 8-9 to 0-8 victory over Kilkenny in the 1903 All-Ireland home final. They then went on to defeat London in the final proper.

Having garnered his third All-Ireland medal in 1929, firing over a mere (for him) three points in a 4-9 to 1-3 defeat of Galway in the final, Aherne's inter-county swan-song came in the epic 1931 championship. The second of the three games it took to separate Cork - now captained by Eudie Coughlan – and Kilkenny in the final is regularly described as the greatest game of hurling ever. Aherne and 13 of his team-mates played every minute of the seven matches Cork endured on their way to that title.

That he became synonymous with the scoring of crucial goals is perhaps best illustrated by the tale of the crowd gathered outside Brabants' Radio Store in Grand Parade one afternoon listening to one of the early broadcasts of matches. With Cork struggling to score, an agitated old man pushed through to the throng and shouted at the radio: 'Please, Sir, tell them to pass it to Gah!'

The best of times, the worst of times

All through Christmas week of 1975, the city of Cork was talking about only one thing. George Best was coming. Not to open a shop. Not even to go on a binge. He was coming to play. Without a club in England, Best was supposed to be 'talking' to Cork Celtic about a contract. As if....

One Dublin journalist of the time dismissed it as 'the greatest fairy story ever to come out of Ireland.' Cork soccer fans were even more caustic about the possibility. Yet, three days after Christmas, 12,000 of them were in Flower Lodge to see George Best make his debut for Cork Celtic.

At that point in his peregrinations through the world game, Best's latest club had been Fourth Division Stockport County. They had reportedly been paying him £300 per game. Cork Celtic were offering him up to £1,000. In that season, the average gate in the Bass League of Ireland was £200. For Best's debut against Drogheda, Celtic switched venues from Turner's Cross to Flower Lodge, bumped up their admission fees to 70p, 50p and 30p (kids) respectively, and took home £6,000.

'Of a dilapidated Turner's Cross, Carl Davenport would say the only time they had a proper shower was when it rained through the holes in the corrugated iron roof,' wrote Billy George in the Irish Examiner. 'When George Best first walked into the dressing-room I hastened to follow, the better to gauge his reaction. He stood in the middle of a suddenly silent room, swept his eyes from top to bottom and said: "It is different."'

Facing page: George Best takes the field for Cork Celtic at Turners Cross in January 1976.

With his new team-mates, Best was quiet and aloof.

At a time when you could buy the Cork Examiner for 7p, George Best was being paid £1000 per game, and the rest of the squad were clubbing together to try to make the dressing-rooms slightly more respectable.

'He seemed to be a bad mixer,' said one former Celtic player. 'He didn't talk very much at all, just came in, went out and played and flew home. I don't even remember him going for a drink with us afterwards.'

That first day, the other players passed to him at every opportunity. Unfortunately, he was as quiet on the field as he was off it.

'At the start we were in awe of him a little bit out there. But once we saw the way he was playing, that he wasn't trying too hard, we weren't in awe anymore.'

That's how one of his team-mates remembers it and the fans have a similar recall. Popular legend portrays Best as being grossly overweight and not managing one attempt at goal. Only the second half of that myth holds true. A couple of typically visionary through passes were the only things he did to excite the crowd. There were no mazy runs. No extravagant flicks. Nothing. Celtic lost 2-0. The fans were disappointed. The management less so.

'Next time we would hope to get him into Cork several days before the game so he can train with the players,' said Celtic manager Paul O'Donovan. 'With a little work, we can make it pay off.'

Best's post-match view was similarly upbeat. 'I am a businessman who just loves to play football. I would like to help Celtic as much as possible.' The previous day, there were 60,000 people at a game in Old Trafford. It was the biggest crowd of the English season. The then 29-year-old Best didn't comment on that. The sincerity of his comments about Celtic were still being debated in the city's pubs when the Daily Mirror broke a story that Cork Hibs were about to sign Rodney Marsh. Nobody was dismissing these rumours as fantasy anymore. Three weeks later, Marsh made his debut.

In the meantime, Cork Celtic travelled to Ballybofey without Best and won 3-0. It was described as 'their best performance of the season'. Still, the club were adamant Best would play in their next home game against Bohemians on Sunday, January 11th. Five days before that match, Celtic had their first training session in preparation. Best wasn't there. It was decided he would fly in the day before fixtures. After that particular work-out, the players established a scheme to improve the dressing-rooms at Turner's Cross.

'We intend to start with the showers,' said their spokesman Bobby Tambling. 'And after that, we will work away on the facilities. We would be very glad of any materials or any other help supporters can give us.'

George Best in action for Cork Celtic against Bohemians at Turners Cross in January 1975.

At a time when you could buy the Cork Examiner for 7p, George Best was being paid £1000 per game, and the rest of the squad were clubbing together to try to make the dressing-rooms slightly more respectable. They started a weekly kitty and decided they would do all the necessary renovation work themselves.

On Saturday January 10th, Best flew into Cork. He stayed at the Silver Springs Hotel and the following morning he had lunch with the other players at the Country Club Hotel. That afternoon, 9,000 people thronged Turner's Cross to watch Celtic defeat Bohemians 1-0. Although Best was again on the periphery of the action, the crowd chanted for him to take the kick when Celtic were awarded a penalty in the second half. He didn't. Bobby Tambling stepped up and missed.

'The prospects are good that he will be staying with us to the end of the season,' said O'Donovan after the game. 'We will talk about it again next weekend.'

The following morning's Cork Examiner ran with that story, declaring 'Best-man to extend Celtic honeymoon' on its front page. Moreover, it also began speculating that if Bobby Charlton signed for Waterford United (which he subsequently did), Best would be opposing his former team-mate pretty soon. The fairy stories just got more and more far-fetched. Well, not really.

Celtic played Shelbourne at Harold's Cross the following weekend. Hoping to get a crowd somewhere in the region of 20,000, the Dublin club had helped their opponents out with Best's expenses to ensure his presence for the game. Just 7,000 paid in though and Best's only significant contribution in a 2-1 defeat was to take the free-kick that Shelbourne's Dermot Shields turned into his own net.

'He will stay with us until the season in America opens in April,' said the redoubtable O'Donovan that day. 'Celtic are confident that their relationship with George Best will flourish.'

Celtic's next game was against Waterford United at Turner's Cross. Bobby Charlton had starred in his debut for Waterford, a 3-2 win over St. Patrick's Athletic, and as the papers built up the forthcoming clash between the England international and his erstwhile United team-mate, it emerged that Geoff Hurst was on the verge of signing for Finn Harps. Of all the rumours doing the rounds at the time, Hurst's was the only one to be off target. In fact, he later replaced Best at Celtic.

Three days before the Cork-Waterford match, Charlton announced he was unable to travel but it was confirmed that Best would definitely play. On the afternoon before the match, a representative of Cork Celtic rang Best's house in Manchester to confirm everything was okay. A few hours later, club officials were at Cork airport, watching the passengers disembark a flight from London. Best wasn't one of them.

A frantic phone call later, it emerged he wasn't travelling at all. He was said to have the 'flu'. After 'Match of the Day' ended on RTE television that night, an announcement was made informing all those intending to attend Cork Celtic's game against Waterford that George Best was unable to play due to illness. The following day, the approach streets to Turner's Cross were hung with posters advertising Best's absence. Some fans turned back when they saw the signs. Two thousand didn't. Four days later, Celtic terminated Best's registration by mutual agreement.

'It was not a success from a playing point of view,' said O'Donovan. 'He just did not turn it on.'

Dinny proves perfect codebreaker

With 14 minutes left in the 1989 All-Ireland football final, Mayo were a point up and had just missed a goal chance when John Kerins' long and accurate kick-out came into the orbit of Dinny Allen. The Cork captain fielded the ball and quickly dispatched it for Paul McGrath to level the scores. A typical Allen moment. Smart, speedy and crucial. Cork would never trail again. After mounting the steps to collect the trophy quarter of an hour later, Allen made a caustic reference to his team's critics in the 'crow's nest' before becoming just the fifth Corkman to lift Sam Maguire.

'Looking back, I don't think I should have said what I did,' said Allen in an interview with the Irish Times a decade later.' It just came out. It wasn't something I'd planned. Basically we had been on the receiving end of comments that we had no bottle, that Meath had beaten us, that we had struggled for a while against Dublin and played poorly against Kerry. I wasn't referring to anyone in particular. People said it was Mick O'Dwyer or this reporter or that reporter. It could have been anyone, I didn't know myself.'

Allen was entitled to vent. The Cork players had taken an amount of stick nationwide following the defeats by Meath in the previous two finals and this was their vindication. At 37, he had travelled a longer and more colourful road than most to reach this destination. Back when his friend and clubmate Billy Morgan led Cork to its previous All-Ireland in 1973, Allen was otherwise engaged, in the middle of a productive flirtation with soccer. His garnering of Sam Maguire was made all the more remarkable coming sixteen years after he won an FAI Cup medal with Cork Hibs.

Dinny Allen scores a goal
Cork Hibs at Flower Lodg

That he would become one of the few men to win an All-Ireland and an FAI Cup is especially appropriate because Allen's sporting life was an ecumenical affair. He played what he wanted to play when he wanted to play it and suffered whatever ridiculous consequences ensued from the various myopic authorities. Fortunately, his movement between codes - as any young person of talent should have been allowed to do - was rewarded with silverware and more importantly still, the recognition of a Cork public who savoured his contributions whether watching him from the City End or from the terrace in Flower Lodge.

One of the most fecund journeys through Cork sport began in Maiville Terrace where Allen grew up and the game du jour there was always soccer simply because of space limitations on the street. However, his first organised matches were on the Gaelic football team at Turner's Cross School, and down at Nemo Rangers, where his father and brother were already involved before him. He won a Munster title with Coláiste Chríost Rí in 1967, and despite a broken leg interrupting his development, featured on the Cork minors that lost to Kerry in 1970, and was a sub on the under-21 team that won the All-Ireland in 1972. By then, Allen was playing senior for Nemo Rangers but had also thrown his lot in with St. Mary's soccer club.

'I helped St. Mary's reach the FAI Junior Cup final against Talbot United but I had a hurling league game with Nemo on the same day, and I chose not to play with St. Mary's,' said Allen in John Coughlan's "100 Cork Sporting Heroes". 'They lost in the final 3-1. To this day, I would put it down as the worst decision I ever made in sport.'

The dilemmas about competing allegiances intensified thereafter. Despite coming to competitive soccer at such a late age, Allen had shown enough promise with Mary's to attract the attention of Cork Hibs. Having grown up so close to Cork Celtic's home in Turner's Cross, he was nevertheless persuaded by Dave Bacuzzi to sign for the rival outfit in January, 1973. A few weeks later, Nottingham Forest came in for Miah Dennehy and Allen was promoted to the first team. Four months after joining the club, he was man of the match in the FAI Cup final replay against Shelbourne.

Dinny Allen raises the Sam Maguire Cup after Cork defeated Mayo in the 1989 All-Ireland Senior Football final.

'The replay at Flower Lodge was made memorable by two outstanding, individual performances,' wrote Plunkett Carter in A Century of Cork Soccer Memories. 'When all else fades into the background, it will be remembered for the brilliance of Cork's Denis Allen and Shelbourne's keeper Paddy Roche. Allen teased, probed and tormented Shels and his brilliant display was equal to the best seen on the lush turf. Despite Cork's total dominance, they had to wait until the 83rd minute for the winner when Carl Humphries ran in towards the near post to flick home a Dave Wiggington cross. Eric Barber had received his marching orders earlier for a foul on Allen and Cork's Noel O'Mahony had to retire with a facial injury which necessitated 12 stitches.'

The most stunning illustration of Allen's ability is the litany of clubs and managers in England that were soon on his trail. Bobby Charlton tried seriously to take him to Preston North End and Brian Clough offered £25,000 on behalf of Nottingham Forest. Tommy Docherty and Dave Sexton were sniffing around too, all for a player who hadn't played a competitive soccer match until the age of 20. He moved from Hibs to Celtic in the summer of 1974, in time to participate in their (admittedly short) European Cup campaign, but a year later, had returned to the GAA fold.

In the summer of 1975, he played for both Cork senior teams, featuring at right half-forward for the hurlers in their Munster final triumph over Limerick and ironically, that was to be his only championship medal for a long time. Having missed out on the 1973 football triumph, he endured eight Munster football final defeats in a row before Tadhg Murphy's last-gasp winner against Kerry in 1983 finally lifted the gloom. A year later, his contribution during those tough times was acknowledged when a team of the greatest players never to win an All-Ireland was selected as part of the GAA's centenary celebrations. Allen was the only one of the hurling and football teams to later shed that tag.

Dropped by the selectors after the 1984 championship, it was October, 1987 before he wore red again. By then, Morgan held the reins and he knew better than anybody that regardless of age, there was no more cerebral forward in the county than his pal. Midway through the second half of the Munster final the following July, Allen collected a canny pass from Colm O'Neill and delivered a clinical finish for a goal that put Cork clear of Kerry and on their way to a second successive title. The faith had been justified.

'I got an accidental knee in the thigh after a collision with Tommy Doyle,' said Allen after the match. 'It started to stiffen up so I had to keep running. Looking back now, that knock proved to be a blessing in disguise. I was in full flight when Colm O'Neill broke down the ball. I saw only the net in front of me. It was the sweetest goal I ever scored.'

Every Cork boyhood is hallmarked by dreams of sporting greatness. Few manage to fulfill as many of them in three different codes as Allen; hurling in a Munster final, man of the match in an FAI Cup final, and captaining his county to an All-Ireland football triumph. Those baubles apart, there were also eight county medals and four All-Ireland club titles with Nemo, and a pair of National Football League wins with Cork. The only problem for anybody trying to juggle the different demands so soon after The Ban had been lifted was the inevitable political ramifications.

When Allen transferred from Hibs to Celtic in the summer of 1974, he was suspended for five months because of irregularities regarding his registration forms. He had been simultaneously suspended from the GAA for playing in America without the necessary clearance. Even after both bans were watered down, Nemo Rangers football selectors still wouldn't consider him for selection although he was hurling away with the club. That sort of bureaucracy has driven good players away from games down the decades but the greatest tribute that could be paid to Allen is the sight of him popping up every couple of years lately at the helm of some Nemo minor football or intermediate hurling team.

Still giving everything, helping others chase their dreams.

Oliver Drew

The purse on offer in the Mercer Street handball court at Jersey City on May 22nd, 1902 was $250. But that was only the second biggest prize. Mike Egan, Galway-born but Pittsburgh-raised, was also putting his world handball title on the line. The challenger was 19-year-old Oliver Drew. From Nicholas Hill in Evergreen, he had sailed out of Cork in February and prepared for the contest by overwhelming local players in warm-ups, occasionally defeating two of them at a time with a flourish that wowed the watching Americans.

The terms for the match-up with Egan were simple. Each game was first to 21 aces and it was the best of 15. The first seven games would take place in Jersey City and however many were required thereafter would be held in Cork. Drew had grown up in the city – his father and brothers were tailors on Prince's Street – at a time when it was the epicentre of world handball. In 1887, the American champion John Lawlor took on Phil Casey from Laois in the first leg of a world title match at Dan Horgan's Court in Duncan Street (now Grattan Street).

Eight years later, Tralee's James Fitzgerald defeated Lawlor in an Irish title contest considered by some to also be for the championship of the world. Throughout this time, players would also travel from the Basque region of Spain to measure themselves against the best Cork had to offer. In such a hot-house atmosphere, Drew was still a student at Presentation College when he was exposed to high-level competition.

At the age of 15, he partnered New York's Jim Dunne in a loss to the highly-rated Cork duo of Willie O'Herlihy (whose family contributed massively to the sport's golden age) and Willie McSweeney. A year later, he teamed up with O'Herlihy to win the prestigious Fermoy tournament and the pair of them pocketed a purse of 20 sovereigns following a triumph in a home-and-away challenge over the great Lawlor and John Corrigan from Dublin.

In Jersey City, five miles across the Hudson River from New York, the contrast between the two individuals on court was striking. Egan possessed such great physical strength that in his youth, he reportedly spent time working out in the training camps of heavyweight boxing champions, Jim Corbett, James. J. Jeffries and Bob Fitzsimons. Far slimmer than his opponent, Drew was a smart and skilful player whose main advantage was his speed and agility around the court. As was the norm at the time, Egan was allowed to serve from the ace line – as per American rules – while the Corkman did so from near to the wall.

'Egan won the first two games by a single ace,' wrote Chris Hurley in "A History of Handball in Munster". 'Drew took the next three games in succession. Egan accounted for the sixth but Drew finished strongly and brought off the final game of the session. The scores were 20-21, 20-21, 21-16, 21-19, 21-6, 5-21, 21-3 in favour of Drew. Drew delighted the audience with his lightning speed and reflexes.'

His fans and the New Jersey media were in shock at the standard of play evinced by the visitor when getting the better of their man. Most observers felt the Corkman unlucky not to be 6-1 rather than just 4-3 ahead.

'Michael Egan, America's handball champion finished in second place in yesterday's match with Oliver Drew, the Irish champion,' wrote the Jersey City Evening Journal the following day. 'No event has ever occurred in handball that created the surprise that followed the local champion's defeat.'

The pity was that the second half of the contest never took place. As per the contract drawn up beforehand, Egan's manager had failed to hand over the first day's receipts to Drew, he withdrew from the match in protest and Cork's best chance of claiming the world champion had gone. Just over a year later, the reigning Irish champion, Tim Twohill from Liscarroll – who played for Cork footballers in the 1897 All-Ireland football final - was routed 8-0 by Egan in another title bout, the clinching game in Kanturk taking just 11 minutes.

Back home in Cork, Drew suffered the only defeat of his singles career on October 19th, 1903 when Willie O'Herlihy upset the odds in a game at the Old Market Place (off Blarney Street) where each competitor had staked £50 each. His response to the setback was to challenge the victor to meet again in any court outside Cork for £100. Drew exacted revenge with a convincing 6-0 win, and afterwards challenged any player in Ireland, including the champion Twohill, to take him on. The two never met - the rules of the time meant that like boxers today, title-holders could avoid opponents if they so wished - and Drew emigrated to America at the age of 21. He died there in 1938.

'Drew won the international championship from Francois Ordozgoili, champion of France and Spain for a stake of $1,500 at Tarrant's Court, New Jersey in 1905, and the championship of America from Denis Sullivan of Chicago at Kennedy's Court, New York in 1906,' wrote Tom McElligott in 'The Story of Handball'. "His career leaves several questions unanswered. Was he a great player who never fulfilled his boyhood promise? We will leave the answer to Father Tom Jones (reckoned by some to be the most gifted Irish player of all) who in a letter written in 1949 spoke of him as "that wonderful and unbeatable Oliver Drew".'

4

From the naming of the finest stadium in the country to the founding of the oldest yacht club in the world, Corkmen have left indelible imprints on the Irish sports pysche. Not necessarily great athletes, these are the stories of those who irrevocably changed the course of some sports and invented others.

Footprints

Sam Maguire

'The Irish heart refused to beat in foreign captive chains -
It never would admit defeat while love and love remained.
With high resolve, with courage bold and zeal that could not tire,
In life and death, in every breath, you were Irish Sam Maguire...'

Séan Morrison, Gaelic Quarterly Review, September, 1936

Among the London team that arrived at the North Star Hotel in Dublin in the early hours of Sunday morning, October 26, 1902 were a talented pair of Protestant brothers from West Cork. Later that day at Jones' Road, Sam and John Maguire could do little to prevent their side losing heavily to double-winning Tipperary in the belated staging of the 1900 All-Ireland football final. With London automatically qualifying each year to play the winners of the home championship, Sam Maguire would go on to play in the 1901 and 1903 deciders as well. That he lost all three is neither here nor there, because in many ways his playing career pales into insignificance compared to what he did off the pitch.

When a group of Maguire's friends and colleagues commissioned the Dublin firm of Hopkins & Hopkins to design an enlarged replica of the Ardagh Chalice in his honour in 1928, they were commemorating much more than the great sportsman they had known. Having captained Hibernians of London in the latter two All-Ireland finals, Maguire turned his attention to administration, becoming such an astute chairman of the board in London that, along with Liam McCarthy (whose father Eoghan had been a noted wrestler and athlete in Ballygarvan before emigrating), he

Facing page: This statue was unveiled in Dunmanway in memory of Sam Maguire.

When a group of Maguire's friends and colleagues commissioned the Dublin firm of Hopkins & Hopkins to design an enlarged replica of the Ardagh Chalice in his honour in 1928, they were commemorating much more than the great sportsman they had known.

is regarded as one of the fathers of London GAA. On an even more historic note, it was Maguire who personally swore Michael Collins into the Irish Republican Brotherhood (IRB) in 1909, and he remained a mentor to, and a trusted agent for his fellow Corkonian for years after.

Born in Maulabracka, just outside Dunmanway in 1879, into a family of seven children, Maguire was a brilliant young scholar at the local Model School and the national school at Ardfield. He moved to London with his brothers after passing the British Civil Service Exams. Once in England, he threw himself into the various pan-Irish activities available to the young emigrant. Although he'd never togged out for Doheny's - his local club back home - he played his part in Hibernians' annexing of four consecutive London championships and juggled commitments to the fledgling Gaelic Athletic Association (GAA) with membership of the Gaelic League and later the IRB.

Before long, Maguire discovered that his status at work in the Post Office headquarters at Mount Pleasant near King's Cross in London gave him unique access to British military documents and he had no compunction about exploiting his professional position to further the political causes he espoused. By intercepting sensitive government material en route through the system, he rose through the ranks of the IRA. In his fine book, "Off the Field and On", Brendan Fullam uses an extract from a 1965 article in the Republican magazine, An tÓglach, to illustrate the extent of Maguire's subterfuge. Maguire held the rank of Major General and was Chief Intelligence Officer in Britain. He was a born underground and enemy-resistance leader. He broke through all barriers of the highest British intelligence departments to get vital information of the utmost value to the IRA at home and which often saved them from falling into dangerous situations. He was not known to Scotland Yard although he worked under their noses in the PO Sorting Office, Mount Pleasant, London. Secret enquiries had been circulated to police stations and intelligence agencies all over England to trace SM (himself) and Sam was laughing with copies of them in his pocket as he went complacently about his business.'

Fullam also quotes a poem written for Maguire by his friend Peadar Kearney, the composer of Amhrán na Bhfiann, which pays tribute to his republicanism while painting a less than pretty picture of his theatre of operations.

Proud to have hailed you friend,
Long years ago!

Amid the fog and fumes of London Town,
An Empire's mart -
Astride the Sluggish Thames,
Building on plundered clans,
Her dread renown!
Strong in your deathless faith
Oh heart of gold!
Your kindly, generous smile
Gave strength to all
Who grasped your hand
In that great brotherhood:
Waiting throughout the years for Eire's call.

An tÓglach's colourful description of Maguire seems appropriate. Daringly operating under the noses of the British authorities, he was heavily involved in gun-running, the planning of a campaign (later aborted) to kidnap and take hostage 25 MPs and in organising the assassination of Sir Henry Wilson in Belgravia in 1922. He also rescued a hit squad in pursuit of Major Percival of the Essex Regiment from certain arrest at Liverpool Street Station in 1921 when he tipped them off about Scotland Yard being on their trail. According to some reports, Maguire was eventually captured and imprisoned for running guns between London and Dublin, a crime that of course meant immediate dismissal from the civil service.

Regarded by many as the mainstay of the London GAA scene in the first 20 years of the 20th century, he served as chairman of the county board, delegate to the Annual Congress and a trustee of Croke Park. Following the end of his professional career in England, he returned to Ireland and got a job in the fledgling civil service. Having contracted tuberculosis, he returned to Dunmanway. He died at the comparatively young age of 47 and is buried beneath a Celtic Cross in the graveyard at St Mary's Church.

Even though the original cup was replaced by a newer model in 1988, Sam Maguire remains the name which dominates the dreams of Gaelic footballers everywhere. His memory has been further amplified by recent events. On September 15th 2002, a statue of him sculpted by the Derry artist Maurice Harron was unveiled in the new town plaza in Dunmanyway; Margaret Walsh has compiled a biography of him; and local singer Charlie McCarthy wrote a song about his life. No more than the recognition he deserves.

Donie Forde

Nobody is quite sure how much time was left in the 1956 FAI Cup final when Cork Athletic secretary Donie Forde decided to leave Dalymount Park in order to fetch champagne for the pending victory celebration. It may have been fifteen minutes before the end. It certainly wasn't less than 12, because that was when the Shamrock Rovers' comeback from 2-0 down began. Three times on his fool's errand, Forde was unnerved by raucous cheers coming from within the ground. Only when the first jubilant Rovers' fans came roaring out through the exits towards him did he finally realise each roar had been to greet one of their goals.

That Forde would have denied himself the last act of a cup final to make sure the players had instant fuel for their post-match celebration goes without saying. Elsewhere in this book, his name crops up in dispatches regarding the flirtations of Raich Carter and George Best with Cork soccer. In sixty years of service to the game, those were two rare occasions when the wider world caught a glimpse of the work Forde did. The rest of the time he was backstage, doing everything he possibly could to keep the production on the road.

'His eyes shone with animation when he isolated the great games and the great characters of the Mardyke,' wrote Billy George in a moving obituary in the Irish Examiner following Forde's death in 2004. 'He never failed to recall the scenes as the thousands unable to gain entry massed on Shanakiel Hill or clung to the railings on the perimeter wall of the Mardyke.
'He'd look you in the eye and tell you there were days when the referee

extended the game as long as was necessary until Cork scored to save a point or produce a win. Donie was still a boy when he was a founder member of the Cork Football Supporters Club, from which Cork United was founded in 1939. He was at the heart of Cork football matter until his death. His benign and efficient influence was seen in every progressive development in the area.The great irony was that the administrative heartbeat of professional soccer in the city was born in Dublin. The Fordes arrived down from Ranelagh in 1932, and the capital's loss was to be Cork's gain. Immediately enthralled with the fortunes of the then Cork FC in the League of Ireland, he was still a student at the North Monastery when he became involved in the aforementioned supporters club. Charting his various roles from the point he became secretary of Cork United in the forties is to plot a route through history.

'Cork Athletic folded in 1957 and Donie went on to forge a life-time association with the Munster Senior League,' said Plunkett Carter in his funeral eulogy to Forde. 'When he joined the MSL it was in a poor state with just a handful of teams competing and during his five decades at the helm it grew to become a vibrant organisation catering for 32 clubs.

'Cork Celtic sought his secretarial services in the sixties and one of the happiest days of his life was when they won the League title in 1974. There was unhappiness too, particularly in 1979 when Cork Celtic, who had been going through very lean times were expelled. Donie was appointed Honorary Secretary of the Munster Football Association in 1964 and filled the position with great distinction until his illness in December 1997.'

He managed all these roles while holding down a full-time job as a supervisor with Rudman's Paint Manufacturers on Blarney Street. The number of soccer-related visitors he gladly received there through the years, not to mention the amount of soccer business conducted on the premises, was a testament to his own innate charm and to his employers understanding. Somebody must have realised they had a living, breathing institution on their premises.

To those of us who never knew him, it's sufficient to know that mass at St. Mary's Church on Pope's Quay and a trip to the bookies were both part of his daily ritual. There is no way to properly gauge how much time he devoted to the cause of promoting the game at all levels, except to say that it can be measured in decades not years. That a stand in Turner's Cross - the ground he loved so well - bears his name is a fitting tribute.

Carbery

Half an hour before throw-in, Patrick D. Mehigan arrived at Croke Park. Beneath the Hogan Stand, he was introduced to the chief engineer and shown the various wires and mechanical devices that had already been put in place. One cable led from there right up to a mahogany box in the press section and that was where they told him to sit. Once in position, they put a leather contraption around his neck and told him to speak into the yellow brass tube once the signal came that he was on the air

With a sheet of paper in his hand, Mehigan began commentating on the 1926 All Ireland hurling semi-final between Galway and Kilkenny and made a little bit of history: it was the first live broadcast of a sports event in Europe. Earlier that summer, the Jess Willard-Jack Dempsey fight had been heard over the airwaves in America but for Ireland and the rest of the continent, this was breaking new ground. Kilkenny won handily but, of course, that was only incidental.

'I fired away and found that I could spout freely enough, particularly as soon as the game that I was familiar with started,' wrote Mehigan of the experience. 'At half-time I had to do a summary of the first half and so on to the end. I was very tired at the finish; they were beaming in the engineers room below and clapped me on the back. They told me I had done fine. I didn't believe them. I knew that I was only a raw recruit and had a lot to learn. Yet, I got a great kick out of it all and was glad to help to spread the light about the loved game of my boyhood.'

Born in Ardfield outside Clonakilty on March 17th, 1884, to describe him as the most influential Irish sportswriter of the twentieth century is actually to do Mehigan a disservice; he was that all right but he was much more too. A prolific poet, and short-story writer, he also penned innumerable columns about nature, politics, emigration and culture. He had been an athlete of renown, playing in two All-Ireland hurling finals, taking the national title in the hop, step and jump and even appears in a photograph of Bandon soccer team from 1906.

At the age of 15, Mehigan was so fresh-faced catching the train from Cork to Dublin that the conductor only charged him half-fare. He arrived in the big city wide-eyed, yet found his niche quickly and was soon rubbing shoulders with the likes of Michael Cusack, Douglas Hyde, and W.B. Yeats. Throwing himself into the various branches of the Gaelic revival, he hurled in the Phoenix Park ever week, attended lectures at the Celtic Literary Society and travelled around Leinster with the Gaelic League.

A posting to London removed him from that fray but in England too, he found an outlet for his energies. He played for the Hibernians in the 1902 All-Ireland hurling final where they were soundly beaten by Cork, that game being played in 1904 to mark the opening of the Athletic Grounds in the city.

'The seventeen that smothered us in that game formed one of the greatest teams ever to win an All-Ireland,' he wrote of the defeat. 'We were much lighter than the Corkmen - Jim Ronayne crushed my life out in the first charge - but they were really a great team.'

Right: PD Mehigan

Relentlessly modest when writing about his own exploits, Mehigan moved back to his home county soon after that. He joined Blackrock, and was good enough to be picked by St. Finbarr's to play for a Cork selection in the 1905 All-Ireland final. Having beaten Kilkenny in the decider, they lost a replay that was ordered because Jim McCarthy, Cork's goalkeeper in the first game, was found to be a British Army reservist. He finally snagged that elusive All-Ireland when an effort of 32 feet, 11 inches won him the standing hop, step and jump title in 1908.

Although he left West Cork at the age of 15, the place never left him. He gained the most of his fame under the nom de plume of Carbery, the barony where he grew up. 'Carbery's Comments' was a staple of the Cork Weekly Examiner for half a century, while Irish Times' readers knew him as their Gaelic games and coursing correspondent, Pat O'. He authored books on athletics, hurling and football and after the first edition of Carbery's Annual came out in 1939 it became a fixture in GAA households up until his death in 1964.

'In the round up of the Irish sporting year there were four fixtures which Murty Morley and I never missed,' wrote Carbery in his book "Mountain Heath". 'The Irish Coursing Cup at Clounanna, the intercounty Beagle Drag Hunt organised by the Fair Hill Harriers from Shandon Steeple and the hurling and football finals at Croke Park.'

The diversion into live radio came at the invitation of P.S. O'Hegarty, then head of Radio Eireann, or 2RN as it was known, which had been launched with a broadcast by Douglas Hyde earlier that year. O'Hegarty knew Mehigan from their time together soldiering with London Hibernians, and he recognised that if this daring new initiative were to take off, it would need a man of a certain calibre.

Two years after his debut on the airwaves, Mehigan was commentating on a boxing match at the 1928 Tailteann Games when he spotted Gene Tunney, heavyweight champion of the world, being ushered to his seat. Spotting the potential for a glamorous guest, Mehigan invited the vanquisher of Jack Dempsey to take the microphone. The first refusal barely registered but the second came laced with an inquiry about the identity of the audience listening. That was the only prompting Mehigan needed.

'I knew Tunney came especially to see his blood relations in Mayo and Cork,' wrote Carbery. 'I spoke my tenderest. "We're hooked up to every homestead in Mayo and every village in county Cork!" His fine eyes softened. Meekly, silently, he walked to the microphone. I introduced him in forty words and he was on the air....'

Father Slattery

On October 9th, 1960, Nigeria entertained Ghana in the final of an international soccer tournament called The Nkrumah Cup. The referee in Lagos that afternoon was Fr. Denis Slattery, a 44 year old priest from Fermoy. One of his linesmen, Nnamdi Azikiwe, would become president of the newly independent country three years later and Slattery himself would enter the nation's folklore. The soccer priest, they called him. Our referee. The father of Nigerian football. Each description reeked of affection and regard.

Fr Denis Slattery (in front with the ball) .

A few weeks after Slattery died in Cork in the summer of 2003, a group of his past-pupils in Nigeria got together to discuss how best to commemorate his influence on their lives. Before they could even properly consider that, they resolved to write to the Irish embassy, and the Catholic archbishop in Lagos. They wanted to know whether it might be possible to have the body exhumed, transported and reburied in the country where he spent half a century as a missionary, preaching the values of education, religion and sport.

That his grave would mean so much to them sums up the contribution he made to a place where he'd first arrived in 1941 when the world was at war.

He was part of a convoy of 50 ships that had sailed 30 days across 4,000 miles of Atlantic Ocean, constantly zigzagging to try to avoid the bombs being rained down by the German Luftwaffe. Twenty-five years old, and a newly-ordained priest, his journey had started out months earlier with the short spin from Fermoy to Mallow to catch the train to Dublin.

'My own father was short in stature, perhaps about five foot four inches, strong shoulders,' wrote Slattery in his 1996 memoir 'My Life Story.' "He was a great footballer and represented his club in the senior division. He had a fine reputation as a sportsman. He was as skilled with his hands as he was with his feet when he stroked the four and eight oar crews for Fermoy. It was from our father that we inherited our skill and love of sports. We were all mad about games: handball, hurling, gaelic football, swimming, soccer, lawn-tennis, athletics.'

Tim Slattery had played for Fermoy in four county senior football finals at the turn of the century, winning and losing two. By all accounts, Denis, the second youngest of eight children, inherited at least some of his father's prowess. A good enough inside-left to play for a "Whitemans' XI" in the Nigerian First Division, it was with a whistle in his hand that he'd leave his true mark on the game.

Invited by the commissioner of a local police training college to referee some intra-mural matches between the students - they reckoned a priest would be impartial - he eventually rose to international standard. As chairman of the Nigeria Referees Association, he was instrumental in bringing through the first generation of native referees as the country moved from life as a British colony to independence.

He coached too. In his first teaching job in Lagos, at St. Gregory's College, he'd managed the first XI. Following a stint in journalism as editor of the Catholic Herald, he founded St Finbarr's College (naming it after the sign at UCC that reads 'Where Finbarr taught, let Munster learn'), and within six years, he'd turned the new institution into a sporting and academic powerhouse.

During his two decades as principal, the school won nine national cups and five of their players went on to captain Nigeria's Super Eagles at senior international level. While Slattery constantly played down his role in the success, his supporters have always insisted that had he been made national coach, the country would have a World Cup title already to its credit. What else would they think? This man once persuaded Stanley Matthews to travel from England to Lagos to train his players? For nothing.

'The name Denis Slattery rings many bells,' went one article in Monthly Life Magazine, 'but the one that chimes loudest is a soccer tune. There is Slattery, the reverend father, there is Slattery, the educationist and Slattery, the journalist. But the Slattery that is a household name with most Nigerians is Slattery, the football administrator.'

He did serve a term as chairman of the Nigerian Football Association. On any other curriculum vitae, that would be the shining light. Here, it is one more title alongside so many others, each offering a glimpse of a different side to his career. As vice-chairman of the Society for the Bribe Scorners, he fought corruption as chairman of the Leper Colony of Nigeria, he campaigned for the worst-off in society and as a founding-member of the Nigerian Union of Journalists, he was almost deported three times for writing fearlessly on behalf of the cause of independence, and regularly thundering 'Nigeria for the Nigerians!' from the pulpit.

'There was no other school in Lagos that feasted so sumptuously as Finbarr's on Independence Day,' wrote Slattery. 'Why? I was a nationalist, a Nigerian Irishman that put the interest of Nigeria before everything except my God and my church. I was present among the crowd in the stadium and watched the solemn lowering of the British flag and the raising of the national flag of Nigeria for the first time. My heart jumped for joy.'

In 1988, the two largest and most important tribes in Nigeria - the Ibos and the Yorubas - both conferred him with honorary chieftain titles in recognition of the contribution he had made to the country's welfare. Fourteen years later, President of Nigeria, Chief Olusegun Obasanjo, made him an Officer of the Order of Niger. Four schools, and three churches list him as their founder, and every time the Super Eagles of Jay Jay Okacha, Nwankwo Kanu et al take to the field, their very presence is a tribute to the foundations he laid half a century ago.

'Sometimes geniuses fail because they cannot work hard while people of lesser talent succeed because they are hard working,' said Slattery once. 'Nobody will ever die of hard work. A lot of people die of laziness, doing nothing and growing fat.'

He worked hard. He did something.

Archbishop Croke

Shortly after the meeting to found the Gaelic Athletic Association was held in the billiard room of Miss Hayes' Commercial Hotel in Thurles, Michael Cusack wrote to Archbishop Croke of Cashel, inviting him to become the first patron of the new organisation. On December 18th, 1884, Croke wrote a letter accepting the position. Cusack had gone looking for an answer from the well-regarded clergy man. What he got back was equal parts manifesto, call-to-arms and mission statement.

'One of the most painful reflections that, as an Irishman, I am compelled to make in connection with the present aspect of things in this country, is derived from the ugly and irritating fact, that we are daily importing from England, not only her manufactured goods, which we cannot help doing, since she has practically strangled our own manufacturing appliances, but, together her fashions, her accents, her vicious literature, her music, her dances, and her manifold mannerisms, her games also, and her pastimes, to the utter discredit of our own grand national sports..."

"...Ball-playing, hurling, football-kicking according to Irish rules, 'casting', leaping in various ways, wrestling, handy-grips, top-pegging, leap-frog, rounders, tip-in-the-hat, and all such favorite exercises and amusements amongst men and boys may now be said to be not only dead and buried, but in several localities to be entirely forgotten and unknown. And what have we got in their stead? We have got such foreign and fantastic field sports as lawn tennis, polo, croquet, cricket, and the like - very excellent, I believe, and health-giving exercises in their way, still not racy of the soil, but rather alien, on the contrary, to it, as are indeed, for the most part, the men and women who first imported, and still continue to patronise them.

"...Indeed if we continue travelling for the next score years in the same direction that we have been going in for some time past, condemning the sports that were practiced by our forefathers, effacing our national features as though we were ashamed of them, and putting on, with England's stuffs and broadcoats, her masher habits and such other effeminate follies as she may recommend, we had better at once, and publicly, abjure our nationality, clap hands for joy at the sight of the Union Jack, and place 'England's bloody red' exultantly above the green.'

So succinctly had Croke captured the very reasons why the GAA was being established that when the first edition of its rulebook was published the following year, it contained a recommendation that his letter should be read at every annual meeting of the association thereafter. Twenty-eight years later, Central Council used monies raised at a tournament played in his honour to purchase a stadium in Dublin called Jones' Road. The GAA named its new national headquarters Croke Park, and almost a century later, the magnificent edifice that dominates the skyline of Dublin's north face is a fitting monument to a figure so central to it surviving the turmoil of the early years. 'Great name, Croke Park,' wrote Carbery in his anthology "Mountain Heath". 'Something of the man Croke himself, thundering a "No-Rent" manifesto from the windows of the Bishop's Palace in Thurles away back in Eighty-two.'

Thomas William Croke was born in the agent's lodge on the Deane-Freeman estate at Dromin, Castlecor, near Mallow on May 19th, 1823. His father William had been given a job there by the Deane-Freemans, well-off relatives of his Protestant mother Isabella. Croke spent the first 12 years of his life at Castlecor before the sudden death of his father necessitated the family moving to the parochial house in Charleville where his father's brother was the parish-priest.

During five years living there, the teenage Croke was educated at the town's classical school and developed a keen interest in sport, especially handball. In 1839, Croke won a scholarship to study theology at the Irish College in Paris. Upon graduation, he taught briefly in Belgium before moving to Rome. In 1847, he was awarded a Doctorate of Divinity by the Gregorian University, ordained a priest and, following teaching stints in Carlow and Paris, was chosen to replace his own brother William as curate in Charleville.

The town of his youth had lost nearly half its population (including William) to the Great Famine and its after-effects, and Croke could not but be affected by the changed circumstances in the country. He soon distinguished himself as an outspoken advocate of tenants' rights, became founding president of St Colman's College, Fermoy, was a vocal campaigner for a 'National System of Education in Ireland', and a member of the constitutional republican group 'The National Association'. Over the next thirty-five years, he served as curate in Midleton and Mallow, parish priest of Doneraile and Bishop of Auckland, New Zealand before being appointed Archbishop of Cashel and Emly in 1875.

From the moment he arrived at the Palace in Tipperary, Croke used his position in society to the benefit of the Home Rule movement and the Land League. Previously the patron for the Society for the Preservation of the Irish Language and its offshoot, the Gaelic Union for the Preservation and Cultivation of the Language, his involvement in the nascent Gaelic Athletic Association was an obvious extension of his interest in pan-nationalist causes. Apart from the stirring letter of acceptance, Croke dipped into his own funds to purchase prizes for the GAA in the early days and spoke resolutely against an early form of the ban - arguing that having people playing some games was preferable to none at all. He recommended no alcohol be sold on or near fields in which athletic sports were held, asked that competitions on Sundays should not start before 2pm in order to preserve Mass attendance and played a role in having a new set of rules drafted in 1895.

Although he had considered resigning in 1887 due to the constant bickering between the GAA and the Freeman's Journal, he played an important conciliatory role after the Fenians hijacked that year's Convention. Having first publicly dissociated himself from the Association's new direction, he then proposed a root and branch restructuring of it, granting each county more responsibility for its own affairs and appointing a central council of appeal. These reforms were implemented at the so-called reconstruction convention in Thurles early in 1888.

'At the same time as he spent his energy and money helping evicted tenants, the Archbishop was equally concerned with what one might call the moral regeneration of the Irish people,' wrote Mark Tierney in his biography "Croke of Cashel". 'It was in this context that he gave his support to the GAA, which he saw as a vehicle for building up the manhood of the nation.'

Which is exactly what it proved to be.

‘Tough’ Barry

During the build-up to the 1943 All Ireland hurling final, newspaper reports suggested that Antrim, surprise victors over Kilkenny in the semis, had a secret weapon which they would employ to defeat Cork. When he gathered his players around him for their first training session before the game, Jim 'Tough' Barry was unequivocal.

'Now we don't know what the secret weapon is, but the only weapon we have is hurling, and fitness, and this is what we're going to produce.'

His confidence was well-founded. Antrim were subsequently devoured by 5-16 to 0-4. The following year, Dublin provided the opposition, the last barrier to the historic four-in-a-row. On the morning of the final, the journalist Carbery met Barry and found him relaxed and confident.

'My lads are good and very good - an obedient, honest lot of boys, who did everything I told them. We'll win alright.' The final score was 2-13 to 1-2.

If anybody could judge when a team was ready, it was Barry. Between 1926 and 1966 he trained 12 Cork teams to All-Ireland titles and co-trained another two. After Cork were knocked out early in 1934, Limerick enlisted his services and they won an All-Ireland as well.

'Jim was not a learned man but he had a natural intelligence and he was a very practical psychologist,' said Eamonn Young, a member of the All-Ireland winning football team of 1945. 'He knew if there was anything wrong with you and that's where his charitable disposition came into play.

He radiated a benevolent personality. He loved people. I remember him saying to me, "I look on all of ye as my sons".'

His record was all the more remarkable because here was a man with no inter-county pedigree of his own. He hurled for Blackrock in his youth but it was as a swimmer and an amateur boxer that he'd enjoyed his best days as an athlete.'You don't have to be a greyhound to train greyhounds,' was his standard response to questions about his own lack of experience at the highest level. A Washington Street tailor by profession, the always impeccably

Between 1926 and 1966 he trained 12 Cork team

turned out Barry got involved with Cork in 1926 as assistant to Packey Mahony. When Mahony finished up three years later, Barry took over. Although never granted a formal say in the selection of teams, his opinions gained considerable weight over time. The job specification may have been to get the players fit but his interpretation of the role went way beyond those parameters.

'Not only did he not play but also I wouldn't ascribe to Jim a very in-depth knowledge of all the aspects of hurling,' said Jack Lynch in an interview with

"Tough" Barry with Christy Ring (centre) and Andy Scannell back in Cork after the 1954 All-Ireland final.

) All-Ireland titles and co-trained another two

Mick Dunne on RTE Radio. 'He had a tremendous ability to bring out the best in the team he was training. He used to do everything. When the training session started, he would go down to the Park to make sure the grass was cut. If it wasn't he would kick up holy murder. He'd make sure the jerseys were washed and the towels were washed. After matches, win or lose, he always made sure that the team were sitting down to a good meal and he wouldn't let anybody interfere.'

To Barry, the welfare of his squad was paramount. If a work situation was interfering with a player's ability to train or prepare for a big game, he would visit the office or factory, most often seeking out the top man to plead the case of his charge. An extremely generous individual, he'd dip into his own pocket regularly to help out anybody on the Cork scene who might have been short a few bob for whatever reason.

'He was a very sound judge of how to get a team right for the day,' said former GAA President Con Murphy, a Cork hurler for 10 years under Barry. 'He wasn't in the least tough, in the sense of being a hard taskmaster. The secret of his success was the way he managed to gain the affection and respect of the players under his charge. He'd know when a player had done enough and he'd tell them not to bother training that night. In the week of a match we'd finish up with his talk to us on a Tuesday or Wednesday night and then he'd tell us not to catch the hurley again until Sunday. He always wanted to keep our appetite fresh.'

During the 12 year famine after Cork's All Ireland win of 1954, Barry's methods came under critical scrutiny from a public starved of success. The most famous adage he contributed to GAA lore was the classic: 'Cork teams are like mushrooms, they come up overnight'. In 1966, the hurlers came from nowhere to win an All-Ireland title. The old warhorse proved right again.

The World's Oldest Yacht Club

At the same time as William Van der Hagen's oil-painting 'Cork Harbour, 1738' was up for auction in February, 2004, the issue of Royal Cork Yacht Club being the oldest such facility in the world also came under review. Michael Clarke, Lough Erne YC's official historian, took umbrage at RTE touting this as a fact, and briefly, it appeared the makings of a controversy was in prospect. It ended soon enough. The RCYC's response was to simply point out that 'proving continuity' was the basis of its claim to a unique place in history.

Nobody could possibly argue that a genetic line can be traced from Sir William O'Brien and his five pals establishing the Water Club of the Harbour of Cork in 1720 all the way to the denizens of the Royal Cork Yacht Club as it exists today. The name has been changed more than once and different locations within the sheltered harbour have been called home but tangible links exist to show one institution descended directly from the other.

Indeed, the only evidence of any club pre-dating O'Brien's new venture is the Flotilla of the Neva in St. Petersburg, Russia. Founded by Peter the Great in 1718, he tried to popularise the fledgling sport by giving away 141 yachts, but the club perished soon after his death in 1725. By that point, O'Brien, the ninth Lord of Inchiquin, had based the new concern in the castle on Haulbowline Island. He and his peers drafted a set of rules, and from the two editions of them still extant, we know that Rule 14 stated 'that such members as shall talk of sailing after dinner, be fined a bumper."In the early years the majority of club sailing activity took the form of sailing in various formations, copying the manoeuvres of the Navies of the day,' wrote Dermot Burns, archivist of the RCYC. 'They communicated with each other by means of flying different flags and firing cannons. Each display and sequence of flags or guns meant something and each owner carried a code book which allowed him to communicate with the other yachts. Paintings from 1738 in the possession of the club show club yachts carrying out such manoeuvres.

'Sometime shortly before 1806 the club moved to the town of Cove as the British Admiralty decided that they had a greater need for Hawlbowline Island than we had. By 1806, the Water Club of the Harbour of Cork had started to refer to itself as the Cork Harbour Water Club. During the 1820s, it became known as the Cork Harbour Yacht Club. Later on that decade it dropped 'Harbour' and became the Cork Yacht Club and in 1831 King William IV granted the club the privilege of using the prefix 'Royal' and it became known as the Royal Cork Yacht Club."

The original premises of the Royal Cork Yacht Club in Cobh.

By that point in its evolution, the club was organised enough to be able to run an annual event which, with its combination of competitive racing and socialising, appears to have been the primitive forerunner of Cork Week.

The 501 boats from all over the world that gathered to compete at that biennial festival of sailing in 2004 were preserving quite a tradition.'The celebrated regatta of Cove takes place in July or August,' wrote Samuel Lewis in his 1837 topographical dictionary “Lewis's Cork”. 'The prizes are numerous and valuable, and many of the best yachts in Ireland, with some from England and Scotland, attend its celebration. Near the Custom-House Quay is a splendid edifice in the Italian style, built by the Yacht club and occupied by its members during regatta season.'

In 1854, the club moved to a new premises in Cobh, one specifically designed by Anthony Salvin, the celebrated Victorian architect who had previously done restoration work on the Tower of London and Windsor Castle. After over a century in that impressive building - today housing the Sirius

Arts Centre - up the quay from the train station, the club moved across to Crosshaven in 1966 following its amalgamation with the Royal Munster Yacht Club.

Approaching the end of its third century in existence, the club has played host to and enlisted as members a litany of illustrious names, from the future King Edward VII - a regular visitor to RCYC events on his competitive yacht Britannia - towards the end of the 19th century, to the Hollywood studio magnate Roy Disney most recently. Beneath the glamorous associations, and rich history however, beats the heart of a club with over 1,500 members on its roster and the sort of competitive culture that spawned, amongst others, Harold Cudmore, and the four-times Olympian Mark Mansfield.

Fireball dingys off Roches Point, during the Fireball Championships,2003. The event was hosted by the Royal Cork Yacht Club.

The First Steeplechase

Like all great sports, this one was born out of one man's desire to prove he was superior to another. Nobody knows the exact date of the conversation but, at some point in 1752, a pair of gentlemen in North Cork had a dispute about the speed of their horses.

'I'll wager my horse is better than yours,' said Edmund Blake. 'I bet he could outrun yours from here to that steeple in the distance.'

The pair of them were by St. John's Church in Buttevant and Blake was pointing to the steeple of St Mary's Doneraile, rising into the sky not quite five miles across the landscape. Cornelius O'Callaghan demanded his friend prove this boast, and just to make it interesting, a cask of wine would ride on the result. When the day of the race came, locals gathered to watch them set off from Buttevant, intrigued by the prospect of this new variation on an old theme. Horses had always raced on the flat. Who'd have thought to have them jump fences on their way from one village steeple to another?

'Away down the slope they ran, jumping a tree log and splashing through the river, stirrup irons clanking as they knocked into each other in the deep water,' wrote Anne Holland in "Steeplechasing - A Celebration of 250 years". 'On up the long hill they galloped, sweat beginning to fleck the hunters' necks as they reached the boreen, a sunken lane at the top of the hill. They jumped off the bank into the lane, one stride and up the bank out of it.

'Here the area known as Cahirmee opened up a little, and on they stretched across open farmland, in and out of more sunken lanes, the riders finding breath to curse and swear at each other if they got too close, or at their horses if they stumbled. They bypassed the boggy ground speckled with marsh marigolds, scrambled up and over more stone walls and somehow kept their seats, picking up their reins and urging their mounts ever faster, even bolder. The crashed through undergrowth and ducked under willows and waded through another loop in the river.'

Action from the re-enactment of the original Buttevant to Doneraile Steeplechase in December 1997.

Beechers Brook at the famous Grand National Course at Aintree, Liverpool, England is callec after Captain Martin Beecher, who lived at Castlecor not far from Buttevant.

The body of water they splashed through was the River Awbeg - commemorated in verse by the poet Edmund Spenser as the 'Gentle Mulla' - one more embroidered detail on a lavish quilt.

To draw a line from Doneraile through Buttevant and on up to Churchtown is to trace one of the richest seams in Irish racing history: eleven miles or so of North Cork that wends through fields that reek of heritage. St Mary's Church was built by the Right Honourable, Sir William St. Leger in 1633. One of his descendants would give his name to the famous horse race that was first run in 1776. Captain Martin Beecher, who lived at Castlecor outside Buttevant, rode in the 1839 Grand National and earned his entry in the history books the hard way.

'A gentleman and a hunting man, just as Blake and O'Callaghan before him,' wrote Denis Walsh in The Sunday Times. 'He was unseated on the first circuit and was pitched headlong into a brook on the landing side of the fence. As the rest of the field flew over his head he lay still. Becher is reported to have said afterwards that he "never knew water tasted so foul without whisky in it." Another legend would have it that he fell at that fence on each of the three circuits they travelled in those days and remounted each time. Either way, Beecher's Brook was born.'

Long before Vincent O'Brien broke through at Cheltenham, Churchtown sent out a couple of Irish Derby winners in St. Brendan (1902) and Loch Lomond (1919) and produced Jack Moylan, one of the leading jockeys of the 1920s. His daughter married Doneraile's Jimmy Eddery, several times Irish champion jockey himself and their son Pat went on to even greater things in the saddle. In the sixties, Jonjo O'Neill used to cycle to seven miles each day from his home in Castletownroche to school in Doneraile.

The night O'Neill returned to celebrate his first jockey's title he did a lap of honour on a pony; the day he and Dawn Run came good on the merciless finishing climb at Cheltenham to win the Gold Cup, Brian Harding was a 13-year-old buoyed by the achievements of somebody from his own home place. Twelve years later, Harding won the Queen Mother Chase at the Festival on One Man. Summoned at the last minute when the grey's usual jockey Tony Dobbin was injured, the Corkman's performance earned him the award for National Hunt ride of the season.

On and on it goes, through the centuries, down the generations. And as to the day it all began. Well, the details of the race between Blake and O'Callaghan were originally gleaned from a manuscript discovered at Turret Hill in Limerick. We have the reason for the race, a flavour of the contest, and the knowledge that their exploits would come to be known forever as steeplechasing. The only thing missing from the narrative is the outcome. Nobody knows who won.

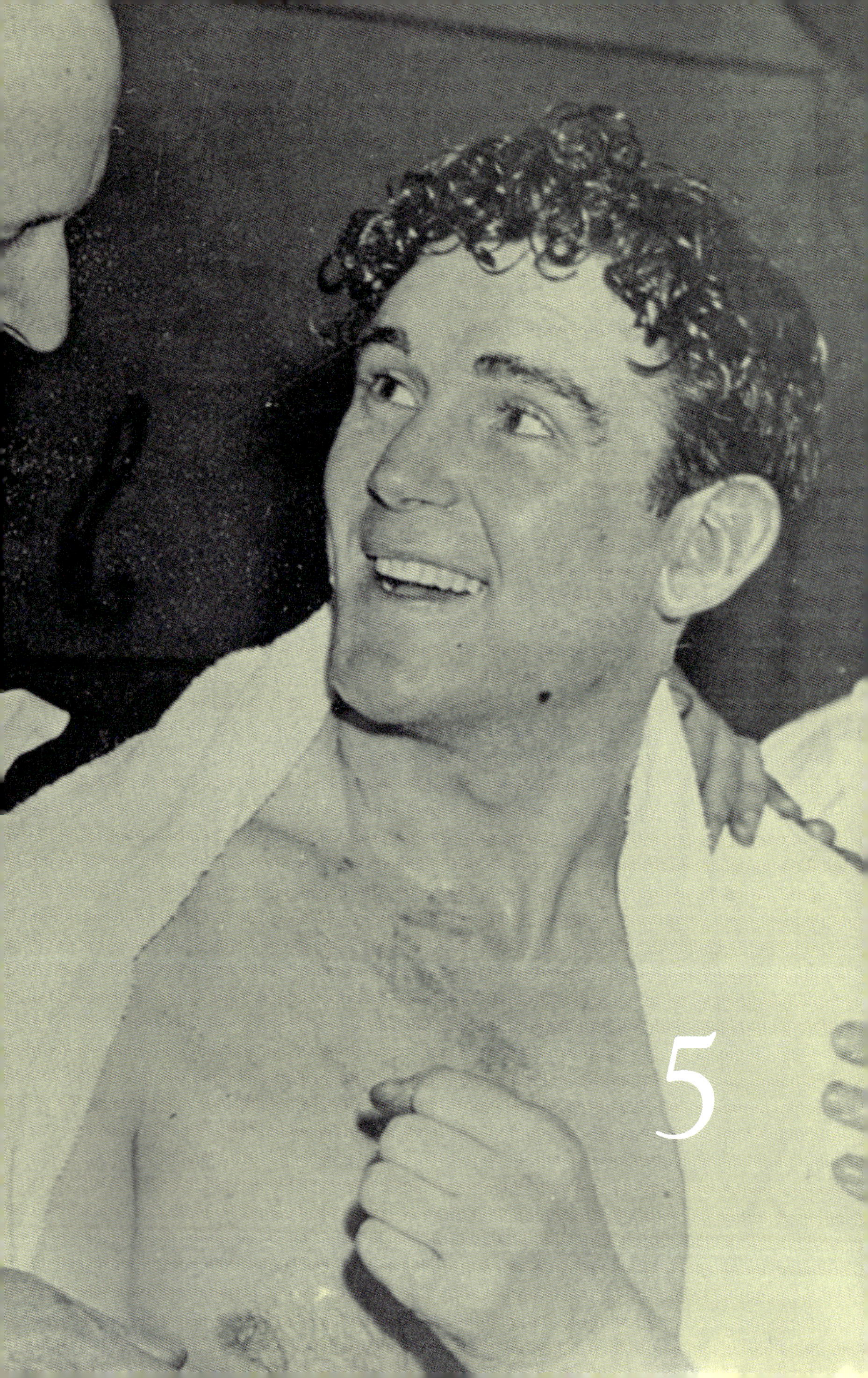
5

They went away. Some of them departed and were soon forgotten. Until now. Others left and we assiduously followed every step of their careers from afar. We marvelled at their triumphs, and mourned their defeats, always insanely proud of the bright light they reflected back on the county that spawned them.

Exiles

Denis Irwin

In April, 2001, shortly after another Premiership title had been secured, Alex Ferguson sat down to talk about Denis Irwin. For close to half an hour, he waxed lyrical about the player he regards as the best full-back he's worked with. When the cameras were finally turned off, Ferguson lingered in his chair.

'What exactly is this for again?' the Manchester United manager asked.

'It's a documentary about Denis's career for RTE.'

'It's about bloody time ye did one,' he replied.

There was a pause, and to fill the silence somebody blurted out that the latest league medal made Irwin the most decorated Irishman to play in English football up to that point. It was the only prompting Ferguson needed. A fuse had been lit. Using the fingers on both hands, he began counting out the trophies with the passion of a schoolboy leafing through a deck of old Top Trumps' cards in search of comforting stats. Listening to him reel off all those league and cup victories he had enjoyed with Irwin brought home the magnitude of the achievement.

'He is a role model to all the players in that dressing room of ours,' said Ferguson. 'They can see him and see how a person can lead his life perfectly. There is a consistent nature about Denis that has allowed him to play until 35 years of age at the highest level. It's very important to stress the point about a person being consistent in their nature. Denis is one of those types who leads his life at the same level all the time.

'One of his main attributes was playing on a very, very good team over the last decade and not needing any publicity for it. He was happy to play his role and be in the shadow of these high-profile players. That's not the say he's any less than these players; he's up there with them all. The nature of the man allows him to live with that, and not everyone can do that you know? But Denis has never been the type to ask for recognition or look for it.'

The manner in which Irwin conducted his football life yielded its own rewards. In an era when his teammates were some of the most recognisable faces in these islands, men who willingly or not sacrificed so much normality on the altar of their fame, he was different. He could watch his son Liam play football, stroll to the local for a drink with his wife, Jackie, and still enjoy the simple things they used to do together when he was an unknown at Leeds United all those years ago. His salary had a few more zeros on the end of it but little else had really changed.

Not for him the common practice among modern footballers of ringing up Manchester clothes shops and asking them to open early so he could buy his clothes before the public arrived. For managing to enjoy the trappings of massive success without letting it impinge on his personal life, Irwin could be described as the luckiest player on that team. Except that would be to suggest the situation was the result of good fortune. It wasn't. It was the consequence of sensible living and a stoic personality that didn't crave attention and could live without back-page headlines.

14-year old Denis Irwin (centre front) celebrates a Munster Colleges Gaelic Football success with his school Coláiste Chríost Rí.

'I've just been able to get on with my life,' said Irwin. 'You always get people coming up to you, but you never get the hassle that the likes of Becksie [David Beckham], or Giggsie [Ryan Giggs] or even Keaney [Roy Keane] can get. I'm just happy to be able to get on with my life. I'm forever grateful for that.'

Later in the filming of that documentary, Jackie Irwin was sitting in the living room of their home in Hale outside Manchester, answering questions about the complexity of trying to rear children properly when their father is lavishly paid to play football for one of the most glamorous teams in the world. Suddenly, there was a thunderclap outside, a flash of lightning and the first few drops of heavy rain started clanging off the windows.

'You'll have to stop this for a minute,' she said, before shouting to her husband in the kitchen. 'Denis, bring the washing in from the line!' From the kitchen, one of the production crew shouted back: 'You're OK. He's already out there looking after it.' Amid the laughter, you realised how much substance there was to Ferguson's psychoanalysis of his player. Denis Irwin the man is exactly like Denis Irwin the fullback. Consistent. Steady. Reliable. Quiet.

'I could never imagine Denis Irwin and Roy Keane sharing a room like they did for all those years,' said Jack Charlton, with a suitably unorthodox interpretation of those virtues. 'Roy never said nothing; neither did Denis. They both waited until you spoke to them to speak to you. They listened but never spoke. Can you imagine two more boring people sharing a room? It's probably just as well that they were both from Cork, because at least they understand each other.'

The presence of two Corkmen in the United dressing room taught Ferguson a lot about the geographic rivalries that divide the city.

'Denis says Roy is from the rough part of Cork, and Roy says Denis is from the rough part of Cork,' said Ferguson. "I don't know exactly who to believe here but there is a little bit of competition in the parts of Cork they come from.' The common background and the parallel career paths have led some to incorrectly conclude that the pair are bosom buddies.

'When I first got into the Irish squad, they put me rooming with Denis,' said Roy Keane 'They knew it would be a help to me and undoubtedly it was. Throughout our lives, throughout our careers, though, me and Denis have been friends, but I would never say we've been that close. He is one of the lads. When the team go for a drink and all that, Denis will be first there and last to leave. But I think Denis knows when to stop, whereas most of us don't, which is a problem. He stays in the background a lot with Jackie and the kids and he deserves a lot of credit for that. There must have been opportunities over the years to make a few bob and exploit himself, but he hasn't done that.'

More than two decades after he swapped the Cork suburb of Togher for Elland Road, the only mystery is how somebody so reserved could stay at the top of such a competitive sport for so long. Undoubtedly, the genes promised some chance of future success. His father, Justin, was an excellent junior soccer player, and his grand-uncle Tom was a top-class cricketer who remains the only man to win an All-Ireland hurling medal and referee an All-Ireland hurling final. From the beginning, one particular quality marked this Irwin out from the crowd.

'Denis hated losing,' said John Keane, a colleague on the Everton schoolboys' team who was also scouted by several English clubs. 'Like most good players, I suppose, he hated losing. He'd get cranky and have to be left alone for a while.'

Whether it was soccer with Maglin Grove, and then Everton, or hurling and Gaelic football for St. Finbarr's or Colaiste Chríost Rí, success presented only one problem. It wasn't unusual for the teenage Irwin to bring home silverware and fling it under the stairs with his gear bag. The first his parents knew about any bauble collected would be when Maura Irwin discovered some glistening trophy clinging to the dirty jersey. Modesty on that scale is not an affectation.

Having received permission to leave class early one afternoon at Colaiste Chríost Rí, Brother Theodore asked the rest of the students to give the departing Irwin a round of applause and their best wishes as he was off to play a schoolboy international soccer match for Ireland. To that point, his classmates didn't even know he was in the squad. 'I remember when Denis had decided he was heading off to Leeds, I thought this was a big mistake,' said Mick Carey, a teacher and coach at Chriost Rí and winner of three All-Ireland club football medals himself with St Finbarr's. 'Here was a very intelligent young man, an extremely good Gaelic footballer, an extremely good hurler. I was trying to explain to him that if he stayed in Cork, he'd play senior hurling for Cork and he'd go to university instead of going to a club in the old second division. How wrong was I?'

Denis Irwin in the famous Manchester United strip. Irwin played 527 first team games during his 12 years the club.

Carey discovered earlier than most that beneath the veneer of humility, there beats a heart pulsating with ambition. Joining up with his first Irish schoolboy squad, Irwin was fascinated to hear the Dublin-based players talk about the various English clubs they had visited for trials. Immediately envious, he wanted some of that for himself. An apprenticeship at Elland Road represented an opportunity to see how he'd measure up at a time when there were still never more than 20 full-time Irish professionals in England. In hindsight, this innate desire to constantly stretch himself may well be the key to his success.

'I was in his house in England when the club rang him to tell him he was included in the Irish senior squad for the first time,' said Irwin's oldest friend, Ray Duffy. 'So I asked him, "Aren't you excited?" And he just said, "I have to go and play now, I have to prove myself." He was totally calm. It was just a case of him deciding he'd have to go and face a different challenge.'

That is the way of it with Irwin. Outwardly cool and unruffled yet privately driven. When Eddie Gray managed Leeds, he had a promising quartet of youngsters on his hands. From a group containing Tommy Wright, John Sheridan, Scott Sellars and Irwin, he worried most about the Corkman's chances of enduring in a professional game that chews up and spits out so many. After Billy Bremner eventually released Irwin, Gray felt certain his easygoing demeanour would militate against him ever recovering from the blow.

Four years later, Gray found himself acting as the player's agent in negotiations with Ferguson at Old Trafford, and marvelling at the manner in which he had battled back. His three pals at Leeds all had good professional careers. He was the only one to become great.

'I felt that it taught them how to think and plan,' said Ted Garvey, a teacher, when asked why he once supplemented the curriculum at Togher national school with chess. 'It was a great mental discipline for them because it taught them how to lose, which I felt was very important, and to be sporting about the losing.'

In learning the taste of defeat, none of his pupils developed as magnificent an obsession with winning as Irwin. Never known for speaking too loudly outside the dressing room, the most singular public manifestation of his extraordinary self-belief came when Mick McCarthy started him on the bench for a friendly against Argentina in 1998. More than three years after the event, he contended it was the Irish manager asking him to prove himself when being introduced as a half-time substitute that rankled most. McCarthy argues that he merely asked Irwin to "prove me wrong". A crucial difference in semantics, the player hung around for one more qualifying campaign after that, seemingly determined not to end his international career on so discordant a note.

During the failed attempt to reach Euro 2000, Irwin was magnificent in the home victories over Croatia and Yugoslavia, two of the better results achieved by any Irish team in modern times. Although in both games, as so often, it was the more headline-friendly contribution of Roy Keane that took the majority of the plaudits, Irwin's understated excellence at the back had been vital. Against Turkey in the first leg of the play-off at Lansdowne Road in November, 1999, it was also his brazen and determined run down the inside-left channel that culminated in David Connolly passing for Robbie Keane to score.

That he missed the return leg and the chance to win his 57th cap due to injury seriously weakened the Irish squad for Bursa because, even if McCarthy was fortunate to have a stock of decent full-backs available, none ever compared to Irwin. To understand the regard his younger colleagues held in him, it's instructive to note the response of Kenny Cunningham to a question about how Wimbledon fans used to feel he was their very own Denis Irwin. 'Ridiculous,' said Cunningham, 'Denis is in a class of his own.'

Despite winning 56 caps, there is a school of thought that his international career never quite matched his club outings in its lustre. Apart from his mishandling by McCarthy, there was a period at the turn of the last decade when Jack Charlton for too long resisted the urge to promote the then Oldham Athletic full-back ahead of the less-gifted Chris Morris. After Irwin starred in an Ireland B team victory over England B at Turner's Cross in early 1990, it was imagined that Charlton would surely bring him in for Italia 90, but the old conservative went for the more experienced option.

Four years later, Irwin suffered in the heat in America and following his suspension for two bookings, failed to dislodge Gary Kelly for the second-round defeat by Holland. How much that experience hurt was most visibly demonstrated on an October night in Skopje in 1999. Seconds after Govran Stavreski headed an injury-time equaliser for Macedonia that robbed Ireland of automatic qualification for Euro 2000, Irwin stomped around the six-yard box, waving his hands and furiously admonishing his colleagues for the slackness of their marking. There was a sense of a player realising his last chance of another major tournament was slipping away. Three months later, the first Irishman to be capped at six levels announced his retirement from international football.

The departure from United was much less painful. After 12 years, 527 first-team appearances, seven Premiership titles, a European Cup, a Cup Winners' Cup, two FA Cups and a League Cup, Ferguson made him captain for his final game at Old Trafford in May, 2002. He was substituted twenty minutes from the end so the fans could acknowledge him properly. The ovation was heart-felt, yet it was arguably surpassed by an incident nearly two years later.

Enjoying a swansong with Wolverhampton Wanderers – where he added a promotion from Division One to the litany of other honours – he came up against his former team at Molineux. As the players lined up for the second half that day, the United away support, a group of fans considerably more knowledgeable and devout than the many corporate visitors to Old Trafford, rose and began chanting Irwin's name. They knew exactly what he did for their club and, though he was wearing the old gold of Wolves, they wanted him to understand how they felt.

In an unlikely 1-0 victory that day, Irwin's typically incisive header set up Kenny Miller's winning goal and during a fierce rearguard action in the last 15 minutes, he was, inevitably, leading by example. Offered the chance by a BBC interviewer afterwards to gloat about putting one over on his former club, he refused to even admit this victory meant more than any other. That was the classy thing to do and class has been the hallmark of his every move this last 20 years. Nobody's holding their breath for the autobiography where Irwin takes a few gratuitous swipes at former United or Ireland colleagues.

Denis Irwin played the last two seasons of his professional career with Wolverhampton Wanderers

On May 15th, 2004, Irwin was substituted one minute from the end of Wolves' last game of the Premiership season against Tottenham. The Molineux crowd gave him a standing ovation as he walked off after his 902nd and final professional appearance.

'The biggest honour I can give Denis,' said the Wolves manager Dave Jones that night, 'is to say that he has trained this week as if it was his first.'

What more would we have expected?

Jonjo O'Neill

Approaching the second last, Dawn Run looked beaten. Even after Jonjo O'Neill guided her successfully over it and briefly back into the lead, Wayward Lad appeared to have plenty in reserve. Using the speed available to a three-time winner of the King George VI Chase, Graham Bradley suddenly found another gear as they raced towards the final jump. Halfway up that punishing hill towards the post, Wayward Lad was clear again, and Forgive 'n' Forget was looming on the outside. It was looking bad for Dawn Run. Until.

'Here comes the mare!' said Peter O'Sullevan, commentating on the BBC. 'She's going to get up! She's going to get up!'

She got up all right. In a way that would forever be associated with guts and stamina and courage, she had won by a length from Wayward Lad. That March afternoon in 1986, it seemed like every Irish person on the course simultaneously flung their hats in the air the moment Dawn Run became the first horse to follow up a Champion Hurdle (1984) with a Gold Cup. Amid delirious scenes, O'Neill and Charmian Hill, the 67-year-old owner of the favourite, were carried around the enclosure by the hordes that had poured through the barriers.

'She made several mistakes, but I can't remember where or when,' said O'Neill to reporters. 'I thought we were beat at the last, but she picked up again on the run-in. She's got so much guts. That was the happiest moment of my life.'

Facing page: Jonjo O'Neill on board Dawn Run after the Cheltenham Gold Cup triumph in 1986.

He retired from the saddle after over 900 winners, two jockey titles, two Champion Hurdles, two Gold Cups, and one particular season when he'd managed 149 wins, including five in one day at Perth in 1978.

A month after the man in the mud-splattered red and black silks put his fist in the air to signal his most famous victory, O'Neill called it a career. He retired from the saddle after over 900 winners, two jockey titles, two Champion Hurdles, two Gold Cups, and one particular season when he'd managed 149 wins, including five in one day at Perth in 1978. Those were the statistical monuments, but punters measure out his achievements by simply dropping names like Alderton, Night Nurse, Sea Pigeon and, of course, Dawn Run, horses with whom he became forever intertwined in the public imagination. A 25-1 win at Navan on Stan Royal had been the first public expression of promise that was only properly fulfilled after a move to England while still a teenager.

'It was before a minor televised meeting at Stratford some 33 years ago that trainer Gordon Richards told us that he had a promising boy riding for him in the opener,' wrote The Daily Telegraph's Brough Scott in January 2004. 'Half-an-hour later I remember doing the replay of what was to be the first J J O'Neill success in an extraordinary career.... Even on that still untidy first occasion you could recognise the inspirational life-force which was always at the centre of Jonjo's riding and which had begun at home in County Cork on the back of a neighbour's pig.

'Without the finesse of John Francome or Richard Dunwoody, he had an irrepressible country boy enthusiasm which made him every inch their equal when the chips were down. It was a quality he has had to draw on through adversity enough to sink an Atlantic liner. Twice he snapped his leg into little more than a bag of gravel. The first time at Stockton it was so bad the bones came out through the boot. The second time at Bangor came in a freakish mid-air accident when his shin was snapped in 36 places by the scissors motion of another horse's flailing hind legs. It took 412 days to get back in action, but back he came, and as Dawn Run was led in at Cheltenham, Jonjo O'Neill was the most popular jockey on the planet."

As Scott so eloquently detailed, success had come at quite a price. When he attempted to come back too quickly from the broken leg at Bangor, he required further surgery in a Switzerland clinic. Before going under the knife there, he had to sign a form of consent, allowing the surgeons to amputate if they thought it necessary. In the wake of Dawn Run's epic adventure then, O'Neill was advised by friends all around the sport to move on to the next phase of his life. He took their counsel, formally retired, and set up Ivy House Farm in Cumbria as his first training yard.

The transition from jockey to trainer had been barely made – he had 18 horses under his hand by that summer - when his new profession had to be temporarily put aside to fight cancer of the lymph glands. When news of his illness broke in August, just five months after his glorious final Cheltenham, The Guardian correspondent described him as ' one of the best-liked men in British and Irish racing'. It was no exaggeration. His relationship with the racing world had been equal parts admiration and affection. Yet, he discovered during the toughest battle of his life that horse-racing was also just a business.

'I just shut down when the verdict was delivered. I could only think of my three children and how I would never live to see them grow up. The treatment was bloody awful and, after a while, you feel as if you can't take any more but you know that if you don't, you will die and you are grasping at every little candlelight there is to live. Situations like that teach you a lot about life.

'Each and every owner promised that the minute I was diagnosed healthy again, I would have their horses back. After the doctors gave me the all-clear, just two horses were returned to the yard. It was no easy task because when you have had cancer, you are a dead man as far as most people are concerned. My whole career - everything I did as a jockey - meant nothing. I had to prove myself all over again.'

Having caught an up-close glimpse of his mortality, O'Neill's resolve was only strengthened. Unlike some of the owners with short memories, he didn't forget the people who tended to him in his hour of need either. Three years after recovering, he returned to Manchester's Christie Hospital and handed over a cheque for £225,000. At various points in his battle, he'd vowed to give back to the medical facility that saved his life and the money was the product of a cancer research fund he'd established. He grew up the son of a grocer in Castletownroche. For him, a debt was always a debt, monetary or otherwise.

These days feted as the first person to ride and to train 100 winners in a single season, his initial progress as a trainer was solid rather than spectacular. By1988/89 however, he had 29 winners, a strike rate of 19 per cent and a burgeoning reputation. In 1990, Gypsy Fiddler gave him his first win at Royal Ascot in the Windsor Castle Stakes, and the following March, the J.P. McManus horse Danny Connors yielded his first Cheltenham triumph in the Coral Golden Hurdle Final.

Such was the young Jonjo O'Neill's passion to own his own pony that he saved his pocket money, earned from delivering milk and newspapers before school each day, in order to buy one.

'This is a fierce buzz,' he said afterwards. 'Even better than the Gold Cup, because this has come after a great team effort. Winning at Royal Ascot with Gipsy Fiddler was something, but I felt like an outsider there. This is home.'

Despite the patronage of high-profile owners like McManus, Michael Tabor and Anne, Duchess of Westminster, the first half of the nineties was a period of stasis. Except in one crucial regard. The trauma of his bout with cancer had been compounded by the subsequent break-up of his first marriage, the divorce from the mother of his three children was even deemed worthy of tabloid newspaper headlines. He met his second wife Jacqui at Doncaster Sales and fittingly, they were married in a suite at Cheltenham racecourse in 1997. The couple have two children.

Throughout this time, his yard kept producing winners over jumps just not at the same rate as before. There was another Cheltenham success in the 1995 National Hunt Amateur Chase with another McManus horse, Front Line, but in 1996/97, O'Neill's strike rate had fallen to ten per cent. Ivy House appeared to most to have developed into a mid-ranking stable, competitive, capable of the odd moment of greatness but not in the highest echelon of the sport.

A fair assessment at the time, it underestimated the character of the trainer. As a jockey, O'Neill's doggedness and persistence were what had distinguished him over the long haul. A decade into his training life, the number of winners started to go up. Much like it had in the second half of the seventies once he'd settled in as a jockey. Between 1996/97 and 2000/01, he ran more horses, won more races, landed bigger prizemoney and nearly doubled his strike rate. That was about the juncture when the path of his training and riding career intertwined again.

When J.P. McManus - still working as a rails bookmaker and professional gambler - began dabbling in horse ownership in the late seventies, O'Neill helped him out by regularly making the trip back to Leopardstown to ride novice hurdlers like Deep Gale for the Limerickman. Nearly quarter of a century later, during which time McManus reportedly had what has been described as 'a life-changing bet' on Dawn Run in 1986, he had a personal fortune estimated at £255m, over 100 horses, and the wherewithal to offer an old friend a unique opportunity to swap Cumbria and the North-East for one of racing's most prestigious addresses.

'I had wanted to train in the south for some time but when I became sick it ruled out a move as the banks didn't want to know me,' said O'Neill upon receiving the news that McManus was buying Jackdaws Castle (former base of the fabled David 'The Duke' Nicholson), near Cheltenham, and installing him there as trainer. 'When the call came from J.P. it was the easiest question I have ever had to answer. I couldn't get here quick enough. It's gone great, we're very lucky to get good horses, better ones than we expected really, and it's just all come together very quickly. Things just happen like that in life sometimes. This is a great place to train. The horses are happy, staff are happy and so am I. I guess if you keep saying your prayers sometimes the man above phones back!'

Since the move to Gloucestershire in 2000, O'Neill's stock as a trainer has continued to rise. In the first 15 seasons of his career, he sent out 407 winners over jumps. It took him less than four campaigns out of the new base to surpass that number. There have been seven more Cheltenham Festival victories too, and the arrival of Tony McCoy as stable jockey in 2004 was regarded as the next step in O'Neill's pursuit of the title of champion National Hunt trainer.

'The idea is to challenge for the championship eventually,' said O'Neill in 2004. 'It is a daunting task, as Martin Pipe is a genius in his own right. But I remember when Johnny Francome was champion jockey and they said a northern lad [he was based in Cumbria at the time] could never beat him, and I did it - twice. So there is hope.'

There is always hope. On a wall in the television lounge at Jackdaws Castle, amid various photographs and racing paraphernalia is a display case containing the metal plate and the various pins deployed to reconstruct O'Neill's right leg in 1980. A chilling reminder of what the man has been through, it puts into perspective a poem entitled "Don't Quit" that hangs in the complex's reception area. The last verse reads:

> 'Success is failure turned inside out,
> The silver tint of the clouds of doubt
> And you never can tell how close you are,
> It may be near when it seems so far
> So stick to the fight when you're hardest hit
> It's when things seem worst,
> That you must not quit!'

He never did.

Jonjo O'Neill seen here with Rhinestone Cowboy (left) and Intersky Falcon just two of the many horses he has trained at his famous Jackdaws Castle, Gloucestershire, England.

Charlie Hurley

When England hosted Ireland in a World Cup qualifier at Wembley on May 8th, 1957, Charlie Hurley paid in at the gate. A promising centre-half with Millwall in the Third Division South, he was reckoned by many to be on the verge of an international breakthrough, so he wanted to check out first-hand what the standard was like. An injury had forced him to turn down a call-up to the Irish squad two years earlier but following a 5-1 defeat in London that afternoon, he was immediately brought in for the return match at Dalymount Park 11 days later.

'That made my father the happiest man in the world,' said Hurley in Séan Ryan's "The Boys in Green". 'He always said I'd wear the green jersey. For four weeks from the time I was picked he never did a day's work. He worked in Fords and the factory was full of Irish. He sat in a corner talking to them all about his son – and the fact that I had a good game gave him the two weeks after. He was king for a month.'

It's not difficult to imagine the pride his father must have felt. The Hurleys had left their home in Devonshire Street exactly twenty years previously. Like thousands more Corkonians in the depressed 1930s, they sailed to England in search of work and a better life. Charlie Hurley wasn't even one year of age when they sailed from Penrose Quay. Now, a few months short of his 21st birthday, he was being invited back to bulwark the Irish defence in a game against the country where his family had made their home.

With fellow Corkonians Pat Saward (then of Aston Villa), and Noel Cantwell (West Ham) also in the starting XI, Hurley's debut was auspicious.

He completely obliterated the threat from legendary English centre-forward Tommy Taylor who'd scored a hat-trick in the Wembley fixture. Afterwards, Liam Tuohy enthused that Ireland had discovered a 'colossus who could grace any international team.' Everybody else noticed too. By the time Ireland gathered for an international again the following October, Hurley had moved to Sunderland for a fee of £20,000.

His first appearance in the red and white stripes was less memorable, a 7-0 hiding at Blackpool. His second was a 6-0 defeat by Burnley. He recovered from those initial setbacks to stay 12 years in the North-East, clocking up over 400 appearances during which he left an enduring legacy. Voted Sunderland's 'Player of the Twentieth Century', the club training ground bears his name, and in 1997, he was given the singular honour of laying a sod from Roker Park in the centre-circle of their new home, The Stadium of Light.'I was the first centre-half to go up for corners,' said Hurley. 'Jack Charlton said he was, but he was lying." Every time Hurley strode forward into the opposing box for a corner-kick, the Sunderland fans would hail his arrival with a chorus of 'Charlie, Charlie, Charlie'. He repaid that faith with goals on twenty-six occasions Which explains why, in the summer of 1999, he received an honorary degree from Sunderland University. After the ceremony, students born long after he retired queued up to get his autograph.

'Remember Charlie Hurley of Sunderland?' wrote Michael Parkinson. 'He could play a bit. He used to give his supporters and team-mates palpitations by dribbling the ball out of the tightest situations. I saw him at Barnsley beat three attackers in his own penalty area and then float a perfect pass out of defence, but not before he first flicked the ball onto his head and down to his instep as if he was centre-stage at the London Palladium.'

Hurley could play with the ball at his feet but it was his bravery and physical presence that endeared him to the Sunderland fans. His reputation for putting his head where others feared to tread was earned the hard way. When the club won promotion from Division Two in 1964, he distinguished himself during a North-East derby against Newcastle United. Following a nasty clash of heads with opposing striker Barrie Thomas just before half-time, Hurley had a gaping wound over his eyes.

'Thomas had a tremendous spring on him and for most of the game I kept banging my head against the back of his. I walked off under my own steam for treatment because you weren't carried off in those days unless it was really serious. There were no substitutes so there was no question about me

The Ireland team that lost 0 - 1 to England in a World Cup qualifier at Dalymount Park, Dublin in April 1957. Charlie Hurley is second from the right in the back row.

staying off. We had a win bonus to claim, we all needed the money. I was sewn up by one of the directors, Stanley Ritson, who was also a surgeon. I remember how his hands shook as he did it. The physio Johnny Watters had to hold his hands to steady him, and he got there eventually, although I don't think they were the neatest stitches in the world - and I still have the scar to prove it! One of my favourite pictures is after that game with my face and shirt covered in blood. There is red everywhere, but underneath it all you can still see my smile.'

The same stoicism informed his attitude to playing for Ireland. As a consequence of his parents' emigration, his accent may have been more Cockney than Cork but his commitment to the Irish cause was exemplary. For more than half his international appearances, he was captain, and for his last three caps, he even stepped into the breach as player-coach, a thankless job at a time when the squad was selected by a group of FAI blazers called "The Big Five". Nobody would have expected less from Hurley given the effort involved in him making it across to Dublin. The trek from Sunderland was often a marathon affair.

'You'd finish at five o'clock on the Saturday and then get a police escort to the station and to the airport,' said Hurley in Paul Rowan's "The Team That Jack Built". 'It was sometimes impossible to get a plane so you'd have to take the boat from Liverpool. I came over on the ferry for the game against Spain in 1965 (a World Cup play-off). It was the most frightening experience I ever had in my life. It was full of queers and everything. You'd pin your arse to the bunk.

'You'd get to Ireland in a terrible state on the Sunday morning. Then, there would just be time for a hot bath to loosen up. I would say that over the 40 caps, if anybody ever earned them it was me. I wasn't one of the guys who ducked out of the big, hard games. There was an awful lot of times I used to turn up on a Sunday after playing on a Saturday and (Johnny) Giles, Tony Dunne, (Noel) Cantwell, a lot of these people got knocks, and couldn't play. I never did that.'

Hurley's character was evident on and off the field. When Bohemians' Willie Browne won his first cap against Austria in Vienna – playing his part in a well-deserved scoreless draw – his amateur status precluded him from receiving his match fee from the FAI in the dressing-room afterwards. Having soldiered alongside the 27 year old newcomer for 90 minutes, Hurley noticed this and took immediate action. He organised a whip-round among the rest of the squad and the joke was that Browne ended up making more money for that game than any of the professionals.

He had his own quirks too. The day before his debut against England, Ireland were training at the Carlisle Grounds in Bray and at the end of the session, Noel Cantwell tried to get Hurley to practice his heading. Always conscious of his appearance, Hurley refused to try a single header because he'd already done his hair that morning and wasn't planning on doing it again until after the match itself

The sad irony of his international career was that a genuine injury prevented him from playing against Spain in the 1965 play-off defeat in Paris. That was the closest the team had come to qualifying for a major tournament during Hurley's era. He called time on his career at international level with typical unselfishness. Against Hungary in May, 1969, he took himself off at half-time and brought on the younger Frank O'Neill in a

tactical reshuffle. A month later, Hurley left Sunderland for Bolton Wanderers and his stint as one of the most highly-rated defenders in England began to wind down.

After finishing his playing days at Bolton, he was appointed Manager of Reading in June, 1972. A tough assignment at a club with little resources, his five-year tenure had its moments too. In 1976, he led Reading out of the old Fourth Division. The point to clinch the club's first promotion in over half a century came at Cambridge United. As the players celebrated on the field afterwards, the travelling support chanted Hurley's name until he emerged from the dressing-room and told them: 'You're the people we do it all for.' A year later, he was gone.

'I won very little as regards trophies as a player,' said Hurley. "In fact, I don't think I won any. I got promotion with Sunderland – but we didn't get a trophy because we were runners-up. Won promotion at Reading – didn't get a trophy. I got a lot of caps. I was voted Ireland's Footballer of the Year. I've been made Sunderland's Player of the Century and I won the first Hall of Fame for Ireland's internationals. But I won those things as an individual and I always wanted to win things with a team. That was my ambition.'

On one trip back to the city where he was born, Hurley was dismayed to find the house where he was born had been pulled down. To his credit, he has never tried to fake excess knowledge about Cork. In an interview in September of last year, he cheerfully confessed to Mike Amos from the Northern Echo that he didn't even know the county had won the hurling All-Ireland, before offering the following description of the sport.
'It's bigger than football in some places but vicious an' all horrible. I was a good footballer and I could mix it if I had to but I wouldn't have fancied hurling.' Still, he retains enough of a connection to be chuffed to return a couple of years ago to receive the Cork Soccer Legends Award. At that function, he told a story of his international debut.

'When I told my father I was marking Tommy Taylor, he replied: 'Don't leave him breathe, boy. Stick to him like glue. Even if he goes to the loo follow him.' I took Dad's advice. I went everywhere with Taylor. Every turn he made I was there in front of him. When he stooped to tie his lace I stood over him. When he was being treated after a tackle, I smiled mischieviously at him. I didn't get to follow him to the loo but when the final whistle blew I noticed that he made a mad dash in that direction.'
A career encapsulated in an anecdote.

Jack Daly

The record book states that Jack Daly scored the second-half try that beat Wales and won Ireland the Grand Slam at Ravenhill on March 13th, 1948. Photographic evidence proves that at the final whistle, the supporters who invaded the field in Belfast ripped his shirt from his back and carried him shoulder-high from the fray. After that, everything gets a little bit hazy but the folklore surrounding him is far too entertaining for us to over worry about the burden of proof.

When the train carrying the victorious Irish team pulled into Dublin, Daly was met by a glamourous woman in a sportscar, carrying a precious fragment of his green jersey from the day before. They drove off together and he stayed so long in her company that by the time he got back to London, he'd been sacked. With no job, he rang up Huddersfield rugby league club, who had been on his trail for a while, and turned professional for a signing-on bonus of £1,000, a basic weekly wage of £6 and double that for every win.

A less salacious version of events involves him ringing his mother down in Cobh the night of the triumph over Wales, discovering that she required £500 for an urgent operation and contacting Huddersfield within the hour. There is also Ulick O'Connor's contention that Daly took the league shilling "through sheer penury and noble rage". That's the way of it with him. The stories are so interesting that various editions of them invariably do the rounds.

'He was an extraordinary character,' says former team-mate Des O'Brien in

Peter O'Reilly's excellent 'The Full Bag of Chips: Ireland and The Triple Crown. 'He joined the British Army and marched right across North Africa with Montgomery. Before the war he played only for fun with London Irish Thirds but, as he departed for combat, he promised: 'When I come back I'll be picked for Ireland'. All through the war he had to carry this heavy wireless equipment on his back, so his upper body strength became incredible. When John ran on to the field he used to do a double somersault. Before internationals he would do double back-somersaults to confirm his fitness.'

Seven minutes into the second half of the '48 decider, Wales had a line-out on their own 25 yard line. When the ball broke loose, O'Brien and Jack Daly hoofed it on towards the Welsh goal-line. With their team-mate Bertie O'Hanlon joining the effort, all three gave chase. Daly's boot connected with it again and eventually he hurled himself over the line and down on to the ball. The man described by the Irish Independent as 'the green tornado'

Jack Daly (centre) with Barney Mullen (left) and Don Hingerty before Ireland played Wales in 1948.

rolled over on his back and clasped the ball to his chest as the 32,000 shoehorned into Ravenhill erupted in celebration. Ireland had taken a 6-3 lead.

'Jim (McCarthy), if we can keep the red blighters at bay for another half-hour,' said Daly, 'I'll be canonised.'

Daly wasn't canonised but his place in history was assured. According to popular lore, many of the fans present wore swatches of his ripped up jersey on their lapels for weeks afterwards. That very night, himself, O'Brien and Paddy Reid ended up in a police cell for their role in an incident with an Orange flute band during which a Lambeg drum was kicked in.

'Daly's whirlwind style and swashbuckling, rollicking approach typified that great team as a whole,' wrote rugby journalist Sean Diffley, 'and JC (John Christopher), with his handsome craggy face and jet black hair, seemed to personify the piratical.

Following an encounter with Daly in a Cork County Junior Cup final between Cobh Pirates and Kanturk, journalist Dave Guiney described being tackled by him as akin to running slap-bang into a four-storey building.

'The friendly face, the super-white teeth, the flashing smile, that smooth, tanned face,' wrote Guiney in 'International Sport'. 'All a cover up for a cunning, incarnate devil. I tracked him with the dedication of Daniel Boone and he hid around corners, waylaying me every few minutes with weapons I had never known of before. It was fire against fire. By half-time there were scorch marks on him. I had the warm feeling that there was smoke coming from my ears.'

The move to the professional ranks appears to have been effortless despite the fact Daly had misguided his new employers about one crucial aspect of his life.

'Jack's age at the time of signing was given as 28 when in fact he was almost 32,' wrote Robert Gate, in a 1989 obituary for 'Code 13: Rugby League History magazine.' 'He gave good value however. He made his debut at blindside prop in a 23-5 win at Featherstone on September 21 1948 in a team which contained not a solitary Yorkshireman, consisting as it did of three Australians, three Cumbrians, three Welshmen, two Scots and two Irishmen, the other being Paddy Reid, one of Jack's Grand Slam colleagues.

'In only his sixth match Jack shared in Huddersfield's 22-3 mauling of the Australian tourists and by the season's end he had earned a Yorkshire League Championship winners' medal and a Rugby League Championship winners' medal. The latter came from Huddersfield's 13-12 victory in a classic final against Warrington at Maine Road, when Jack scored the opening try. At the end of his first season, Jack was selected for a British Empire XIII which played two games in France during May 1949. This was the prototype for the celebrated Other Nationalities team which was instituted the following season and for which Jack would be capped seven times (1950 to 1953).'

In 1951, he made the short journey to West Yorkshire where he signed for Featherstone Rovers, a young team looking for experienced hands. Daly left his mark there too in the club's first great side, one that lost the 1952 Challenge Cup final, a game distinguished for being the first televised live by the BBC. The rollicking prop that fans and players alike knew affectionately as 'Paddy' is best remembered for his contribution in the semi-final of that campaign, a bruising encounter with Leigh at Maine Road.

As the hooter blared to signal Featherstone's 6-2 victory after a war of attrition, every player on the field slumped to the ground exhausted, too shattered by the physical toll to even contemplate exuberance. Except one. Daly ran to where most of the Featherstone supporters were gathered, and to their delight, performed his trademark standing forward somersault celebration. The code had changed. The showman remained in place.

Frank O' Farrell

Approaching the six-month anniversary of his appointment to the manager's chair at Old Trafford, things could not have been going better for Frank O'Farrell. By the middle of December, 1971, Manchester United were top of the table, five points clear of their nearest rivals and the bookies' favourites for the title. Lining out in an attack-minded 4-3-3 formation, they lost just once in their first thirteen outings and George Best and Denis Law had bagged 28 goals between them. The mood around the club was predictably effusive.

'Frank is my last great signing,' said Busby of the man he'd personally headhunted the previous summer, 'perhaps the greatest of the lot.'

Almost exactly twelve months later, on December 19th, 1972, O'Farrell was sacked. At the board meeting where chairman Louis Edwards informed him of his dismissal, Busby kept his head down, refused to make eye contact and never spoke a single word. When first offering him the job, the Scot had informed O'Farrell that the directors fully realised the task of revitalising United would take the new manager some time. Now, not even two years later, Busby's silence spoke volumes. Like Wilf McGuinness before him, O'Farrell had been put to the sword by the former manager who just couldn't bear to relinquish the reigns.

'Perhaps with more time and with Best out of the way O'Farrell might have reversed the fortunes of the club,' wrote Stephen Kelly in "Backpage United'. 'Busby's presence was also a continuing intimidation and the whole episode had been one of the most shameful in the club's history.'

Born in Cork on October 9th, 1927, the journey to the Old Trafford boardroom had begun on a grassy patch in Douglas. Living in Turner's Cross, he captained Christ the King Gaelic footballers and his first organised soccer game was with Nicholas Rovers. From there, he progressed through minor ranks with Clapton Celtic and Western Rovers, showing enough along the way to catch the eye of the professionals.

'O'Farrell started work on the railway at 16, the first steps towards his ambition to become a train driver.' wrote Plunkett Carter in "From the Lodge to the Box". 'In 1947, Cork United signed Frank to replace Tommy Moroney, who had joined West Ham. With Cork United, he had the best possible soccer education as he played alongside such stars as Owen Madden, Seanie McCarthy, Florrie Burke and Davy Noonan, and was paid £3 per week for the pleasure.'

He learned so quick that soon he was following Moroney to Upton Park, taking the *Innisfallen* from Penrose Quay to the big-time in January, 1948. It took him a couple of years to establish himself as a first-team wing-half but eventually he became club captain and an Irish international. That he won just nine caps may have had something to do with his principled stand alongside Peter Fallon during a tour of Norway and Germany in 1955. Fallon kept his jersey after a match, and with O'Farrell backing him up, refused to give it back to the FAI until they agreed to pay the £2 per day pocket money that was the standard for international teams. The FAI's solution was to let them keep the jerseys. Fallon was never capped again, and O'Farrell got just four more.

After nearly 200 appearances for West Ham, he moved to Preston North End in November, 1956. Four years into his time at Deepdale, he was offered the player-manager's job at non-league Weymouth, and so began the

Frank O'Farrell with his record signing Ted McDougal.

typical climb up the managerial ladder. He led Weymouth to the Southern League title and an historic trip to the heady reaches of the fourth round of the FA Cup. Torquay United came calling then, and during his three-and-a-half-year tenure with them, they were promoted to Division Three and came within two points of a ticket to Division Two in 1968. Despite the failure their campaign had earned them a first appearance on BBC's Match of the Day, and brought O'Farrell to national attention.

In December 1968, he succeeded Matt Gillies at Leicester City. It was a job in the top division but a tough assignment. The club were fighting a relegation battle that they eventually lost, that pill tasting all the more bitter as it was also accompanied by a defeat in the FA Cup final against Manchester City. O'Farrell steadied the ship however, and secured Leicester's return to Division One in 1971. Unlike so many others, he didn't have to sacrifice his principles to do so either. His team played attractive, open football.

Leicester's style on the field and O'Farrell's penchant for discipline off it – he once dropped Peter Shilton during a contract row – caught the eye of Busby. When Jock Stein and then Dave Sexton turned down the United job, the Corkman got the call.

'Frank O'Farrell's integrity was well-known in the game,' wrote Eamon Dunphy in "A Strange Kind of Glory". 'In this age of dodgy deals and Flash Harrys, O'Farrell played by the rules and eschewed big talk. Catholics like O'Farrell do not, as most do, regard their faith as some kind of convenience food for the soul. Their Catholicism is a way of life, its values inherent in everything they do. Frank O'Farrell's character was formed by this rigorous interpretation of God's intentions. He is a man of absolute honour, unworldly to a degree.'

His virtues may have been the very elements of his personality that left him ill-prepared for a club rife with politicking, struggling badly to cope with the aftermath of Busby's move from manager to director in 1969. O'Farrell's first glimpse of that problem came during his contract negotiations. Busby told him the salary was £12,000 per year plus a Jaguar car. A fair enough deal for the era. However, once Louis Edwards got involved in the talks, O'Farrell discovered the salary on offer was actually £15,000. Either £3,000 had slipped Busby's mind or this didn't bode well for the way he conducted business.

There was another disturbing cameo on his first day at Old Trafford that portended future discord. O'Farrell discovered the manager's office, the most symbolic piece of real estate in the ground, was still occupied by Busby and that he was expected to make do with a smaller, less auspicious space down the corridor. Befitting a man of certain beliefs, he took a stand on the issue, and to the utter shock of many United employees, the elder statesman moved out. A little victory. Perhaps the sort that left a lingering scar.

'It was a tough moment but I proved I had the courage to face it,' said O'Farrell. 'I was nobody's puppet.'

Despite the giddiness surrounding United's impressive run during the opening months of his first season in charge, O'Farrell was a shrewd enough judge to realise their league position at Christmas was false. In truth, a bad team was being carried by the genius of George Best. Later, it would be commonly asserted that O'Farrell didn't grasp the nettle quickly enough when Best started to misbehave off the field. But what could he do? Best was the sole reason the side was punching above its weight, taking over top spot in October for the first time in three years. Without him, this was a mediocre outfit.

'There were world-class players coming to the end of their careers either through time – like Bobby [Charlton] and Denis [Law] – or choice – like George – playing alongside players I did not feel were good enough to get into Aberdeen's reserve team,' said Martin Buchan who arrived from Scotland in March, 1972. 'Now that might seem a harsh thing to say. But we played Aberdeen in a friendly as part of my deal and we lost up there 5-2 so maybe I wasn't far from the truth.'

By that stage in the season, United's title bid had already faltered, disappearing on the back of seven consecutive defeats after Christmas. The morale-sapping effects of the slump were exacerbated/caused by the antics of Best. Although still capable of miraculous feats with the ball, the wayward winger was beginning to serially break the rules, embarking on the downward spiral off the field that would truncate the rest of his career. Yet, one of O'Farrell's first acts as manager had been to improve Best's wages which were seriously lower than the sums being earned by Charlton and Law. He wanted to acknowledge a fundamental truth; a player should be paid according to his worth.

Best's first disappearance on O'Farrell's watch was prior to a cup-tie at Southampton. A fine was imposed but he still started the game. It ended in a draw and during the replay back at Old Trafford, United were in trouble until Best chipped in with a couple of wonder goals. The dilemma facing the manager was acute. How could he possibly discipline the troubled talent and teach him a lesson without fatally damaging the team's prospects and endangering his own job?

This problem was more serious because his failure to act on Best's proclivities provided fuel for his critics within the dressing-room, most especially senior pros who resented the outsider coming in with a new approach. The senior pros referred to the manager as 'little boss' because to them Busby was still 'big boss', and mocked O'Farrell's religious piety by calling him Father Frank behind his back. Denis Law famously complained later that the manager had arrived as a stranger and left as one too, his refusal to cosy up to the senior pros more significant perhaps because many of them golfed with Busby on their off-days.

'I suppose with hindsight there was a fair bit of scheming around,' said Martin Buchan in Jim White's "Always in the Running". 'There were others more interested in destroying Frank than the good of the club. Under Sir Matt, they had grown up with the philosophy of go out and enjoy themselves. That's all very well but you can only enjoy yourself if you are doing the job right. I think a lot of them resented the efforts of Frank and Malcolm [Musgrove, O'Farrell's coach] to bring a bit more organisation to the team. The trouble was, at the time, all the other teams were getting organised.'

Although many in the squad complained later that the manager didn't spend enough time on the training ground, the player who least needed to work on his game had a peculiar take on matters. 'Frank tried to improve the side by individual coaching,' said Best. 'But the good ones among us didn't need to be taught, and resented it, and some of the others were just not good enough to be taught anything.'

The signing of Buchan – who threatened to leave if O'Farrell was sacked - was to prove the Corkman's enduring legacy to the club. He played over 450 games for United and captained the FA Cup-winning team of 1977. Indeed, his initial impact had been so significant that Alex Stepney contended that had the Scottish defender arrived earlier, O'Farrell's debut season could have culminated in silverware rather than an 8th place finish in the league. It ended, instead, with a curious postscript. Best repaired to Marbella from where he announced his retirement from football the day before his 26th birthday. 'He is, like all other geniuses, difficult to understand,' observed O'Farrell at the time. "I don't think he can cope with his own problems and there is nobody he can really lean on for help. He is like a boy lost. He needs someone to help him. We at Old Trafford have done everything possible to help him.'

Two weeks later, O'Farrell met Best in Manchester and persuaded him out of retirement. Even with Best back in the fold, his second campaign in charge began in contrasting style to his first. It took United ten games before they won their first league game, and his other ventures into the transfer market failed to bear fruit. A gamble that Ted MacDougall could score as freely in the top flight as he had for Bournemouth in the third was too little too late, Wyn Davies failed to live up his reputation for goals, and Ian Storey-Moore, a gifted winger from Nottingham Forest, couldn't deliver on initial promise due to an injury that eventually ended his career.

At a combined cost of close to half a million quid, that trio made just 62 appearances between them for United. Of the factors usually cited to explain O'Farrell's demise, the poor quality of his purchases is perhaps the most justified. He made more bad signings than good, and the failure to land Alan Ball when he became available was a crucial oversight.

As the team lurched from bad to worse in the autumn of 1972, O'Farrell demonstrated his mettle by dropping the fast-fading Charlton, but the Best problem continued to loom large. That November, he went off the rails completely, and on December 5th, he was suspended for a fortnight and transfer-listed by the club. The soap opera surrounding Best's every move wasn't helping the manager's own cause. When Busby re-instated Best without consulting O'Farrell, the writing was on the wall. Banquo's ghost had hovered long enough over proceedings. His presence had just been felt.

Nine days before Christmas, United were torn apart by Crystal Palace, losing 5-0 to one of the worst teams in the league, an outfit that were relegated at the end of the season. Ranked by some as the club's most abject performance of the post World-War II era, it was the game that sealed the manager's fate. When John Aston, the chief scout, came to pick up O'Farrell on the way to the seismic board meeting on December 19th, the manager quipped: 'A nice day for an execution.' The one-liner would later become the title for a book O'Farrell wrote but didn't publish about his experience at United. The trauma of being

fired was exacerbated by United's crass handling of his severance. They reneged on an initial promise to honour the remaining three and a half years of his deal and forced him to take legal action.

'They could sack me all they wanted,' said O'Farrell. 'That happens. But then to humiliate me and force me to go on the dole, that's what really hurt. From the time I'd left school I never had to go on the labour but I was suing the club for breach of contract and my solicitor told me I had to do it.' There was life after Old Trafford. It was pitched in a lower key but eventful all the same.

'It was 18 months in a 74-year lifespan," said O'Farrell in a 2001 interview with The Sunday Times, 'which, when you think about it, is only a small thing.'

Once United had been forced to pay up, his comeback began at Cardiff City, a job that curiously segued into two years managing Iran. With a national stadium housing 120,000 and the Shah bent on turning the nation into a soccer power, O'Farrell delivered early. Aside from his weekly visits to the palace in Tehran to coach the Shah's son, he managed the national team to a win over Israel in the final of the Asian Games, a victory that earned him his place in the country's folklore. When he departed in 1976, he had also trained his own successor.

'I, for one, benefited greatly from the teachings of Frank O'Farrell,' said Heshmat Mohajerani, the Iranian who succeeded the Corkman and brought the side to the 1978 World Cup finals.

Two further stints at Torquay – where he now lives - were punctuated by a return to the Middle East where he spent six months in charge of El Al Shaab, a club in the United Arab Emirates. He stepped off the managerial treadmill for the final time in 1982, and his priorities in retirement have always been clear. Apart from occasional work as a scout for Bruce Rioch, football took second place to his charity work. Although still revered at Plainmoor, he was unable to make a reunion of the promotion-winning team of 1966 in May of 2000. He had a prior commitment to a religious charity walk in France that weekend and couldn't possibly renege on it. Nobody would have expected anything less.

Marcus O'Sullivan

Marcus O'Sullivan was 12 years old when the teachers at Colaiste Chríost Rí made a simple announcement to the students. Unless a doctor's note could be produced, every boy was to come out for the cross-country run. There were over 100 kids there but when it was over, he got a tap on the shoulder. Somebody had spotted some potential in one of the smallest competitors in the race. Twenty-four years later, 3,000 miles from Turner's Cross, he ran around an indoor track at Madison Square Garden, New York in 3 minutes, 58.10 seconds and became just the third man in history to clock 100 sub-four minute miles.

That the other members of that exclusive club are the legendary New Zealander John Walker, and Steve Scott, America's finest middle-distance runner of modern times, sums up the breadth of his achievement. Although six of his sub-4 miles were at the Cork City Sports in the eighties, maybe too much of his best work was done too far from home for us to properly grasp the impact he had. As he caught his breath that night in Manhattan's most famous arena however, 18,000 New Yorkers rose to give him a standing ovation. Kenya's Laban Rotich had actually won the 1998 Wanamaker Mile but third-placed O'Sullivan had made off with their hearts.

'I've been privileged to know some great days in my career and this surely was one of the best,' he said afterwards. 'Before the race, I kept asking myself if anybody really cared other than myself and my family if I ran under four minutes. The roar that went up as I crossed the line, however, told me all I wanted to know. Unlike

Marcus O'Sullivan in actic in the National Track and Field championships 1996.

me, the crowd knew immediately that I'd got the time and they were magnificent. Afterwards people kept asking who really won the race. That was unfair to Laban, but I suppose it reflected the hype and the general build-up to the race. I was a little concerned I wouldn't do it. I wanted to get it here. I was running with a priority - I had to. There were too many people here from Ireland watching.'

More than two decades after he left Cork to take up an athletics scholarship at Villanova University, it's easy to forget the hard road he travelled. As a teenager at Leevale AC, he'd come under the spell of Donie Walsh, a Villanova alumni who had once run for Jumbo Elliot, the former coach of Ronnie Delaney and Eamonn Coghlan. Walsh filled his head with stories of the American scene but it took a stroke of good fortune for him to gain entry to the college.

'An incoming scholarship athlete changed his mind about coming here and in the middle of August I got a call,' said O'Sullivan in an interview with Villanova Magazine. 'I really came as an afterthought but Donal Walsh told me, "When Jumbo sees you he'll know what I'm talking about". Jumbo's strength was the understanding that the psychology was to pair very good athletes with very, very good athletes and that competition would make everyone better. But don't kill them in the process with over-training. Just bring them along nicely. I earned Jumbo's endorsement in about six months. Someone told me he thought I was good. And for him to say that, you had to be good. He complimented the work and the commitment and in my mind that could take me to the pinnacle.'

For O'Sullivan, the transition from very good to very, very good wasn't particularly smooth. Early in his collegiate career, he was anchoring the Villanova team in a 1,600-metre distance relay at the prestigious Penn Relays. Before a crowd of nearly 14,000 at Franklin Field, Philadelphia, he had a narrow lead coming into the final backstretch. Between there and the finish, he inexplicably faded to sixth and the next morning's New York Times described how he 'walked across the line in despair'.

'That was the most humiliating time of my career,' said O'Sullivan said. 'For Villanova, the Penn Relays are like a home meet and a great tradition. I wanted to do well, but maybe I hadn't put in the proper training. That nearly ruined me.'

The reasons why it didn't ruin him are obvious. There is the sense about his entire career that other Irish athletes before and since have been blessed with far more natural talent yet significantly less courage and determination. Being outsprinted so emphatically by his peers might have damaged any other runner beyond repair. O'Sullivan is made of sterner stuff. He returned to the event the following year, anchored Villanova to victory in the 6,000-metre relay with a record split and also ran a leg on the Wildcats' winning 3,200-metre relay team. Knocked down. Brushed off. Stood back up. The metaphor for his sporting life.

'Ignorance is bliss,' he said. 'I may not have been aware of the significance of the mile. I was an average athlete, not great. I think that's why, 15 years after I ran my first sub-four-minute mile, I'm still doing it. I'm a slogger. There have been days when I didn't feel like running, like people who don't feel they want to go to work. But I've done it.'

Every Irish runner arriving at Villanova comes weighed down by certain expectations that have lingered since Delaney and Coghlan ran into history. O'Sullivan was no different. He just appeared better able to cope with that pressure. It may have helped that he didn't arrive in America as a vaunted talent. He came instead as somebody with a little more focus than most.

Before running the 2004 New York City Marathon alongside former Irish international Frank O'Mara, and some other contemporaries, O'Sullivan was asked a question about the previous longest distance at which he'd competed. He proceeded to tell a story of a 10 mile race he ran during his early days in Philadelphia. Desperate to get back to Cork for a visit, he entered an event in which the first two finishers bagged return flights to Ireland. An American Olympic 10,000m specialist called Greg Fredericks took first ahead of O'Sullivan. A charming story yet one that underlined too the difficulty involved in uprooting at 18 and gambling everything on the ability to compete as an elite athlete in a foreign country.

Indeed, his standing in the sport in the early days was such that in 1982, his coach had to beg Howard Schmertz, the director of the Millrose Games, to take a chance and give the unknown O'Sullivan an entry into the Wanamaker Mile, then the most prestigious race on the indoor calendar. Eventually, Schmertz relented and the 20 year old finished a credible fourth behind Coghlan, who was in the midst of the imperious 'master of the boards' phase of his career.

O'Sullivan would never claim that title from him but he eventually came mighty close to emulating his compatriot's run of seven victories in the event. After that debut, he ran 15 more Wanamakers, won five, finished second four times and dipped under the four minute mark there on 11 occasions. In 2002, he was inducted into the Millrose Games Hall of Fame.

In truth, Millrose probably meant little enough to people in Ireland and Cork. Beyond the athletics community in his homeland, O'Sullivan's various feats have never been properly acknowledged because indoor races are regarded as inferior to the outdoor track. Perhaps his finest hour outdoors came in Dublin on the night he, Coghlan, Frank O'Mara and Ray Flynn broke the world record for the 4 x 1 mile relay in a fund-raiser for the charity, GOAL. O'Sullivan was good in the open air, good enough to participate in four Olympics, and to finish 8th in the 1,500m final in Seoul. Indoors, he just happened to become great.

'I wasn't even going for the first world indoor at Indianapolis, because I was thinking of the outdoor season ahead,' said O'Sullivan. 'But a friend of mine said I should strike while the iron is hot.'

Between Indianapolis in 1987 and Toronto in 1993, he captured three world indoor championships in the 1,500 metres and broke the world record in 1989 with a time that remains in the top five best-ever performances. His personal best of 3.50.9 in the indoor mile is also still among the top five in history. While O'Sullivan was busy amassing titles and breaking records, Ireland often appeared oblivious to his success. Perhaps only now, at a time when no Irish male athlete has come close to gold at the world indoors since O'Sullivan departed the fray, can his achievements be properly appreciated.

'This championship victory has given me great satisfaction, not least for the Irish supporters who travel everywhere with us,' said O'Sullivan following his victory in Toronto in 1993. 'I feel really pleased for them. But for the future, if I could sneak a bronze in a major outdoor championship, not a gold, just a bronze, and if I could run a 3:32 for the 1,500 metres, I could walk away from this sport happy.'

The outdoor medal never came. He had to find other motivations and the menial task of cleaning out his basement led him towards the one of which he is arguably most proud. The discovery of an old trophy reminded him of the first time he broke four minutes for the mile – 3:58:84 at Chapel Hill, North Carolina in January, 1983 – and started him counting all the others. He was at 76 then and knew that a century was doable. What better monument to the doggedness that fueled his initial drive than that?

'I'd say that the 100 sub-four minute miles is something I feel particularly proud of. In a way it reflects the consistency throughout my career, but more importantly John Walker and Steve Scott are the only two other men that have done it. They were always the two guys that I really looked up to and still regard as the last of that sort of old-school generation.'

As a student at Villanova, O'Sulllivan met and married Mary Spinks, a nursing major at the university. The couple live with their two kids in Havertown, Pennsylvania but also have a 60-acre farm in New Jersey. Having enjoyed near enough two decades at the top of professional athletics, he was diligent enough with his lucrative earnings, and cannily uses his spare time to add an MBA in Finance to his accounting degree. Upon retiring from competitive running in 1998, his ambition was to go into business and he was interviewing for jobs with various corporations when his alma mater came and asked him to coach.

'I certainly never wanted to coach and I'm not going to pretend I did. All through my running days on the track circuit, myself and Frank (O'Mara) would talk about what we'd go into down the road. We were very close and always aspired to some kind of business where we could use our skills as well as our competitiveness. The idea of going into coaching wasn't even mentioned. The irony of the whole thing is that the CEOs, and all the people I was interviewing with, said that I had to try this. Tom Donnelly, my coach for 12 years, was another important factor because he showed great confidence in my ability to coach at this level. Finally, there was the family support. Putting everything into the mix in the decision-making, it really seemed like the appropriate choice.'

Jumbo Elliot's last Irish recruit returned to campus with the official title of Head Track and Field Coach, with a staff of six assistants working under him. For his efforts in revitalising the programme there, he has already been voted Regional Coach of the Year in the Mid-Atlantic Conference three seasons running. On September 18, 2004, a plaque in the shape of a winged track shoe bearing O'Sullivan's name was unveiled at the Villanova Stadium Wall of Fame. The day Elliot's afterthought finally took centre-stage.

Marcus O'Sullivan with 1984 Los Angeles Olympics marathon silver medallist, John Treacy.

Harold Cudmore

The scene was the deck of Lionheart, a 12-metre yacht competing in trials for the America's Cup in the early 1980s. Harold Cudmore was at the helm, growing frustrated with the way the spinnaker was being handled by his crew on the bow. With no way of reaching any of them, he decided to vent his anger at the nearest body he could find. Hunched intently over the charts, navigator Andrew Spedding was the unlucky recipient of a ferocious kick in the backside.

'What the hell's that for?' asked Spedding.'Just pass it on. Pass it on!' shouted Cudmore.

On an Australian boat he was skippering another time, an erroneous bowman was the cause of his ire. Having tolerated enough mistakes, Cudmore abandoned the wheel and decided to let the bowman know how he felt.

'You have got to be the most (expletive deleted) useless (expletive deleted) idiot I have ever seen on a boat anywhere in my entire (expletive deleted) life,' blared Cudmore at his crewman. As he suddenly realised the man whose collar he had grabbed, was bigger, stronger and younger than him, his grip loosened and his tone softened. 'And I hope, that you will take this as constructive criticism.'

There is a canon of stories about Cork's most famous sailor that span the globe from Crosshaven to Cowes, Saint Tropez to San Diego. Beyond the passion and intensity that gained him a place in dockside lore, Cudmore was also one of the finest yachtsmen of his generation. The winner of five world championships, twelve international match-race titles, and twice skipper of the top-scoring yacht in the Admiral's Cup, he was also the first foreigner to win the Congressional Cup, a California race second only in standing to the America's Cup.

Still, merely listing victories such as leading Ireland to its first serious international ocean racing triumph in the 1991 Southern Cross Cup serves only to paint a black and white picture of his achievements. Far better to observe him in glorious technicolour.

'"Fast Harry" has been knocking on the door for years as one of the world's best match-racers." wrote John Bertrand in Australian newspaper, The Advertiser in April, 1986. 'His nickname comes as much from his off-the-water style as from his on-the-water speed. He's a fast-talking, leg-pulling Irishman with the swagger of a Mick Jagger and the irreverence of a Dave Allen - a charming rogue with a brogue, a Rolling Blarney Stone. As a skipper, he's very, very sharp. He has excellent reflex actions - which means years of ingrained experience. He loves the high drama and excitement of one-on-one match-racing.'

That lively character portrait is conveyed not by a journalist but by a fellow sailor. Bertrand was the iconic skipper of Australia II, the yacht that took the America's Cup back from the United States in 1983, breaking their 132-year stranglehold on the event. To understand the level Cudmore reached, it should be pointed out many aficionados of the sport felt that he, Bertrand, and the legendary American skipper Dennis Conner were the three greatest skippers in the world during the 1980s.

Unlike the other two, Cudmore never won an America's Cup, in part at least because he was never able to muster a boat with sufficient financial backing to compete to the finish. He did skipper White Crusader, Britain's America's Cup challenger in 1986-87, but it was knocked out before the semi-final stage. In 1992, Bill Koch's America 3 retained him as a full-time adviser to their programme and ended up winning the trophy. Apart from sharing his experience, Cudmore was also a sparring partner, preparing Koch's crew by racing against them – and, by all accounts, regularly defeating them in private contests.

Facing page: Harold Cudmore and Chris Bruen sailing in a 505 at Crosshaven in September 1968.

'Meet this copper-haired yachtsman at a harbourside bar and you are greeted by a charming, witty companion,' wrote Barry Pickthall in The Times in 1993. 'Get in his way in a race and you are met by expletives and fist-waving from the legendary ogre. He rides rough-shod over friend and foe in order to win. The aggression vanishes once he crosses the finish line, just as if some malign spirit on his shoulder has returned to a drawer along with the charts. For those sailing with or against him for the first time, it can seem an abrupt change. Suddenly, the man who has been berating you throughout the race is there shaking you warmly by the hand and thanking you for your efforts.'

The boy who would grow up to be christened 'King Harold of Cowes' by the denizens of England's most famous sailing town was born in Cork in 1944 into one of the city's best-known business families. His father and name-sake was an altruistic politician constantly working for the betterment of the city, and a man with sporting passions of his own. A former President of the Munster Motor and Cycle Club and a founding Trustee of Vernon Mount, Harold Cudmore senior had also been flag officer of the Royal Cork Yacht Club and Irish Cruising Club.

Showing plenty of early promise on the water, the son followed the father and became the youngest member ever to be elected to the Irish Cruising Club. In tandem with Chris Bruen, son of the golfer Jimmy, and later, Richard O'Shea, he began carving out his international reputation. O'Shea and himself finished 17th in the Flying Dutchman class at the Munich Olympics.

Four years later, his campaign to qualify for the Montreal Games was hampered by the Irish Yachting Association so he turned his attention instead to the World Half-Ton Cup at Trieste. Having dragged a trailer across Europe with a car that could only be stopped from overheating by keeping the bonnet open, he guided Silver Shamrock – designed by Ron Holland, the New Zealander who came to Cork in the early seventies - to an impressive victory. The manner of his win showcased all of Cudmore's skills and his services have been in demand ever since.

'Harold's significance within sailing was that, along with Dennis Conner in America, he was really almost the first of the modern professional skippers,' says Keith Wheatley, Sunday Times' sailing correspondent between 1985 and 2004. 'Yachting had been dominated by wealthy amateurs pre-Cudmore. He hated that. Despite his background in the Cork establishment, Harold was always clear that he wanted to earn his living as a sailor.

'In the late '70s that was somewhere between revolutionary and impossible but he blazed the trail. He showed owners such as Edmund de Rothschild and Peter de Savary that expensive high performance yachts needed a professional approach to winning races. He transformed events like the Admiral's Cup with his insistence that the old days of a rich owner plus his toff mates were over. Harold was the perfect link between the new generation of younger Olympic sailors, athletes with attitudes and the blazeratti, because, at bottom, he is a subversive toff with a lot of brains.'

Having spent most of his career sailing under the flags of other nations, an inevitable consequence of life as a professional at the top of the sport, Cudmore skippered Atara to the 1991 Sydney to Hobart race, his win in that 630 mile event clinching an Irish team triumph in the six-race Southern Cross series. His third Cross victory, this one was different. He was competing for Ireland, alongside friends, the other two boats on the team being skippered by Cobh's Joe English and Gordon Maguire from Howth.

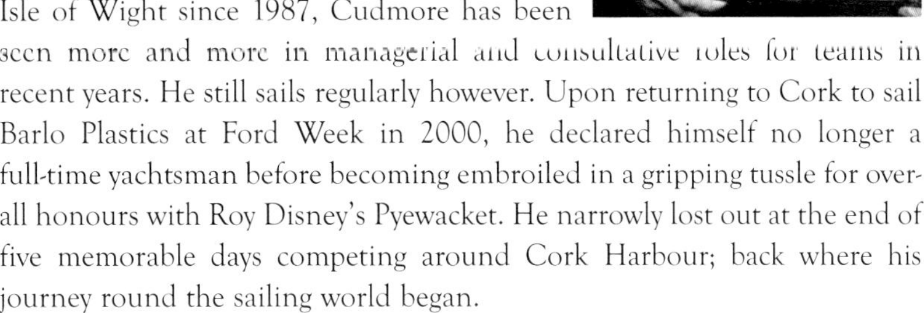

'For this regatta, we got together old sailing friends from Ireland and showed we could do it for ourselves,' said Cudmore afterwards. 'This opportunity came up to take a team overseas to represent Ireland. It was nice to get a result and the enthusiasm back home was great.'

Based in Cowes on the northern shore of the Isle of Wight since 1987, Cudmore has been seen more and more in managerial and consultative roles for teams in recent years. He still sails regularly however. Upon returning to Cork to sail Barlo Plastics at Ford Week in 2000, he declared himself no longer a full-time yachtsman before becoming embroiled in a gripping tussle for overall honours with Roy Disney's Pyewacket. He narrowly lost out at the end of five memorable days competing around Cork Harbour; back where his journey round the sailing world began.

Noel Cantwell

The most famous photograph of Noel Cantwell shows him casually tossing the FA Cup above his head at Wembley. Having just led Manchester United to a 3-1 victory over Leicester City, there is a look of manic glee on his face. On either side, his team-mates Bobby Charlton, Tony Dunne, David Herd and Albert Quixall appear visibly stunned by the brazen act of celebration. They are staring wide-eyed, mouths agape, at their captain casually flinging about the most revered trophy in English football. The date was May 25th, 1963, and moments later, Cantwell got a tap on the shoulder from a stadium commissionaire reprimanding him for his cavalier treatment of the precious silverware.

'Don't worry,' replied Cantwell. 'I knew I would be able to catch it because I play cricket for Ireland.'

That sort of innate self-confidence was one of the reasons Matt Busby had appointed him captain almost as soon as he signed from West Ham United in 1960. By the time three years later that United had salvaged a disastrous season – relegation had been a real possibility for long spells - by defeating Leicester in the showpiece of the English season, Cantwell was leading a side containing outzised characters like Charlton, Paddy Crerand, Johnny Giles, Denis Law, Dunne, and Bill Foulkes. Nobody doubted he was equal to the task. At Upton Park, he'd practically been manager Ted Fenton's first lieutenant for years.

'Basically, Ted let the players get on with it,' recalled Vic Keeble, West Ham striker of the time. 'Noel, our skipper, would always be the one to start us

The Cork Athletic Team of January 1951. Noel Cantwell is fourth from the right in the back row.

off. We'd have a talk at the beginning of the week and talk about Saturday's game. Ted would always ask Noel what he thought.'

On one occasion, Fenton had sought Cantwell's counsel about a particularly thorny selection problem. A few weeks into the 1958 season, an injury crisis meant there were only two choices to partner Cantwell in the centre of defence. Newly-promoted to Division One, the manager was torn between recalling Malcolm Allison, a veteran recently recovered from TB, or handing a first competitive start to an untried 17 year old called Bobby Moore. Cantwell and Allison were best pals but that didn't colour his judgment. Moore made his debut that weekend and Allison never got to start a single match in the top flight.

Born on December 28th, 1932, Noel Euchuria Cornelius Cantwell grew up near the Mardyke, an appropriate address for one who would become both a soccer and cricket international. Having cut his teeth in schoolboy football with Western Rovers, he captained the Irish Youths' team before making a peculiar transition to the senior ranks. According to legend, he was working on his batting stroke in the nets at Cork County Cricket Club when a messenger from Cork Athletic was dispatched to find him in a hurry. Athletic, for whom his older brother Frank played, were a man short for a Shield game against Waterford United and Cantwell's proximity earned him his debut.

The move from Ireland to England came in equally odd circumstances. 'West Ham had two players from Cork, Tommy Moroney and Frank O'Farrell, who used to come home during the summer and play friendlies

to boost the coffers of the local schoolboys' association,' said Cantwell. 'I played with them for the representative team and used to do reasonably well, but I never had big ambitions or intentions. But they asked if I'd be interested in coming to England and recommended me to Ted Fenton. I was getting £3 a week playing for Cork when Ted came over to try and sign me. He negotiated a fee of £750, of which I got £150 and I felt like a millionaire.'

He must have felt like a millionaire because he'd been supplementing his football earnings with work in a Birmingham factory when Fenton came calling in the summer of 1952. Although in time it would appear the Londoners had picked up a bargain, the early going was tough. Living in digs with Moroney, the 19-year-old new arrival spent his first season in England failing to convince as a centre-forward in the club's A team.

'I didn't have many qualities as a centre-forward other than aggression. I was thin and skinny and there was nothing to excite anybody so I spoke to Tommy about my lack of progress and said I was probably more suited to being a defender. Ted Fenton gave me a try at left-back, I showed promise and he blooded me in the first team at the end of my first season.'

How quickly he progressed in the course of 12 months was demonstrated by his selection at centre-half for his international debut against Luxembourg in October, 1953. Over the course of eight years at Upton Park, Cantwell played 263 first-team games, and scored 11 goals. He captained the side that won the old Division Two in 1958, and the same year, played on a star-studded London XI (including Johnny Haynes, Danny Blanchflower and Jimmy Greaves) that was beaten in the two-legged final of the Fairs Cup by Barcelona. In those fledgling days of European competition, it was a tournament so novel and prestigious that the games at Stamford Bridge and the Camp Nou were watched by over 100,000.

It was during his stint in East London that Cantwell spent the close-seasons indulging his other sporting interest and earning that rarest of accolades, international honours in two sports.

'Two of his brothers, Frank and Gerry, played interprovincial cricket for Munster,' wrote Ger Siggins, Irish cricket historian. 'But he picked up five Ireland caps from 1956 to 1959 when he was summering back home in Cork. A left-hand bat with Bohemians, his second cap against the 1957 West Indians saw him record a glorious dismissal - caught Frank Worrell bowled Garfield Sobers 0. His highest score came against New Zealand the next summer when he made 40.'

Facing page: Noel Cantwell throws the FA Cup in the air after Manchester United's victory over Leicester City in the 1963 final.

There was a contract offer to play county cricket for Essex but Cantwell reportedly turned it down because it would have meant spending 12 months a year in England and deprived him of his restorative summers in Cork. In any case, he was blossoming on and off the field at West Ham. He had fall-en in with a cerebral bunch of footballers who thought seriously about the game they played, had certain ideas about changing it and time on their hands to debate the process.

After training every day, they would repair to Bienvenuto Al Cafe Cassettari, an eaterie near Upton Park for which the club had provided them with vouchers. At various times, the members of what became fondly known as the West Ham Academy included Cantwell, John Bond, Dave Sexton, Malcolm Allison, Frank O'Farrell and Jimmy Andrews, all of whom would go on to manage with different degrees of success. Using salt cellars and pepper shakers, they questioned every orthodoxy.

'We were getting away from the big hobnailed, toe-capped, dubbined boot and soon we were playing in lightweight boots and the day had gone when we had big shin pads,' said Cantwell. 'Teams didn't warm up before games – they got stripped five minutes before they went out and embarrassingly kicked the ball around – but we would go into the gym at quarter past two and have a fairly good work-out and come back out then and get prepared. The weight-training gave you tremendous confidence. You felt stronger and you felt good. How one looks and how one appears is always very important. I think it helped when we got away from the baggy shorts and got all the good gear.'

That holistic approach meant Cantwell would even bring his own shorts to wear on Ireland duty because he reckoned the international kit was sub-standard. When Manchester United paid £29,500 - a then record for a full-back – to bring him to Old Trafford in November, 1960 , they were getting some-body with a burgeoning reputation as a leader, and a man of character. With United still in rebuilding mode after Munich, the new boy was shocked at the old-fashioned way the fabled club was being run. He had moved from the middle of a modern footballing revolution to a place firmly rooted in habits that were pre-War.

'One afternoon Noel Cantwell started chatting to me in the bath after train-ing,' wrote Eamon Dunphy in "A Strange Kind of Glory". ' "Is that it?' he asked of the training routine. I told him it was. He was incredulous. I was Irish, he could confide in me. Doesn't anybody ever talk about the game here? Why isn't the training organised...what about ballwork...do you ever see Busby...doesn't anybody think about the game. Was that it? A bit of running, head-tennis, and "round the back" for a bloody free-for-all. The frustration poured out of him. He shook his head in disbelief as I assured him that, yes, that was it, and no, there wasn't any talking about the game.'

Cantwell overcame the initial shock and endeared himself to the fans by doing emergency service at centre-forward, left-half, inside-left, outside-left and centre-half. Within a couple of seasons, he was being talked about in hushed tones as a possible replacement for Busby when the great Scot finally chose to call it a day.

'He was almost like a general on the battlefield,' said Matt Busby. 'He was a great and versatile player, a wonderful marshall. He was one of the best informed theorists and thinkers in the game. His influence on other players ran right down the line, from the top internationals to the lads on the ground staff. He successfully "fathered" greats such as Denis Law, Harry Gregg, Pat Crerand, Johnny Giles and Bobby Charlton. And talking of versatility, he was the personification of the word. One day, he would be at full-back for United and two days later, at centre-forward for his country. One day, he is going to carve himself a new future as a great manager.'

The 1963 Cup final victory was followed by a row over money, perhaps inevitable at a notoriously low-paying club where all first-teamers were on £25 per week plus a fiver for every league match played. Later the following season, Cantwell was involved in a personal showdown with the team trainer Jack Crompton, the dispute stemming from dressing-room unrest about the primitive training techniques.

"It was a strange dressing room, when you think about it,' said Cantwell of United in the sixties. 'You'd be standing, stripping and talking to people every day, maybe five days a week and half of them did not get on very well together.'

In any case, his influence was fading. In 1965, he became the first Cork soccer player to write an autobiography - "United We Stand" - but by then he had been relegated to the status of a fringe player, managing just two starts in the league-winning campaign that season. Although his tally of 144 appearances over seven years tells the story of an Old Trafford career that began to fade over time, he had done enough to be commemorated in song, his personal hymn was rendered to the tune of 'The First Noel'.

'The great Noel...Matt Busby would say...would captain United on cup final day...in '63...we beat Leicester City...Noel Cantwell our skipper that day...Noel, Noel, Noel, Noel...that was the name of our hero Cantwell....'

With Ireland fans, his popularity arguably peaked on the occasion of his 30th cap at Dalymount Park on May 5th, 1965. Up to the 63rd minute of a World Cup qualifier against reigning European champions Spain, Cantwell had struggled to make an impact. Pressed into service from the outset as an emergency centre-forward – a tactic so successful he finished his international career with a stunning 14 goals in 36 appearances – he waited in the penalty box for Frank O'Neill to send in a free-kick from the right. O'Neill put the ball too close to the keeper Jose-Angel Iribar but Cantwell made a play for it anyway.

As was his style when in the opposing area, he had earlier charged into Iribar and got a mouthful of abuse back. This time, he ran straight at the Spanish custodian, shouting insanely as he did so and causing the visitor to fumble the match-winning goal into his own net. The Spaniards were outraged at the manner of the defeat, and the embarrassment caused to Iribar, a player reckoned at that time to be second only to the Soviet Union's Lev Yashin in his position. They exacted sweet revenge later that year, beating Ireland 1-0 in a play-off held in Paris, denying Cantwell his last chance of reaching a major finals.

'Matt Busby didn't always approve of us going off to play for Ireland, especially if it was a friendly and United had a midweek match,' said Cantwell by way of explaining a few of his untimely absences from squads. 'You might develop a twinge you never knew you had.'

During his last season at Old Trafford, Cantwell's leadership qualities were acknowledged in another forum when he was elected chairman of the Professional Footballers' Association (PFA). He relinquished the union job in 1967 to succeed Jimmy Hill as manager of Coventry City. Effectively, his task was to keep a newly-promoted but very average City side in Division One. He promoted fellow Corkonian Pat Saward from coach to assistant-manager, and having avoided relegation in his first two seasons, Coventry finished sixth in 1970. Their highest-ever league position, it also earned him one more distinction: the first and only manager to have qualified the club for Europe.

Their stint in the Fairs Cup wasn't enough however to save him from the sack in 1972.Later that year, he took over Peterborough, an outfit then rooted at the bottom of the fourth division. The worst-placed club in England, Cantwell brought some brio even to that humble role. 'There is only one way to go now,' he said to the press, 'and that's up!' He was true to his word. At the end of his first full season in charge, they won the Fourth Division

championship. Contemporary newspaper reports describe him celebrating afterwards with champagne in hand and a massive cigar in his mouth. He may have been off-Broadway but he still had the flair for the big stage.

After close to five years at Peterborough, Cantwell followed a lot of veteran players of the era out to America to sample the opportunities on offer in the country's then booming NASL. He managed the New England Tea-men and Jacksonville Tea-men before returning to Peterborough for two more stints in the late eighties. Having served for one match as interim Ireland boss back in 1968, he was interviewed for the job the time Jack Charlton edged out Bob Paisley. He later sampled life as a professional publican before Dave Sexton made him part of the English FA's scouting team whose job it was to run the rule over players and opponents for Sven-Goran Eriksson.

A huge crowd turned at Flower Lodge to watch Manchester United play Bolton Wanderers in a friendly in February 1963. No games could be played in England because of "the big freeze" In the picture Harry Gregg saves as Noel Cantwell looks on.

An unsentimental character who put most of his football medals up for auction in 1995, the one constant in Cantwell's peregrinations appears to have been Cork. Right up until his death following a battle with cancer in September, 2005, Cantwell never forgot where he learned the game. Whether it was to play a testimonial for a League of Ireland player or to present trophies for the Cork Schoolboys' League, he was always readily available to fly home. Back in his pomp at Old Trafford, he'd once persuaded Matt Busby to allow him represent a select XI in a friendly match against a Jerry Lane XI at the schoolboy pitch in Togher. What better example of his silver tongue and common touch?

Jack Doyle

'I want to fight like you and sing like John McCormack,' said Jack Doyle.

'Wouldn't it be just too bad,' replied Jack Dempsey, 'if you could only sing like me and fight like Count McCormack.' - Pompton Lakes, New Jersey, 1935.

The traffic around White City was so bad that with half a mile still to go, Jack Doyle had to get out of the taxi and walk to the stadium. Well-wishers clapped his back every step of the way and one over-zealous female fan even clipped a lock of his hair as a keepsake. By the time, he reached the dressing-room, Doyle was almost giddy, laughing, joking and reading the plethora of good luck telegrams he'd received. Outside, 70,000 people were teeming into London's one-time Olympic venue to watch a 19 year old from Cobh challenge for the British heavyweight championship.

A raw talent that first became apparent in frantic childhood fistfights in his home-town quarry; he now stood six-foot-five and weighed just above 15 stone, and wore glamorous green satin shorts with his initials embroidered in gold along the side. Numerous impromptu punch-ups on the most famous waterfront in Ireland and a devotion to studying Jack Dempsey's instruction manual "How to Box" had put him top of the bill on a night when, win, lose or draw, he'd pocket £3,000. For a child reared somewhere between poverty and hardship in the Holy Ground district of Cobh, it had been some rise.

Facing page: The Gorgeous Gael, Jack Doyle. Over 70,000 came to the White City venue in London to see him fight for the British Heavyweight Championship.

Numerous impromptu punch-ups on the most famous waterfront in Ireland and a devotion to studying Jack Dempsey's instruction manual 'How to Box' had put him top of the bill on a night when, win, lose or draw, he'd pocket £3,000

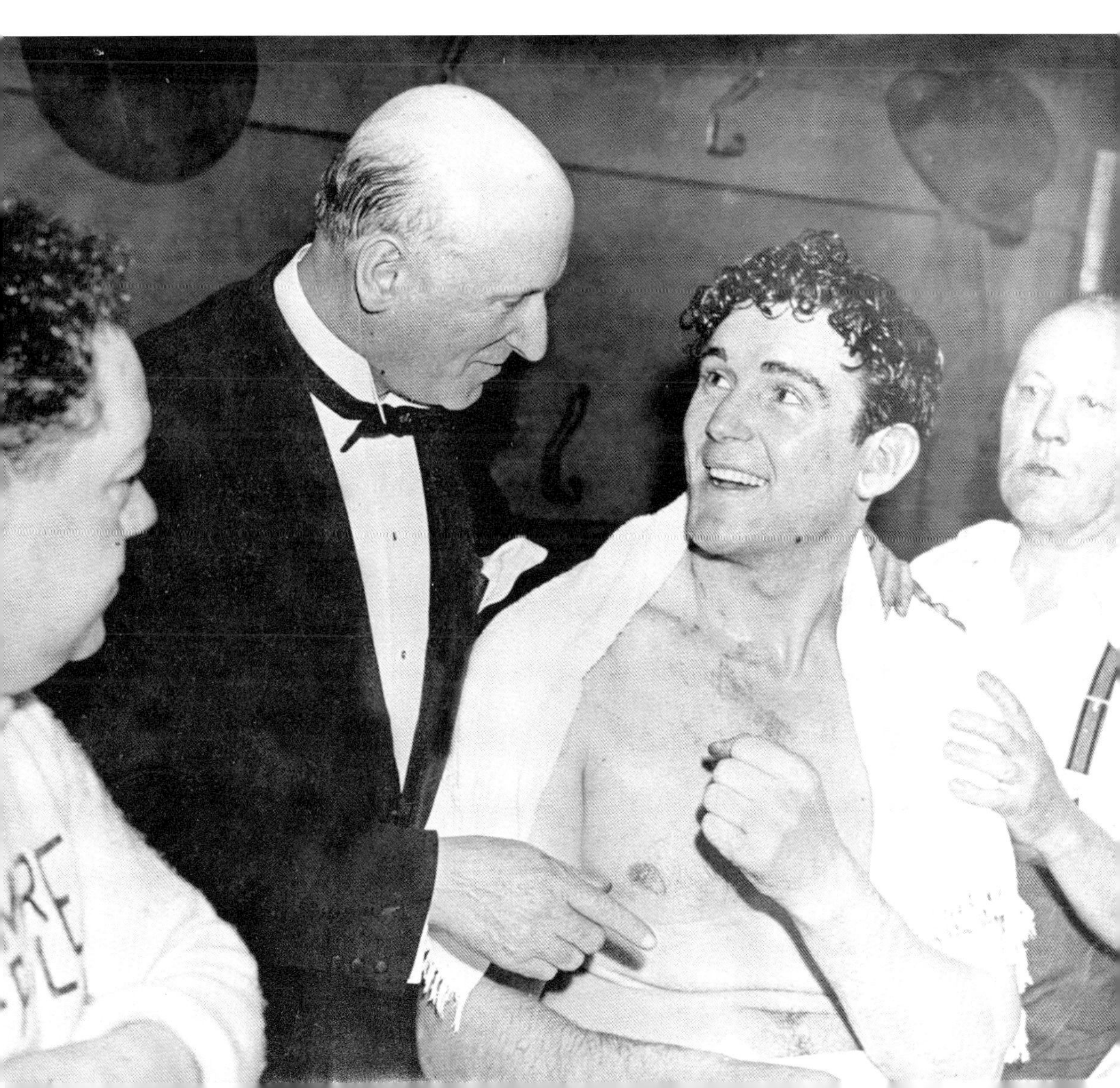

CIENT ENGINEERING Co
CORK EXAMIN
LIGHTING
HEATING
LONDON & NEWCASTLE TEA Co
YS STOUT.
LE CHATEAU
94

O'FLYNNS
OFFICE

Previous page: While Jack Doyle fought Jack Petersen at the White City, back in Cork huge crowds waited outside the offices of the Cork Examiner newspaper to hear news of how he fared.

When he was born on August 31st, 1913 at 12 Queen's Street, Joseph Doyle had weighed 14lbs. The extra girth would be a natural aid to him as he grew up in tough circumstances. His father Michael was invalided out of the Merchant Navy and ended up half-blind following an accident in a quarry, so his mother Stacia had to work several jobs just to keep her children clothed and fed. A boyhood of pitch and toss, and chester cake came to an abrupt end around the age of 12 when Jack, as he was affectionately called, got his first job on a farm.

That segued into a stint unloading the coal boats down at the quay, and when that trade was slack, he carried suitcases for the rich American tourists after they docked. None of it was easy work but it must have felt better to have a few bob than to be tramping, sometimes barefoot, to school. As a teenage worker, he honed his fighting skills in impromptu bare-knuckle bouts of the sort that were plentiful in the port town. Whether it was British soldiers over from Spike Island or co-workers in the coal trade irked by his good fortune at cards, he downed them all.

Turned down by the Free State Army at 16 because he was two years too young, he took the Innisfallen to Pembroke where he enlisted in the Irish Guards by lying about his age: he pretended to be 14 months older than he actually was. Less than two months after joining up, he had his first amateur bout in the army. He won with a second round knock-out and began in earnest the journey that brought him to national prominence. Three years after seeking out the Irish Guards' recruitment officer, he was out of uniform and had sold out White City.

The first sight of him entering the arena elicited huge cheers that grew louder still after he climbed through the ropes, stripped off his robe and unveiled a golden torso to compliment the handsome face. He chatted casually to the referee but after a few minutes the small talk gave way to nerves. As champions often do, Jack Petersen had let Doyle stew in the spotlight until he was good and ready to make his entrance. By the time, the referee Pickles Douglas brought the two boxers together, the challenger's early anxiety had given over to anger. He wanted to make the cocky Welsh champion pay in the same way he'd inflicted punishment on his previous ten professional opponents.

There was only one problem with that intention. Petersen was better than anybody he'd ever faced before and Doyle should not have been anywhere near a boxing ring that July night in 1933. He was suffering from a bad dose of the clap – history has yet to confirm whether it was gonorrhea or syphilis – that had left him in no physical condition to go 15 rounds against a tough, unbeaten veteran of 23 fights. Apart from anything else, the venereal disease he contracted earlier that summer following an encounter with a woman he met in the West End had seriously affected his ability to train properly. In the days before penicillin, his title chances had been effectively destroyed the night he entered a shady late-night establishment called Murray's Club.

From the bell, Doyle still went on the offensive. He knew his only chance was to put Petersen down early. Even before incurring his STD, he'd never been past the second round in a professional contest before. His method was unorthodox, raining punches on the Welsh champion from every direction and headed to every destination. A huge number strayed below the belt but Doyle didn't heed the warnings from referee. A frantic first round culminated in the pair of them duelling toe to toe in the centre of the ring.

Home is the Hero. Jack Doyle arrives in Cork to celebrate his 21st birthday in August 1934.

The sort of action beloved of spectators, it nonetheless brought Douglas to the Doyle corner before the start of the second. His ultimatum was stark and fair. Any further punches below the belt would merit instant disqualification. Less than a minute of the second round had elapsed when Douglas called a halt to proceedings. He had a reputation as an officious referee and another stray Doyle punch persuaded him to invoke the rule book. The fight was over. Doyle had lost. The decision was greeted by a sustained chorus of boos in the stadium, and back in Cork, the crowd gathered outside The Cork Examiner offices in Academy Street were stunned at the news that the local boy had failed ignominiously.

'I fouled Petersen in the first round,' wrote Doyle in the Sunday Pictorial in 1939. 'I admit that now freely. I was warned that I should be disqualified if I persisted. I did persist. I fouled him again in the second round more than once. I was ordered back to my corner, disqualified and disgraced. Why did I do it? Why did I ignore the warning I got? The plain honest fact of the matter is that I was ill, so ill that I should never have been in the ring.

Jack Doyle won each of his first ten professional fights inside two rounds. This lack of experience of going the distance did not help his cause in his British Heavyweight title fight against Jack Petersen.

'I could have refused flatly to go in the ring at all. I put the public first. I did not want to disappoint the tens of thousands who were waiting for the "match of the century", not just the huge crowd who watched, remember, but the peoples of Britain and Ireland. I knew I had only one chance. A knockout in the first two rounds. My strength would not last beyond that.

"At all costs, I must knock Petersen out in six minutes. I left my corner reckless and desperate, my mind obsessed by just one thought – I must hit and keep on hitting. In this way I became fighting mad. I did not know what I was doing. I saw red. "Hit and keep on hitting" drummed through my dazed mind and not until I had been forced back to my corner did I realise what I had done.'

There was a chaotic aftermath to the bout as the British Boxing Board of Control ordered his purse withheld pending their investigation into the circumstances surrounding his disqualification. Eventually, they suspended him for six months and required him to forfeit £2,740 of the money due to him. The rest was to be paid at a fiver per week each to Doyle and to his mother back in Cork. It was a draconian penalty, far in excess of the usual levied for such an offence. Worse again was that after taking the case to the High Court and winning, the BBBC had the decision overturned on appeal. He would box again after Petersen but really, his time had already passed.

While the legal shenanigans played out, his second career, and the one for which he would arguably become far more famous, took off in earnest. Deprived of his right to box for six months, he turned to the only other gift he had – his voice. A tour of a revue in which he showcased both his talents equally, singing songs in the first half and working out to music in the second, began at the Theatre Royal in Dublin. For four weeks, every one of its 3,600 seats was filled twice daily and he was pocketing £600 per week due to a clause guaranteeing him a share of the gate. The arena had changed but the Doyle name remained box office.

'His voice was a captivating blend of Doyle soprano and McCormack tenor,' wrote Michael Taub in his classic study "Jack Doyle: Fighting for Love". 'His material struck a perfect balance between pure schmaltz and acceptable sentimentality and his delivery, as in the boxing ring, was executed with a perfect sense of the dramatic. He set up his audiences perfectly with perennial favourites like The Hills of Donegal and The Rose of Tralee and then knocked them out cold with his emotional rendering of Mother

Machree. Having been held spellbound by The Voice, the fans were now transfixed by The Torso as Jack pushed his massive frame through a series of calisthenics and shadow-boxing routines. The physical side to the show was designed not only to keep Jack in fighting trim during his enforced absence from the ring, but also to arouse the women in the audience.'

The show moved to the Cork Opera House in September, 1933. There, he was greeted as the returning hero who had suffered a great injustice in England. They paraded him through the streets and hung on his every word as if he had won and not lost the title. Therein, always, lies the problem with Doyle. There is a good argument for not featuring him in a sports history of Cork at all. Even in a county that has never excelled at producing boxers, there are pugilists with equally good careers. Between Packey Mahoney (later to earn distinction training Cork and Glen Rovers) fighting for the British heavyweight title back in 1913 and Kieran Joyce boxing in two Olympics, Mick Leahy defeated Sugar Ray Robinson in September, 1964. Admittedly, the greatest pound for pound fighter of all time had turned 44 at the time of the bout.

Doyle's record was a reasonable - 17 victories and six defeats - but he was disqualified in the only title bout he ever fought. He was punched all over Dalymount Park by Mullingar's Chris Cole during a 1943 comeback and according to one account, reportedly begged Cole to throw the fight beforehand. If he had such a great boxing talent - and pundits differ about everything beyond his punching power - he was guilty of squandering it.

That is the sober assessment. The truth is that in a place that hasn't boasted a world champion boxer since the 19th century, Doyle is the most famous we have ever produced. More than quarter of a century after his death, he lives on in the most vibrant ways, each a tribute to the romance of his rise, the operatic tragedy of his fall. Apart from Michael Taub's superb biography, there is a stage-play, a beautiful Jimmy McCarthy song (poignantly titled 'The Contender') and of course a statue still standing down in Cobh. Sporting lives filled with medals, and overflowing with achievement slip through the cracks, yet this tale endures.

Why? Because it was the story with everything, a handsome leading man involved in a melodrama that spanned continents and decades and teemed with equal portions of pathos and passion. The rags to riches element of his early life; the injustice meted out by the British Boxing authorities; the voice that could move an audience to tears; the glamour of his liaisons with a slew

Fans that were unable to get tickets for Jack Doyle's concert at Cork Opera House were treated to an impromptu recital in Emmet Place. Acts like this helped raise Doyle's status to that of a returning hero who had suffered a great injustice in England.

of women; the failed comebacks; the divorces and the break-ups; and the final, terrible, descent into alcoholism and penury.

After threatening but never achieving boxing glory and embarking on a cabaret career, the highlight of which was The Punch and Beauty show he put on with Movita, the Mexican Hollywood starlet he married - Doyle dabbled in wrestling, once drawing 22,500 to Tolka Park. He filmed three movies, and during his foray into acting, stole a woman from Marlon Brando, drank with Errol Flynn and Clark Gable, starred in The Belles of St. Trinians, and sampled as many Hollywood starlets as his appetites would allow.

By the winter of 1978 however, he was homeless and penniless and on the way out. After a spell dossing on the streets of London, wandering at times barefoot from pub to pub, he died on December 13th. He'd been put up just the night before by John O'Sullivan, a Corkman working on the railway, who couldn't bear to see Doyle in such a pitiful state. The funeral was, inevitably, an epic production. Between London and Cobh, three requiem masses were said, and the coffin's journey stopped traffic in Dublin and Cork before he was brought back, brought home to the Holy Ground.

Tony Mullane

A gifted skater, boxer, musician and singer, his legion of fans in baseball knew him as either 'The Apollo of the Box' or 'The Count'. The Sporting News preferred to describe him as an intolerant racist and 'a man of the most sordid nature'. A canny promoter in Louisville, Kentucky witnessed the effect his good looks had on women and used him to introduce the notion of a Ladies' Day at the stadium. In a Cincinnati divorce court, one of his wives admitted to hitting him with a potato roller, but only after he had cut her with a knife and had smashed a water jug over her head. For a sober individual who never smoke or drank, Tony Mullane cut quite a dash.

At the age of five, his parents Dennis and Elizabeth (nee Behan) brought him away from their native Cork to live in the new world. They settled near Erie, Pennsylvania, and eight decades later, their son's death after illness would be marked by obituaries in the New York Times and the Chicago Daily News. Between 1881 and 1894, he was arguably the best pitcher in American baseball's major leagues, winning a total of 285 games, a statistic that still ranks him among the top 25 players in that position of all time. He was also the first player ever to throw the ball both right- and left-handed in the same game, a feat so remarkable that only three others in the history of the game have replicated it.

'A. H. Tarvin, the Louisville historian, has traced the custom of ladies' day back to the eighties, saying that the originator of the practice was Aaron S. Stern, a clothing manufacturer who owned the Reds,' writes Lee Allen in his baseball history 'The Hot Stove League'. "Pitching for Stern's team was Tony

Mullane, a handsome fellow. Stern noticed that although a few ladies were always on hand, they were out in abundance whenever Mullane was scheduled to pitch. Seeing an opportunity to increase attendance, the owner then decided that Mullane would always pitch on Monday and that all ladies with escorts would be admitted free.'

Although remembered most for his ambidexterity, his turbulent career teemed with incident. Once he realised how good he was, Mullane began demanding a salary commensurate with his talent. A revolutionary notion at a time when players were bound to a team until the team decided otherwise by an oppressive contractual stipulation known as the 'reserve clause', the Corkman was the ultimate contract rebel. After two immense seasons with the St. Louis Browns, he tried to move across town to the St. Louis Maroons for more money. When the Browns' owner sneakily lured him back by stumping up the cash before then forcibly transferring him to a lesser club, Mullane signed for the Cincinnati Reds instead, and suffered a one year suspension from the game for his temerity.

'The flamboyant Mullane scrambled from club to club in pursuit of higher pay, but clearly he was worth it,' writes William Curran, in "Strikeout: A celebration of the art of pitching". 'He should easily have reached 300 career wins had the American Association not suspended him at the height of his career for jumping his contract. All the same, The Count's frequent moves fetched him salaries many times what a good position player commanded in that era. It is suspected that in his best years Tony received under-the-table bonuses as well. Mullane's career illustrates that, even as early as the 1880s, a proven winner could almost write his own contract although few other hurlers seemed bold enough to press their advantage.'

At one point, Mullane was drawing down $5,000 a year, more than six times the average wage in the sport. He was worth every penny. Apart from being the most formidable pitcher of the age - his physical strength befitting somebody who spent his teenage years fighting in the bareknuckle boxing rings of Pennsylvania - he could fill in competently at every other position on the field. If that was a truly noteworthy gift in a game where players specialise in one position from an early age, Mullane was a highly unpopular figure among contemporaries. Despite lavish earnings, his lust for more caused him to sit out another half a season late in his career as a protest against league-wide pay cuts. Then there was the matter of his unreconstructed racism.

'Moses Fleetwood Walker was the best catcher I ever worked with, but I disliked a Negro and whenever I had to pitch to him, I used to pitch anything

I wanted without looking for the signals,' wrote Mullane of Walker, his former team-mate with the Toledo Blue Stockings. 'One day he signalled me for a curve ball and I shot a fast ball at him. He caught it and walked down to me. He said: "I'll catch you without signals but I won't catch you if you are going to cross me when I give you signals." And all the rest of the season he caught me and caught anything I threw. I pitched without him knowing what was coming."

Once his pitching power faded, Mullane worked a couple of seasons as a professional baseball umpire - once famously having to be escorted off the field by police in Nashville, Tennessee after giving too many unpopular decisions - before serving more successfully as a Chicago policeman until retiring at the age of 65. He married several times but only had one child, a daughter. Even though his obituaries twenty years later contained no mention of his racial prejudices, they did hurt him later. In 2003, baseball's Veterans Committee placed him on a list of 200 former players who were under consideration for entry to the sport's distinguished Hall of Fame. His career statistics made him look like a posthumous shoo-in but the rules expressly state that voters must consider a person's character and integrity as much as their playing ability. No surprises then when he didn't make the cut.

The Cincinnati Reds, Tony Mullane is second from the left, back row. At the height of his powers, Mullane was earning $5,000 a year, this was more than six times the average wage in the sport.

Hugh Alexander

In September, 1939, Hugh Alexander was in Buenos Aires attending the Chess Olympiad when World War II broke out. Six rounds into the tournament, the reigning British champion immediately withdrew from competition, and returned to London by boat. A mathematics teacher by profession, he volunteered for national service, and was quickly assigned to the elite code-breaking unit at Bletchley Park. At the conclusion of the war in 1945, Winston Churchill would credit four cryptographers there with shortening the duration of the conflict by two whole years; Alexander was one of them.

Conel Hugh O'Donnell Alexander, to give him his rather distinctive full name, was born in Cork on April 19th, 1909. His father was a professor of civil engineering at UCC, and the family lived on Connaught Avenue. They moved to England when he was just eight years old but Alexander would always tell people he regarded himself first and foremost as an Irishman. Even if his decision to embark on a career in the higher echelons of British intelligence meant he could never hope to properly fulfill his talent on the chess board, there seems little enough argument he was the finest player to whom this country could ever lay claim.

'I have many times had the pleasure of meeting Alexander over the chessboard,' wrote Mikhail Botvinnik whose reign as world champion lasted 14 years. 'On one occasion (in 1946) I suffered a crushing defeat. He was a real paladin, sans peur et sans reproche.... With his urge for overcoming and taming opposition, with his enthusiasm for uncompromising struggle, Alexander pioneered the way for British players to modern, complicated and daring chess; chess players will never forget him.'

Hugh Alexander (left) and the Russian Grandmaster, David Bronstein, are deep in concentration during the 13 hour epic chess game in 1953.

Although he attained the level of international master in 1950, Alexander's peculiar choice of job precluded him from competing with enough regularity against the greats like Botvinnik. In the decades after World War II, the British government would never allow him travel anywhere behind the Iron Curtain to compete against his most illustrious contemporaries. London was riddled with Russian spies at the time, and it was feared that if Moscow got wind of the presence of such an important Cold War code-breaker on their territory, he would be either killed or imprisoned.

'He was unique in his profession,' said Dr Lou Tordella, deputy director of the US National Security Agency. 'He was the best at what he did and probably better than any of his NSA counterparts in terms of sheer aptitude and accomplishment in the subject of cryptanalysis.'

Befitting somebody who followed up a prodigious schoolboy career by winning the prestigious Cambridge University chess championship four years running, he still found enough opportunities to leave an indelible mark on the sport. In 1953, he defeated the Russian grandmaster David Bronstein in an epic contest at Hastings that lasted 13 hours and took three days to complete. Alexander's dogged triumph over the higher-rated opponent garnered front-page headlines in the English papers, made him a household name, and led to his taking on the job of chess columnist with The Sunday Times.

'Alexander could well be described as the greatest Irish player of all time,' wrote Enda Rohan in a contribution to Mark Orr's excellent Irish chess archive website. 'He wrote to me in 1957 saying: 'I do think of myself as an Irishman, not an Englishman, in spite of my long time here'. We had many friendly arguments during the 1957 Dublin Zonal (a world championship qualifying event) where there was great local interest in his performance, though officially he was representing England.'

In many ways, Alexander was a man with a foot in both camps. For the duration of the war, he had billeted his Australian wife Enid, and their kids at a safe house in Donegal while he got on with the work of cracking German codes for the Allies. Given an OBE in 1945 for his success in that regard, he was promoted to CBE ten years later. More honours were to follow. Shortly before his retirement from the intelligence corps, he was made a Companion of the Most Distinguished Order of St. Michael and St. George - an individual award conferred by the Queen in recognition of his unique contribution to the country's foreign affairs.

"I think the best way for the player to begin to understand and enjoy problems is through using the chess skill he already possesses to solve them simply as chess puzzles,' wrote Alexander once, explaining his philosophical approach to the sport. 'While it is the struggle in a game of chess that is the central element, most players get pleasure from the ideas that occur in a game and not just from winning; so, although at first some may find problems rather bloodless, there are few who will not grow to enjoy them. In any event, I am sure that it is worthwhile at least making the attempt to widen one's range of chess experience.'

When he retired, the American government tried desperately to lure Alexander across the Atlantic to bring his vast experience of code-breaking to bear in the Pentagon . A lucrative offer was turned down in favour of devoting more time to writing books about chess and promoting the sport. Unfortunately, he became seriously ill just a few months into this new vocation and died on February 15th, 1974.

'I am not going to recite his triumphs at chess, or try to describe his immense services to British chess over forty years,' wrote Stuart Milner-Barry, a close friend of his, in the book “The Best Games of CHO'D Alexander”. 'Nor would I be the right person to describe his work at GCHQ since the War. But I would like to say something about him as a colleague and a friend. He had a full, happy and successful life, left behind him a famous name, and memories that will always be treasured by his friends of all ages.'

Quite a name all right. Quite a life too.

Jack McAuliffe

Although born in Meelin on March 24th, 1866, nobody seems to know exactly how old Jack McAuliffe was when his family swapped a townland in North Cork for a fresh start in Bangor, Maine. All that can be said for certain is that by the time they moved south to Williamsburg, Brooklyn in the early 1880s, he'd already discovered a talent for fighting. Just after his 16th birthday, he dismantled an English sailor in a bareknuckle contest in the basement of a Bangor storehouse. Not an official bout but a comprehensive enough victory to give him a first inkling he could forge a career with his fists.

Once in New York, the teenage McAuliffe began working in a cooperage. There, he befriended a Kildare immigrant and future world middleweight champion, Jack 'non-pareil' Dempsey, and in this company, he started learning how to box properly. Turning pro with a 17th round knockout of Jack Karcher at the age of 18, he embarked on an undefeated run that would stretch for well over a decade. A mere two years and ten days after that auspicious pro debut, he annexed the vacant world lightweight championship with a 21st round dismissal of Billy Frazier in Boston.

'As champion, he liked the high life, good food, and fine clothes,' writes Tracy Callis, historian at the International Boxing Hall of Fame. 'He also loved the racetrack and was addicted to gambling. Accordingly, he did not take to training too well and never over-trained. On a number of occasions he came in heavier than planned - but he was such a talented fighter, it usually did not matter.

'A heady, crafty, intelligent boxer, who (like Gene Tunney years later) studied the every move, tactic and tendency of his opponents. He was blessed with that wonderful, natural gift of extreme quickness, was light on his feet and employed springy, bouncy, brisk movements. He was a master strategist, not a terribly crunching, power-hitter but possessed a wicked, sharply driven, straight left jab that cut opponents up.'

Jack McAuliffe was known as "The Napoleon of the Ring" because of his peculiar stance.

Variously known as "The Napoleon of the Ring" because of a peculiar stance, and "Dapper Dan" for his sharp-dressing, the defining fight of McAuliffe's life came just a year into his lengthy reign. A contest with the British champion Jem Carney took place in clandestine circumstances that have since become part of boxing lore. To keep one step ahead of the law, the fight was billed to start at 1am, and the location - a twenty-four foot ring erected inside a barn in the rural town of Revere, Massachussetts - was a closely guarded secret right up to the first bell.

'The invited guests arrived in pairs at a designated hotel, and after each had passed muster, he was permitted to remain until the march to the stable under the guidance of the hotel proprietor who led the way with a lantern,' wrote Nat Fleischer and Sam Andre in "A Pictorial History of Boxing". 'At the barn the spectators found a Salvation Army group practicing hymns, and their presence helped throw the police off the trail. Carney tipped the scales at 129lbs and McAuliffe at 126lbs.

'Throughout the early rounds, the men hooked and jabbed, landing few blows of any consequence. McAuliffe was dropped in the seventh round but came back strong. When the 60th round arrived, McAuliffe showed signs of fatigue. His backers, fearing the loss of their wagers, became unruly. The break came in the 70th frame when Carney scored a clean knockdown that looked like a finisher. Only interference by McAuliffe's friends saved him. Order was restored and the bout went on until the 74th round when Carney again put him down. The spectators rushed the ring again....'

Fearing the imminent arrival of the local constabulary, the referee stopped the fight, declared a draw and got McAuliffe off the hook, his unbeaten record and his grip on the title preserved. The dubious ending didn't detract too much from the epic nature of the bout, and if anything, it probably only added lustre to his legend. Fully twenty-seven years later, Carney and himself - by then a pair of balding, flabbier, middle-aged men - donned oversized gloves and re-enacted their fabled encounter for a theatre audience in London.

A couple of other dodgy decisions went his way too. Despite struggling with a broken bone in his arm for much of the fight, his title bout with Billy Myer on February 23rd, 1889 in North Judson, Indiana was declared a draw after 64 sapping rounds. Objective witnesses felt Myer had the better of things that night but the decision allowed McAuliffe to keep a tenuous grip on his crown. Five years later, he barely landed a serious blow on Young Griffo (an up-and-coming Australian contender) yet was still awarded the decision.

At the Carnival of Champions held in New Orleans in 1892, the event which supposedly marked boxing's entry into polite society, McAuliffe had a far more convincing win over his old nemesis Myer before subsequently working as a corner-man for John L. Sullivan during the latter's defeat by Gentleman Jim Corbett. Following his own embarrassing loss to the younger Corbett, the legendary heavyweight warned his Cork pal to quit the sport while he was ahead.

McAuliffe heeded the advice but - like every other deluded fighter - he made a couple of comebacks, most likely motivated by a desire to keep earning fresh cash to replace all he'd squandered. After a spell working as a vaudeville entertainer, he eventually set up as a bookmaker himself. Newly prosperous, he even mounted an unsuccessful run for a seat in the New York State Assembly in 1934, dipping his toe into politics at the age of 68, more than half a century after first climbing into the ring.

Seventeen years after his death at Forest Hills, Queens, New York in 1937, he was among the first class of fighters inducted into Ring magazine's Boxing Hall of Fame. No further explanation of his standing in his sport required.

Patsy Donovan

In July, 1914, Patsy Donovan's job as a scout for the Boston Red Sox had him tracking the Baltimore Orioles. The Sox owned an option to buy the contract of a promising young pitcher by the name of Babe Ruth and the club wanted Donovan to verify the kid was the genuine article. Sitting in the stands, ostensibly to watch Ruth pitch against a side from Montreal one afternoon, he saw the 19-year-old phenomenon pick up the bat when his turn came and dispatch a home run that he said later 'looked as if it had left this world'.

Donovan contacted the Red Sox owner Joe Lannin immediately, related the story, and the most famous baseball player the game would ever know was on his way to the big leagues. Charles Donovan recounts his father's bit part role in that little swatch of sporting history in an unexcited tone. It is, after all, just one more memorable cameo in a life that teemed with them.

'My father was born in Queenstown in 1864. He was three years old when his mother Hanora brought him to America, following his father Jeremiah who had come over first. They were motivated to leave by the poverty they faced back home. By the time my father was 13, he was out of school, earning 90 cents for working 12 hours a day in a woollen mill in Lawrence, Massachusetts. He freed himself from the morass by playing baseball. By 1903, he was the highest paid player in the game, getting $8,800 a year from the St Louis Cardinals.'

Jeremiah Donovan worked on the Boston and Maine Railroad and Hanora busied herself rearing seven children. It was a strict house where the parents cautioned the kids about the need to seize every opportunity the new country afforded them. Leisure activity for boys in the town consisted mainly of baseball in the summer and skating the Merrimack River in winter. Although his only formal education was at St. Patrick's Grammar School in Lawrence, and a life in the mill appeared his destiny, Patsy had earned a reputation in the local leagues as an excellent baseball player.

The sport was still in its infancy then and he would be all of 25 years old when he finally turned professional with a club in London, Ontario. From

Patsy Donovan finished his base career with an impressive batting average of .301. In 1903 he was Baseball's highest paid player earning $8,800 from the St Louis Cardinals.

there, he was picked up by the Boston Beaneaters, and would go on to spend 17 years in the major leagues with the Brooklyn Bridegrooms, Louisville Colonels, Pittsburgh Pirates, the Cardinals and the Red Sox. For nine of those years, including the last two seasons before the Red Sox moved to their current home of Fenway Park, he combined the roles of player and manager – that feat alone making him stand out among his contemporaries.

In a game where statistics are the sine qua non, and .300 has always been regarded as the benchmark separating the good hitters from the rest, he finished his career with a batting average of .301. Usually playing as a right-fielder, he totalled 2,253 hits, another impressive number, and stole 518 bases. The minutiae of his career are important because in the absence of footage, they are the only material evidence Charles possesses to back up his contention that his father deserves to be posthumously inducted into baseball's Hall of Fame. Having first raised the issue with the relevant authorities in 2000, he succeeded in having his name put on a ballot of old-timers in 2005, but it was unfortunately turned down. Patsy Donovan passed away on Christmas Day, 1953, yet more than half a century later, his son, a man of 84 years, remained on a serious quest to have his father's achievements recognised.

Donovan had no shortage of people willing to testify on his Dad's behalf either. One of his father's last jobs in the sport was as high-school coach at Phillips Academy in Andover, Massachusetts. An aspiring first baseman named George H.W. Bush was among his charges during that stint, and when the time came to speak up on behalf of his former coach, the 41st American President wasn't found wanting either.

'When I was a young high school baseball player, my life intersected with Coach Donovan's,' wrote Bush in a letter to the Hall of Fame. 'His interest in baseball was every well known in the Massachusetts area, and he was, indeed, of the highest character. ... I enthusiastically second the motion for nomination.'

When Patsy married Terese Agnes Mahoney in 1910, the Red Sox gave the newly-weds a wedding present of a trip to Europe. Donovan reputedly saw the county of his birth from the deck of the boat that took him to England on the first leg of that journey. That it was the nearest he ever came to going home, says his son, was always a source of great sadness to him.

Cork is a sports mad county as seen by the passion of the Cork hurling fans.

Bibliography

Allen, Lee: The Hot Stove League, Barnes Place, New York, 1955

Beecher, Sean: Day by Day - A Miscellany of Cork History, Collins Press, Cork, 1992

Carter, Plunkett: A Century of Cork Soccer Memories, Greenmount Rangers, Cork, 1995

Carter, Plunkett: From the Lodge to the Box, Greenmount Rangers, Cork, 2002

Carthy, Brian: The Football Captains, Wolfhound Press, Dublin, 1998

Corry, Eoghan: Catch and Kick, Poolbeg, Dublin, 1989

Coughlan, John: 100 Cork Sporting Heroes, Evening Echo, Cork, 2003

Crick, Michael: Manchester United; Betrayal of a Legend, Pan McMillan, London, 1990

Crosbie, George F: The Bruen Loop, Mercier Press, Cork, 1998

Cronin, Jim: Cork GAA - A History, Coiste Chontae Chorcai, Cork, 1986

Cronin, Jim: A Rebel Hundred, Coiste Chontae Chorcai, 1997

Cronin, Jim, Barry, Brendan, Arnold, John and Smyth, Jimmy: GAA Ballads of Rebel Cork, Coiste Chontae Chorcai, Cork, 2001

Curran, William: Strikeout: A celebration of the art of pitching, Crown, New York, 1995

De Burca, Marcus: The GAA - A History, Gill and MacMillan, Dublin, 1999

Desmond, Gerry and Galvin, Dave: Between the Picket Fences, Munster Senior League, Cork, 1999

Dorgan, Val: Christy Ring, Ward River Press, Dublin, 1980

Dunne, Sean: The Cork Anthology, Cork University Press, Cork, 1993

Dunphy, Eamon: A Strange Kind of Glory, Heinemann, London, 1991

Edwards, Gareth: 100 Great Rugby Players, Queen Anne Press, London, 1987

English, Alan: Stand Up and Fight, Yellow Jersey Press, 2005

Fitzsimmons, Walter J: The Cork Motor Races 1936-38, Dreoilin, Meath, 2000

Fleischer, Nat and Andre, Sam E: A Pictorial History of Boxing, Citadel Press, New York, 1959

Fullam, Brendan: Captains of the Ash, Wolfhound Press, Dublin, 2002

Gilleece, Dermot: Breaking 80, Poolbeg Group Services, Dublin, 2002

Gleeson, John: Fyffes Dictionary of Irish Sporting Greats, Etta Place, Dublin, 1993

Griffin, Marcus: Fall Guys; The Barnums of Bounce, Reilly and Lee, Chicago, 1937

Hammond, Roy: Media Memories of Cork, Leprechaun Productions, Cork, 1994

Hannigan, Dave: The Big Fight, Yellow Jersey Press, London, 2002

Hannigan, Dave: The Garrison Game, Mainstream Press, Edinburgh, 1998

Hayes, Liam: Out of our Skins, Gill and MacMillan, Dublin, 1992

Hayes, Liam, Hogan, Vincent and Walsh, David: Heroes of Irish Sporting Life, Medmedia Ltd, Dublin, 1995

Holland, Anne: Steeplechasing, Little, Brown and Co, London, 2001

Horgan, Tim: Cork's Hurling Story, Anvil Books, Dublin, 1977

Houlihan, Con: Now Read On, Sportsworld, Dublin, 1992

Keane, Colm, Hurling's Top 20, Mainstream Publishing, Edinburgh, 2002

Keane, Colm: Ireland's Soccer Top 20, Mainstream Publishing, Edinburgh, 2004

Keane, Roy: Keane, Michael Joseph, London, 2002

Kelly, Stephen: Backpage United, Queen Anne Press, Harpenden, 1994

King, Seamus: A History of Hurling, Gill and MacMillan, Dublin, 1996

Lewis, Samuel: Lewis' Cork, Collins Press, Cork, 1998

McElligott, Tom: The Story of Handball, Wolfhound Press, Dublin, 1984

McElligott, Tom: Six O'Clock All Over Cork, Wolfhound Press, Dublin, 1992

McGee, Eugene: Classic Football Matches, Gill and MacMillan, Dublin, 1993

McGarrigle, Stephen: The Complete Who's Who of Irish International Football, Mainstream Publishing, Edinburgh, 1996

McRory, Seamus: The Voice from the Sideline, Blackwater Press, Dublin, 1997

Mehigan, P.D: Fifty Years of Irish Athletics, Gaelic Publicity Services, Dublin, 1943.

Mehigan, P.D: Vintage Carbery, Beaver Row Press, Dublin, 1984

Mehigan, P.D: Mountain Heath, The Kerryman Ltd, Tralee, 1944

Moran, Mary: Cork's Camogie Story, Cork, 2000

Murphy, Sean: A History of Handball in Munster, Munster Handball Council, 1984

Naughton, Lindie, and Watterson, Johnny: Irish Olympians, Blackwater Press, Dublin, 1992

Nolan, Pat: Flashbacks; A Half-Century of Cork Hurling, Collins Press, Cork, 2000

O'Hehir, Michael: My Life and Times, Blackwater Press, Dublin, 1996

O hEithir, Breandan: Over the Bar, Poolbeg Press, Dublin, 1984

O'Mahony, T.P: Jack Lynch - A Biography, Blackwater Press, Dublin, 1991

O'Reilly, Peter: The Full Bag of Chips, O'Brien Press, Dublin, 2004

O Se, Paidi, and Potts, Sean: Paidi, Townhouse, Dublin, 2001

O'Tuama, Liam: Where He Sported and Played - Jack Lynch, Blackwater Press, Dublin, 2000

Power, John: Cork Book of Champions, Cork, 1945

Power, Vincent: Voices of Cork, Blackwater Press, Dublin, 1997

Quinn, Mark: The King of Spring, The Liffey Press, Dublin, 2004

Rafferty, Eamonn: Talking Gaelic, Blackwater Press, Dublin, 1997

Roberts, James B. and Skutt, Alexander G: The Boxing Register, McBooks Press, New York, 2002

Robinson, Patrick: Horsetrader

Rousmaniere, John: Fastnet Force 10, W.W. Norton, New York, 1980

Rowan, Paul: The Team That Jack Built, Mainstream Publishing, Edinburgh, 2004

Ryan, Sean: The Boys in Green, Mainstream Publishing, Edinburgh, 1997

Slattery, Fr. Denis J: My Life Story, West African Book Publishers, Lagos, 1996

Smith, Raymond: Complete Handbook of Gaelic Games, Sporting Books, Dublin, 1993

Smith, Raymond: The Football Immortals, Aherlow Publishers, Dublin, 1983

Smith, Raymond: The High Rollers of the Turf, Sporting Books, Dublin, 1992

Spillane, Pat and McGoldrick, Sean: Shooting From The Hip, Storm Books, Dublin, 1998

Taylor, Rogan and Ward, Andrew: Kicking and Screaming, Robson Books, London, 1996

Taub, Michael: Jack Doyle - Fighting For Love, Stanley Paul, London, 1990

Tierney, Mark: Croke of Cashel, Gill and MacMillan, 1976

Toibin, Niall: Smile and be a Villain, Townhouse, Dublin, 1995

Ulyatt, Michael E: The Fighting O'Kellys, Cherry Burton, Hutton, 1991

White, Jim: Always in the Running, Mainstream Publishing, Edinburgh, 1996

Wolff, Alexander: Big Game, Small World, Warner Books, New York, 2002

Young, Eamonn: Rebels at the Double, Mainstream Publishing, Edinburgh, 1990

Newspapers and Periodicals

The Evening Echo, Irish Examiner, Irish Times, Irish Independent, Sunday Tribune, Sunday Times, Sunday Independent, The Guardian, The Independent, The New York Times, The Racing Post, The Evening Press, The Journal of Olympic History, Code 13 Rugby League History Magazine, Basketball Ireland, Polo Quarterly International, Ring Magazine, Galesburg Daily Register, The Limerick Leader, Fairway and Hazard, Daily Telegraph, Villanova magazine, Sunday Pictorial, Seanchas Duthalla, Seattle Police Department Yearbook, Horse Latitudes, Journal of the Horse of the Americas, Gaelic Quarterly Review, Wisden, Cork Holly Bough

Index

All photos in this publication are the property of Evening Echo Publications (Cork) Ltd. except the following:

Danno O'Mahony 20 (Boston Public Library)
Dr. Pat O'Callaghan 30 (John D. Kelly, Clonmel)
Vincent O'Brien and Nijinsky 38 (Inpho)
Jack Lynch 62 (Colman Doyle)
Roy Keane 72 (Inpho)
Frederick Barrett 116 (Danny Hicks)
Denis Horgan 122 (Pat Murphy)
Tom Horan 157 (Cricinfo.com)
Eddie O'Sullivan 186 (Inpho)
Gearóid Towey 191 (Inpho-Patrick Bolger)
Norman Williamson 200 (PA)
Royal Navy 233/234 (PA)
Beecher's Brook 277 (PA)
Denis Irwin 285 (PA)
Jonjo O'Neill 290 (PA), 293 (John Grossick), 295 (PA)
Charlie Hurley 299 (PA)
Marcus O'Sullivan 313 (Inpho)
Cincinnati Reds 343 (Baseball-almanac.com)
Jack McAuliffe 348, 349 (Elmer Chickering)
Patsy Donovan 352 (Baseball-almanac.com)
Noel Cantwell 325 (Inpho)

Design and layout by Marguerite Kiely,
Graphic Artist, Evening Echo Publications.

Printed by City Print, Victoria Cross, Ireland.